The Refuge Abyss is a one of those rare books which come along and name the world with such exquisite precision, theoretical acumen and methodological discernment, that they are genuinely paradigm-shifting. In this necessarily painful articulation of the abyssal state to which people labelled 'refugees' are condemned, Hyab Teklehaimanot Yohannes offers a sublimely theoretical voice and a poetics of relation and decoloniality.

Alison Phipps, *UNESCO Chair for Refugee Integration through Education, Languages and Arts, University of Glasgow*

If you are interested in the refugee condition, this is the book you should read. Not only inspired by but also reminiscent of seminal contributions to postcolonial theory, its dark and gripping narrative draws its urgency from lived experience. Few scholars today have the courage to write so poetically, and few books manage to combine theoretical sophistication with emotional depth. In the myriad of academic publications on the subject, *The Refugee Abyss* stands out!

Katja Franko, *Professor of Criminology, University of Oslo*

This deeply moving book demands our commitment from the start. We learn from people who have experienced some of the worst that humans can inflict on one another. We are invited to listen, to see, and to feel. It is a profound and ultimately uplifting experience, despite the horrors described.

Mary Bosworth, *Professor of Criminology, University of Oxford*

This book plumbs the depths of some of the darkest places in human experience. But rather than leaving us there, it offers to lift us from the pit by gathering the poetic traces through which we can find restoration and relation. It is essential reading for anyone who cares about human relationships.

Fergus McNeill, *Professor of Criminology and Social Work, University of Glasgow*

In this powerful and timely intervention, Hyab Yohannes performs the urgent task of unsilencing voices, recovering stories buried deep in the 'refugee abyss'. In the process, he counters the anonymising, dehumanising, depoliticising conditions of this oppressive necropolitical reality. The book deploys Edouard Glissant's acentric, relational thought in pioneering ways that transcend geographies and histories. Challenging stubbornly oppressive grammars of coloniality, The Refugee Abyss ultimately asserts poetry and poetics as steadfast traces of an emergent political imaginary.

Charles Forsdick, *Drapers Professor of French, University of Cambridge*

The Refugee Abyss

In defiance of the refugee abyss, this book presents the flesh of pained bodies and the breath of displaced voices, contributing to the thread of traces yet to be forged and the politics yet to emerge, in a world where Relation takes precedence.

The book unfolds in several traces. First, open wounds and scars represent the refugee abyss, revealing the onto-epistemic chains that silence displaced voices. These voices, through embodied subjects, recount their struggles in a world marked by violence. Second, the book questions the rights-based order, revealing how the human rights project is a new incarnation of the colonial civilising mission. It claims to elevate humanity, starting with those deemed uncivilised. Yet, its mask of benevolence, once upheld in the metropoles of empire, now appears hollow. Third, the book theorises the nation-state as a womb-abyss, a matrix that both births and consumes life. Fourth, it explores the refugee abyss as a realm of confinement and destitution, where lives are commodified, exploited, and destroyed. Fifth, it shifts from open wounds to the poetics of refuge, illustrating how life persists in the shadows of rights and laws, while death is inflicted through them. Finally, it reflects on untamed life, emerging from wounds and scars as a proclamation of the unfamiliar and enduring.

This book will be of interest to students and scholars of criminology, criminal justice, and refugee studies. It will also appeal to political scientists and policymakers interested in issues of citizenship, human rights, and decoloniality.

Hyab Teklehaimanot Yohannes, Lecturer in Forced Migration and Decolonial Education at the University of Glasgow, researches decoloniality, poetics, and political theory.

Routledge Studies in Criminal Justice, Borders and Citizenship

Globalizing forces have had a profound impact on the nature of contemporary criminal justice and law more generally. This is evident in the increasing salience of borders and mobility in the production of illegality and social exclusion. *Routledge Studies in Criminal Justice, Borders and Citizenship* showcases contemporary studies that connect criminological scholarship to migration studies and explore the intellectual resonances between the two. It provides an opportunity to reflect on the theoretical and methodological challenges posed by mass mobility and its control. By doing that, it charts an intellectual space and establishes a theoretical tradition within criminology to house scholars of immigration control, race, and citizenship including those who traditionally publish *either* in general criminological *or* in anthropological, sociological, refugee studies, human rights and other publications.

Edited by
Prof José A. Brandariz, ECRIM, University of A Coruña
Prof Maggy S Y Lee, The University of Hong Kong
Katja Franko, University of Oslo

Border Criminologies From The Periphery
Cross-national Conversations on Bordered Penalty
Edited by José A. Brandariz, Giulia Fabini, Cristina Fernández-Bessa and Valeria Ferraris

Ambivalent Humanitarianism and Migration Control
Colonial legacies and the Experiences of Migrants in Mexico
Erika Herrera Rosales

The Mobility Control Apparatus
Getting to the Core of Crimmigration in the Schengen Area
Maartje van der Woude

For more information about this series, please visit: https://www.routledge.com/criminology/series/CJBC

The Refugee Abyss

Hyab Teklehaimanot Yohannes

Routledge
Taylor & Francis Group
LONDON AND NEW YORK

First published 2026
by Routledge
4 Park Square, Milton Park, Abingdon, Oxon OX14 4RN

and by Routledge
605 Third Avenue, New York, NY 10158

Routledge is an imprint of the Taylor & Francis Group, an informa business

British Library Cataloguing-in-Publication Data
A catalogue record for this book is available from the British Library

ISBN: 978-1-032-56794-5 (hbk)
ISBN: 978-1-032-56795-2 (pbk)
ISBN: 978-1-003-43719-2 (ebk)

DOI: 10.4324/9781003437192

Typeset in Sabon
by KnowledgeWorks Global Ltd.

As a defiance
of the abyss that stretches—past, present,
and imagined future—we offer this book:
a flesh of pained bodies,
a breath of displaced voices,
to the traces yet to be forged,
to the politics yet to be born,
in a world where Relation
takes precedence.

Contents

Un-Foreword *x*
Acknowledgements *xi*
Series Editor Introduction *xiii*

Introduction 1

1 Open Wounds and Scars 10

2 The Right of the Rightless 27

3 The Nation-State as a Womb-Abyss 50

4 Realities Within the Refugee Abyss 77

5 From Sea-camp to Metropole 105

6 Poetics of Refuge 133

Conclusion 165

Index *175*

Un-Foreword

This book is born from flesh and bone,
disfigured faces, tears unknown,
displaced voices, underground cells.
So too lies the true book cover:
in this un-foreword, beneath the surface
of the publisher's prescribed design.
From this cover – this un-foreword –
begin the poetic traces that unfold.

Figure 0.1 Original book cover designed by Robel Solomon, commissioned by the author.

Acknowledgements

Our deepest gratitude begins with the people whose stories, witnessings, testimonies, and poetic traces have revealed the open wounds and enduring scars, the stifled grief and silenced rage, the unmarked graves and forsaken bodies within the depths of the refugee abyss. We are profoundly thankful for the courage, humility, and grace it has taken to unearth these poetics, digging into the marrow of flesh and bone to shape the very essence of this book. The open wounds, the scars laid bare, the tears shed, and the rage and joys celebrated form the foundational pillars upon which this work stands. Equally, we are moved by the trust placed in us to give voice to these shared experiences.

To our parents and families—both those present and those who have become ancestors—our gratitude is immeasurable. Words cannot fully capture the depth of their guidance, love, and presence in both life and loss. We humbly acknowledge this inadequacy and refrain from attempting to encapsulate what transcends expression.

We extend our sincere thanks to Professors Alison Phipps and Fergus McNeill, our mentors and exemplars. They have been our steady points of reference, sources of inspiration, and unwavering support, offering wisdom that is as personal as it is professional. Their constancy has been a gift beyond measure.

We are profoundly grateful to the friends, institutions, cultures, and languages that have made this book possible. Among many, we offer heartfelt thanks to Dr. Samson Maekele Tsegay, Dr. Tesfalem Habte Yemane, and Zeraslasie Redie Shiker, whose friendship and scholarship have enriched this work immeasurably. We are also deeply thankful to Dr. Camillia Kong, Dr. Tawona Sithole, Dr. Esa Aldegheri, Dr. Sarah Stewart, and Pinar Aksu for their steadfast support, invaluable feedback, and insights into the conceptual and philosophical discussions that underpin this book.

Our deepest appreciation also extends to the UNESCO Chair in Refugee Integration through Education, Languages, and the Arts, the School of Education, and the University of Glasgow for providing the resources, intellect, and shared joy that have made this study possible. Lauren Roberts, Bella

Hoogeveen, Jennifer McArthur, and Rebecca Rae, your past and present contributions to this work are appreciated beyond words.

We extend our gratitude to Robel Solomon for his thoughtful and inspiring cover design, which emerges from beneath the surface of the publisher's prescribed design, unfurling its own unique beauty and poetics. Our heartfelt thanks also go to Karen Gorden, whose carefully curated photographs enrich the book with depth and beauty. Both the book cover and photographs were made possible through the generous support of *The Chancellor's Fund* at the University of Glasgow. We are deeply grateful for both the funding and the flexibility it afforded us.

A special thank you to Professor Katja Franko for her unwavering support throughout the writing, editing, and publication of this book. We are equally grateful to Professor Katja Franko and Dr. Teresa Piacentini for their guidance and examination of the PhD research that laid the groundwork for this book.

To the publisher, Routledge, along with the administrators, copyeditors, and series editors, we extend our gratitude for your collaboration, support, and tireless efforts in bringing this publication to life. It has been a privilege to work alongside you on this journey.

To the friends, colleagues, and strangers we have not named, we extend our deepest gratitude, for you have contributed to this work in ways both seen and unseen.

Series Editor Introduction

Routledge *Studies in Criminal Justice, Borders and Citizenship* showcases contemporary studies that connect criminological scholarship to migration studies and explores the intellectual resonances between the two. It provides an opportunity to reflect on the theoretical and methodological challenges posed by mass mobility and its control. Inaugurated in 2013, the series sets out the cutting edge of scholarship in the field of border criminology and related disciplines.

Hyab Teklehaimanot Yohannes's *The Refugee Abyss* offers a unique, deeply moving and thought-provoking examination of the lived experiences and unacknowledged voices of refugees, displaced people and those seeking asylum, primarily from Eritrea. Through first-hand accounts of the ordeals, vulnerability and healing, expressed through poetry and other forms of displaced voices, Yohannes raises key questions about 'who has the right to be heard' in a period of hardening politics, rhetoric and law. The chapters highlight the ongoing impacts of colonialism and neo-colonialism on border control and mobility and the racialised systems of precarity, violence and indignity inflicted upon non-citizens in multiple sites, stretching from the deserts and sea-camps to shantytowns and the metropoles. More significantly, the book is a poignant reminder of the politics of knowledge production and the importance of supporting people on the move to write and tell their own stories and pushing the boundaries of academic scholarship on borders and citizenship.

Maggy Lee
The University of Hong Kong

Introduction

'Does the world know we exist?'

This profound question haunts this book, urging us to reflect on a condition we term the refugee abyss. It emerges from the increasingly pervasive experience of this abyss, voiced by those whose existence has become undesirable in a world that is not only indifferent to their suffering but often predicated upon their death. Drawing on Édouard Glissant's *Poetics of Relation (2009)*, the 'abyss' is understood as both a site of profound suffering and a space of potential transformation and relation. Glissant emphasises that the abyss is ungraspable and opaque, embodying both devastation and possibility. The refugee abyss represents a state where life is torn apart by deep, open wounds and enduring scars. It also reflects an existential questioning of one's own being and the process of becoming-with.

The refugee abyss is imposed upon refugees—ourselves included, as former and current refugees—through a series of meticulously orchestrated stages. In fact, the pronouns 'us' and 'we' are used throughout the book as plurivocal carriers of both the participants' and the primary author's voices. The refugee abyss, which we confront through a plurivocal voice, first manifests as the loss of safety, home, and self. This begins with the stripping away of human dignity in homelands and places of belonging, driven by organised violence, uncontrollable terror, or relentless disaster. Among the most devastating forms of organised violence, and the primary focus of this book, is state violence perpetuated by oppressive regimes. This violence extinguishes the possibility of a dignified life, forcing people from their homes and communities while offering no shield against the obliteration of lives, livelihoods, and futures. At its worst, state violence leads to the horrors of ethnic cleansing, genocide, civil wars, and religious persecution. It plants deep terror in the hearts of those who can no longer live safely in their own lands or among their own kin and communities. State violence, underpinned by the shadows of colonial histories, is a major driver of forced displacement, particularly in what Mbembe (2001) terms the 'postcolony'. Eritrea provides a poignant case study of such organised and generalised state violence, with the mechanisms of its brutality and terror explored in subsequent chapters.

DOI: 10.4324/9781003437192-1

It is important to note from the outset that the widespread violence in Eritrea occurs in a context where the notion of being a rights-bearing subject or the rule of law is completely absent.

Equally destructive is the violence wrought by armed groups and terror organisations. These forces, emerging from the vacuum left by collapsing governments or through invasion, conquest, and domination, perpetuate horrors against which states are powerless or unwilling to act. The forced displacements in Sudan, Ethiopia, and Libya illustrate the devastating consequences of such violence, leaving countless lives shattered and communities torn asunder. These countries are among the major destinations and transit hubs for Eritrean refugees, whose realities are explored in this book.

Unabated disasters further compound these tragedies. Extreme poverty, environmental catastrophes, climate change, global inequality, and failing humanitarian systems consign millions to the limbo of forced displacement. Refugee camps across Africa, East Asia, and the Middle East are stark reminders of a world unable—or unwilling—to address the conditions that devastate lives, cause forced displacement, and extinguish hope.

With their very existence at stake, those afflicted by violence, terror, and disaster are driven to flee their homelands in search of safety and the hope of a dignified life elsewhere. Yet, fleeing does not end their suffering; instead, it ushers them deeper into the refugee abyss, where they bear existential wounds and scars. Forced displacement condemns them to a state where, as Fanon (1986) poignantly explains, humanity is severed from the body, with the former becoming the first victim of murder. This severing of the human from the body reduces displaced people to mere flesh and bone, stripped of any life beyond their biological condition. These bare bodies are then cast into the darkest corners of existence—suffocated at brutal borders, left to vanish in desolate camps, tortured to death in spaces of horror, claimed by lifeless deserts and treacherous seas, hunted by state and non-state actors in cities and slums, confined and murdered both in movement and in immobility.

The refugee abyss is unending. The murder of humanity creates a condition in which corporeal bodies lose control over their own movements, faces, sexualities, and identities. Violence is inflicted to ensure that even the smallest expression of joy is accompanied by shame, humiliation, fear, and pain, culminating, inevitably, in death, even if it is death in life. Such bodies are reduced to flesh that embodies the cry, scream, and wail, their voices silenced except in expressions of suffering. They experience the world fractured into zones of disposables and zones of humans, where the torment and destruction of bare bodies are seen as necessary to maintain the political order and its accompanying values and rights. The zones of disposability, which this book refers to as the belly of the refugee abyss, are spaces where calculated, contained, and deliberate death is enacted.

It is worth noting that colonial fantasies, once confined to distant lands, are now re-enacted within the nation-state and the metropole, under the guise of asylum. What was once inflicted upon so-called 'savages' in the plantation, the jungle, and the colonial frontier is now visited upon displaced people seeking refuge. The nation-state and its seat of power, the metropole, have become a new nomos, a womb-abyss, where violence unfolds in broad daylight for all to witness. Daily border violence, police brutality, the cruelty of the asylum system, the legitimisation of harm through law, and forced removals have become normalised spectacles. The asylum process itself is deployed as a confessionary system, designed to reduce those seeking refuge to accessible and transparent bodies that can either be granted asylum or forcibly removed at the will of a legislative body. In this new reality, the wounds of colonial violence are reopened and lived anew, ensuring that no refuge remains for those cast into the refugee abyss, as was the case with the Windrush scandal in the UK (Gentleman, 2019).

The refugee abyss, however, is not without its survivors, for it does not necessarily lead to absolute annihilation. In truth, the very existence and endurance of the abyss hinges upon the (de)humanisation and (de)existence of survivors as its necessary condition. It is equally true that one must exist to ask and confront existential questions: Does the world know we exist? The very act of posing such a question reveals a weariness in the authors, worn by the world we inhabit. These authors are victims and survivors of the refugee abyss, bearing witness to both their death and survival. Their experiences shape their awareness of their own being and becoming, and of the others they encounter. In other words, they do not merely express radical dissent; they also extend an invitation to imagine a new world, a new life, and a new form of knowledge.

Thus, this book is an invocation of what has been silenced and erased, an effort to grieve what has been rendered ungrievable and to give voice to what has been deemed unsayable. It stands not only as a lament for lost lives and displaced knowledge but as a 'displaced voice' itself, challenging colonial logics and structures of power, existence, and understanding. At its heart lies a journey through the open wounds and enduring scars of those forced into exile, tracing their experiences through the abyss of forced displacement, dispossession, and dehumanisation while imagining the possibility of dignity and life beyond the refugee abyss. It seeks to offer conceptual, empirical, and practical reflections where fixed and rooted identities dissolve, colonial structures are contested, and new ways of being and relating emerge. The book follows displaced people from the open wounds of profound indignity to the scars that remain as markers of victimhood and survival. It seeks not only to examine the enduring pain inflicted by histories of violence but also to reimagine a path toward relational co-existence, even amid the difficulties of the refugee abyss.

Through poetic traces, the book confronts the precarious realities of forced migration, cautiously linking the 'open boats' of the Atlantic slave trade to the precarious migrant boats crossing treacherous waters today, and to the sprawling metropoles that continue to haunt the world. It examines the realities of refugees, displaced people, and those seeking asylum—primarily from Eritrea—while reflecting on the broader condition of the refugee in our time. These labels, though shifting, illuminate the same reality: a state of forced displacement, a relationship gripped by violence, and a paradox that perpetuates a racialised gaze and a grammar of coloniality. The realities these labels describe create a condition where one breathes without truly living, where one suffers the consequences of an abyss that has not yet been grasped, if it is even graspable at all.

The Journey

Conceptually and structurally, this book offers original insights into how poetic traces can inspire a shift from violability, coloniality, and destitution to healing, restoration, and relationality. It employs an investigative, relational, and non-exclusive poetic approach, which we have termed the 'Journey', integrating philosophical concepts into poetic expressions for decolonial inquiry. In the Glissantian sense, the Journey signifies a wandering through the abyss, moving from open wounds and scars to acentric relationalities. As an approach, the Journey not only exposes the disfigurement and pain wrought by the refugee abyss but also envisions relational futures. It calls for a physical and metaphysical reorientation of the foundations of knowledge, being, and power across temporal, spatial, aesthetic, and historical dimensions. It is an undertaking in the poetics of restorative thinking, tracing, creating, being-in-common, and becoming-with in the world (Mbembe, 2022).

In this Journey, the book spans an unyielding vocation to uncover bodies, voices, and sedimented traces buried deep within the refugee abyss. The poetics of the book do not belong to one author alone. It is not a singular claim nor an absolute song, but rather poetic traces woven from many lives. It is an account of lived experience, embodied knowledge, and displaced voices drawn from over a hundred participants who have lived through—and continue to live in—the ordeals of the refugee abyss. The book contains stories that dominate its pages with poignancy, alongside others whose silent conditions and perishability resonate through them. The primary author has folded their own story, as a former refugee, into the anonymous accounts of all the participants of the study. Each trace has been intertwined, anonymised, and studied as a displaced voice. For this reason, we choose the pronoun 'we' over the singular 'I', as this work breathes through collective efforts. Throughout the writing, we intentionally move from the collective experiences of refugees to the specific participants and our unique stories. We weave between the poetic and the political, never with the intention of being autobiographical. At all times, the authors' position remains fluid, for our poetics is not focused on the individual, but rather on the multiple and the relational. Our shared poetics, stories, and narratives, as Glissant (2009) writes, 'are perhaps like long breaths without beginning or end' (p. 38). They defy any notion of fixed and singular identities.

In sharing our ordeals and poetics, we endured the unbearable, listened to each other's grief and joys, and contemplated together. The participants, including the primary author, have survived underground cells buried deep beneath the surface, crossed borders ravaged by violence, endured the barren tents of refugee camps, and lived on the edges of shantytowns. We have wandered police cities shadowed by unyielding forces, traversed deserts that devour lives, followed rivers that stretch across borders, and crossed sea-camps that cradle both life and death. We live in the margins and depths of the abyss of the womb-abyss, where all things seem to both begin and end, caught in its unrelenting violence. From these depths, we reflect not only on what is but also on the possibilities that lie beyond, however unrealistic they may appear. From traces of incompleteness, silence, tremors, ruderal landscapes, and the vulgarity of certain ordeals and lost lives, our displaced voices emerge, crying out in a desperate call to reimagine the world anew from a position of acentric relationality.

At times—in fact, so often—we found ourselves brimming with words, descriptors, and stories, yet they remained fragmented, haunted, stunned, and often hopeless. Making sense of these traces of poetics has been a trembling experience, resonating with the tremors of those who carry knowledge, bearing the wounds and scars from which we long to heal. At other times, writing this book led us to moments when words eluded us entirely. In these instances, we turned our gaze to the sites of our open wounds and scars, including those on the body, at the borders, on our faces, in unmarked graves, exhumed remains, in movements, and within systems, searching for poetic traces amid the ruins and carceral spaces. We often experienced that language does not fully describe the depth of conversations punctuated by tears, silences, and hugs. Hence, we turn to poetry and poetic forms of expression to name the unspeakable and to endure the unendurable. We even formatted our stunned revelations in poetic forms (Badwan and Phipps, 2024), sketching traces and rhythms of breath, capturing the essence of our displaced voices.

The formatting of our revelations in poetry serves multiple purposes. First, it seeks to disrupt the grammar of coloniality that portrays the refugee as both a paradoxical figure of vulnerability and suffering on the one hand, and a threat to the principles of the nation-state on the other, one that must be swiftly contained by any means (see Agamben, 1995; Yohannes, 2023). Against such grammars of coloniality, we remain steadfast in our poetry and poetics. Our poetic traces enable us, as Agamben (2014) writes, to destitute the 'communicative and informative function' of language, 'in order to open it to a new possible use' (p. 70). This new use, we hope, opens onto an irreducible relation grounded on shared vulnerability and responsibility towards one another. Second, suffocated in our breath and feeling the pain of our open wounds deep in our bones, we sense we have nothing to lose. Our only option is to trace and express our poetics from this position, for our poetics are the breaths through which we emerge, as Maldonado-Torres (2008) eloquently writes, 'out of the impossibility of demanding anything whatsoever' (p. 136). In fact, as we write this book, many friends, colleagues, and participants in this study confront the spectre of death in war zones and perilous journeys. With humility and vulnerability, we present their poetic words, inviting engagement through care, curiosity, and critical reflection. Finally, in alignment with Lorde (2018), we 'feel' and relate beyond breathlessness and pain so that we 'can be free' (p. 4).

Book structure

The Journey of this book unfolds in seven *traces*: the open wounds, the rights of the rightless, the womb-abyss, the refugee-abyss, from Sea-camp to Metropole, the poetics of refuge, and untamed life. Each trace corresponds to a chapter (with the last one serving as a conclusion to the book), which we summarise succinctly below.

Chapter 1, the *first trace*—Open Wounds and Scars, begins by recounting open wounds and enduring scars. The book intentionally refuses to start from the system or the systemic, instead foregrounding embodied knowledge by tracing the lived, felt, witnessed, (un)marked, and forgotten experiences, including those left behind or perished without a trace. The open wounds and scars, as signifiers of the refugee abyss and its onto-epistemic shackles, are the sources of displaced voices through which embodied subjects express their ordeals and engage with the world in exteriority. The displaced voices represent poetics of ceaseless transformation, where emergent epistemic utterances arise. Foregrounding these displaced voices and the poetics they evoke is essential for recognising refugees as 'questioning, speaking, writing, and creative subject[s]' (Maldonado-Torres, 2016, p. 29). This approach opens the possibility of shedding the masks that conceal the open wounds, excavating their layers, and exploring the questions buried beneath the constraints of systematic knowledge.

Chapter 2, the *second trace*—The Right of the Rightless, interrogates the foundations of the rights-based order, examining its roots in 'coloniality' and raciality. Coloniality refers to the creation of 'zones of being human and not being human or not being human enough' (Maldonado-Torres, 2016, p. 13). Emerging from the abyss of slavery and colonisation, coloniality has evolved to obscure its mechanisms of inflicting open wounds while continuing to project its physical and metaphysical matrices of power on a global scale. Coloniality underpins the systems of knowledge, power, and existence that classify and differentiate humanity along racial lines, deeming some lives more valuable than others and relegating others to the realm of what we term the refugee abyss. It describes the refugee as a form of (de)humanity and (de) existence within the confines of the rights-based order. From this perspective, the chapter fundamentally challenges the foundations of the rights-based order and its embedded grammars of coloniality.

Chapter 3, the *third trace*—The Nation-State as a Womb-Abyss, has two aims. First, it offers a theoretical conceptualisation of the nation-state as a 'womb-abyss' in the Glissantian sense, a matrix that simultaneously births and consumes life. It explores how the womb-abyss underpins the nation-state, functioning both as a juridico-political system and as a condition of existence that shapes human experience within and beyond its borders, along with the abyss it perpetuates. The central question here concerns how state power is formed, administered, and projected within the womb-abyss, regulating the (im)mobilities of populations in an era of global (b)ordering. Second, the chapter examines Eritrea as a postcolonial example of the womb-abyss. Following its independence, Eritrea descended into a self-colonising state, prioritising its sovereignty over the lives of its people. Through this case study, the chapter explores modalities of punishment and control, where life itself and its inevitable perishability (death) are subsumed by systems of sovereignty and governmentality asserting power over both life and death, existence and de-existence. Together, these objectives provide insight into the refugee abyss, both within and beyond the belly of the womb-abyss.

Chapter 4, the *fourth trace*—The Refugee Abyss, presents the refugee abyss in a poignant and often poetic manner. The chapter examines the circumstances that compel people to risk their lives in the hope of finding safety elsewhere. This is primarily driven by the relentless deprivation of rights, home, and community, followed by violent (b)ordering regimes that devour the essence of life itself. In the refugee abyss, movement entails risking one's life in the hope of finding it elsewhere or facing death. To remain immobilised is to endure death in life. The belly of the refugee abyss confines lives, stifles cries of protest, transforms dreams into nightmares, and perpetuates destitution through limited resources and extreme poverty. Within the belly, refugee lives are treated as disposable commodities, sold to the highest bidder, subjected to sexual abuse, and sometimes killed for no reason other than the act of killing itself. Some are buried alive, while others vanish without a trace, forever lost. By exploring the belly of the refugee abyss, stretching from places of origin to the sea-camp, the chapter traces the conditions that first inflicted the open wounds and scars.

Chapter 5, the *fifth trace*—From Sea-camp to Metropole, traces the perilous journeys of refugees from the sea-camp to the metropole. The chapter demonstrates that, just as the plantations represented the 'belly' of the slave abyss (Hartman, 2016), the 'asylum colonies' stretching from the deserts and sea camps to the borders and metropoles exemplify the belly of our times (Yohannes et al., 2024). Asylum colonies are marked by a 'double negation': the denial of existence, where refugees' lives are reduced to conditions of 'unliveability and ungrievability', and the denial of recognition, where their precarious (de)existence remains unknowable and unacknowledged (Yohannes et al., 2024, p. 11). Much like the abyss of the open boats in the trans-Atlantic slave trade, the inflatable boats in the sea-camp symbolise an abyss marked by unending cycles of floating and sinking, appearing and disappearing, and giving rise to both life and death. Children are born on migrant boats only to perish in the blink of an eye. Similarly, the metropole, with its bordering and asylum regimes, constitutes the ultimate expression of the refugee abyss, one that incessantly dehumanises those seeking refuge and suppresses their claims to asylum. With displaced voices uttered but unheard, people seeking asylum are treated as nobodies with no voices in the colonial grammars of the metropole.

Chapter 6, the *six trace*—Poetics of Refugee, marks a significant shift in the Journey, transitioning from open wounds and scars to the poetics of refugees and acentric relationality. In this chapter, the border, the camp, the desert, the sea, and the destination lands are not entirely barren; they are spaces through which the trace runs, connecting not only the suffering of open wounds but also the displaced voices and poetics that emerge from these seemingly hopeless places. Even in the darkness, violence, destitution, and solitude of the refugee abyss, as Glissant (2009) poetically expresses, 'the trace was lived as one of the places of survival' (p. 9). The trace of life in spaces devoid of rights and laws shows that life was not lived outside of rights and laws, but rather in their shadows; death, on the other hand, was inflicted with rights and laws. We encounter, here in the place of habitation and destination, traces that connect us with the poetics of 'over there', from where we come. The trace of our scars runs through the fragments of ruderal spaces where healing and restoration begin. These seeds of survival reorient the Journey away from the violence perpetuated by the structure and conditions of the refugee abyss, towards what we call acentric relationality.

Final chapter, the *last trace—the Untamed Life,* concludes the book by reflecting on what we call the untamed life, which implies that which emerges beyond open wounds and scars. The untamed life proclaims the unfamiliar and the emergent, birthed from the traces of open wounds, scars, ruins, and (de)existence. The conclusion offers poetic gestures and humble invitations.

Finally, we must note that this book comes with a warning, dear reader. You are being invited to bear witness, through our words, poetry, and images, to profound vulnerability, cruelty, and vulgarity, but also to resourcefulness, creativity and new orientations for being, knowing, and relating. We assure you that if our words leave you feeling raw and emotional, you are not only justified but courageous enough to meet the demands of our times. These are the times in which we all, including you, dear reader, live and die. So, keep reading—if you can. Keep lamenting, praying, singing if you can, and crying. Even better, express yourself through poetry, move your body in dance or song, or connect with nature. Do not forget to make coffee, step away, and then return.

If your intellect and instinct tell you that these wounds and scars are too unbearable to witness through our words and poetics, we understand, provided you try to engage with our invitations and our outstretched hands waiting to meet yours in irreducible poetics of relation. You will find our invitations and waiting hands in the last two chapters, where you will encounter little resistance from our calloused hands, wounded bodies, disfigured faces, and haunting memories, all striving to heal and transform into liveable lives.

If you still resist, we will remain with our cherished 'opacity' and honour your own. As Glissant (2009) reminds us, 'opacity' is our shared principle, and through it, we remain in relation.

References

Agamben, G. (1995) We Refugees. *Symposium: A Quarterly Journal in Modern Literatures*, 49 (2), 114–119.
Agamben, G. (2014) What Is a Destituent Power? *Environment and Planning D: Society and Space*, 32 (1), 65–74.
Badwan, K. and Phipps, A. (2024) *Keep Telling Of Gaza*. Berlin: Sídhe Press.
Fanon, F. (1986) *Black Skin, White Masks*. London: Pluto Press.
Gentleman, A. (2019) *The Windrush Betrayal: Exposing the Hostile Environment*. London: Guardian Faber.
Glissant, É. (2009) *Poetics of Relation*. Ann Arbor, Michigan: University of Michigan Press.
Hartman, S. (2016) The Belly of the World: A Note on Black Women's Labors. *Souls*, 18 (1), 166–173.
Lorde, A. (2018) *The Master's Tools Will Never Dismantle the Master's House*. London: Penguin Books.
Maldonado-Torres, N. (2008) *Against War: Views from the Underside of Modernity*. Durham, North Carolina: Duke University Press.
Maldonado-Torres, N. (2016) *Outline of Ten Theses on Coloniality and Decoloniality*. Paris: Frantz Fanon Foundation.
Mbembe, A. (2001) *On the Postcolony*. Berkeley, California: University of California Press.
Mbembe, A. (2022) *The Earthly Community: Reflections on the Last Utopia*. Rotterdam: V2_Publishing.
Yohannes, H.T. (2023) Refugee Trafficking in A Carceral Age: A Case Study of the Sinai Trafficking. *Journal of Human Trafficking*, 9(1), 33–47.
Yohannes, H.T., Yemane, T.H., and Wangari-Jones, P. (2024) Chapter 1: The Hostile Environment, Covid-19, and the Creation of Asylum Colonies in the UK', in G.K. Bhambra, L. Mayblin, K. Medien, and M. Viveros (Eds) *The Sage Handbook of Global Sociology*, pp. 3–16. London: SAGE.

1 Open Wounds and Scars

Introduction

To breathe life into this book and make its poetics possible, we must scratch into our own lacerated bodies, disfigured faces, and unmarked graves, drawing forth blood, fibre, and bone in search of meaning, reason, and relation. Clearly, scratching injured bodies is endlessly and intolerably painful, yet nothing remains to provide this work with a starting point or an anchor to reveal its poetic traces, except open wounds and scars. Among us (at least among the participants in this study), there is no body left unscathed; no face not disfigured. No part of us remains uninjured by the forces that inflict lacerations and scars. Each of us bears the weight of both physical and mental wounds and scars. Open wounds and scars are indelible markers fixed deeply into our bodies and souls by the torments of the refugee abyss, with life suspended between the fragility of survival and the imminence of death.

While the effects of the refugee abyss may vary among displaced people, we are profoundly marked by open wounds and enduring scars. The wounds recounted by the participants in this study are countless, each bearing witness to unspeakable suffering. Among the most immediate and visible afflictions are languishing in underground cells, enduring the agony of physical and psychological torture, bearing the cruelty of rape and sexual violence, starving to death in merciless deserts or inhospitable camps, succumbing to malnutrition and the slow deterioration of the body, illnesses caused by neglect and harsh conditions, the relentless exhaustion of struggling to stay alive, and injuries from violence such as gunshots, beatings, or explosions at borders.

Moreover, forced displacement from our homes and communities left us battered by the chaos of escape. Separation from loved ones inflicts wounds of profound grief. Many remain trapped between borders, caught in a liminal existence with no clear path forward. Death at the hands of human traffickers or during perilous journeys claims the fate of far too many. Beyond physical suffering lies a deeper, more insidious pain: the loss of identity and belonging, a severance from cultural and social relations, and a sense of alienation that tears at the spirit. The self becomes fragmented, splintered by displacement and the rupture from one's history, culture, and heritage. Trauma from the

DOI: 10.4324/9781003437192-2

abyss lingers both within and beyond the refugee experience, carrying the existential pain of invisibility, unintelligibility, and unworthiness it imposes.

The racialised experiences and the constant fear of being othered gnaw at the soul. Dehumanisation strips away dignity, leaving us unable to live fully, mourn our losses, honour our dead, or preserve our memories. Dreams shatter, aspirations for a better life dissolve, and personal and collective histories are disturbed. Once-flourishing communities are left adrift, bereft of a past, trapped in the pain of the present, and denied a future. Hope withers under cycles of despair, endless waiting, and confinement. The human spirit erodes under the relentless weight of systemic oppression and marginalisation.

These wounds are not only borne by our bodies but also by the very essence of our existence. They rob us of our status, recognition, and humanity itself. Perpetual uncertainty and instability become the rhythm of life, with the wounds and scars of violence inscribed too deeply for time to heal. Even in moments of fleeting joy, in laughter or shared jokes, these open wounds and scars remain ever-present. They run deep, cutting to the core of being and entwining with whatever future we might dare to imagine.

The question of what meaning, reason, and relation can be derived from open wounds and scars is the focus of this book, explored through poetic reflections in each chapter. Now, let us turn to the stories of those who bear these wounds and scars, along with the questions they invite us to consider. Behind every story we tell, deep wounds cut through flesh and bone, and tears resonate with memories as profound as the abyss itself.

Open wounds and scars

We present the following stories that exemplify open wounds and scars, and illustrate the questions addressed in this book.

The story of Medhin

Medhin is an Eritrean mother who, at the time of writing this book, lived in exile. In a face-to-face meeting, Medhin agreed to tell us her family story in detail. She began by sharing that her husband had passed away a few years prior after battling a chronic illness for almost a decade. Together, they had three sons and a daughter, all of whom tragically died. The three sons lost their lives in the successive wars with Ethiopia, with one falling during the battle for liberation and the other two in the recent border conflict. Sadly, her daughter drowned in the Mediterranean Sea while attempting to cross to Europe.

Medhin had never contemplated leaving her hometown, where she received love and support from childhood friends and close relatives. She had no desire to leave Eritrea, but circumstances forced her to do so after her only daughter fled the country to avoid the draft. She followed her daughter to a neighbouring country, where they lived together until her daughter made the fateful decision to embark on a risky journey that tragically claimed her life. Now, having lost her entire family, Medhin resides in exile and is cautious of returning to Eritrea due to the 'irregular' manner in which she left the country.

Losing her entire family one by one over the past decades, Medhin has endured immense grief. It has been challenging for her to come to terms with the fact that she was unable to bury any of her children. The death of her daughter has been particularly painful, as she had hoped to have her by her side in her old age, especially considering her declining health. Alone in exile, Medhin admitted to us that she had endured unparalleled grief. Comparing her life in exile to her childhood, Medhin lamented that she was born among 'mamets and hanetay' and that she had been a mamet herself before becoming 'an abandoned creature'. She expressed that frustration and a sense of guilt for being alive dominated her life. For her, simply existing was a nightmare, and this feeling was intensified by the fact that she was not alone in experiencing such a precarious existence as an Eritrean. When tracing her family history over the past 50 years, she recounted over a dozen relatives, both young and old, who had lost their lives in wars and perilous journeys to exile. In Medhin's view, perpetual war and inevitable exile were conditions of (de)existence that had been imposed on generations of Eritreans. When we asked her about the reality faced by Eritreans, she responded with a thought-provoking question: 'Where are our mamets and hanetays?' With this poignant question, Medhin directed us towards a socio-cultural interpretation of the grim reality Eritreans endure and the underlying events that led to it.

Translated literally, Medhin's question means 'Where are our heroines and heroes?' However, the words 'heroines' and 'heroes' do not precisely describe the meaning of the Tigrigna words mamet and hanetay. Mamet and Hanetay (in their singular forms) are archaic epithets that symbolise deep socio-anthropological meanings and social roles. The epithet of hanetay has a long history and is still prevalent in some parts of Eritrea. Hanetay is a masculine figure associated with a rare feat of killing a lion, which demonstrates semantic, metaphorical, and conceptual higher qualities. It is associated with courage, strength, ingenuity, and, to some extent, wisdom. For these reasons, a hanetay constitutes a higher social status; such a man is offered a special seat and dinner on ceremonial occasions, and his death generates the most poetic mourning. Hanetay is also dressed in specially designed costumes, some of which come from his victim's (the lion's) mane. Thus, Hanetay is an epithet of nobility that embodies what Bourdieu (1989) calls 'symbolic power' to articulate one's social status in relation to others. Nevertheless, if a war or an attack by an enemy were to happen, the hanetay is expected to protect his community like any other member. In traditional Eritrean patriarchal society, ethnic groups and subgroups functioned as subnational autonomous entities, and their sustained existence hinged on the willingness of their members to make sacrifices for the collective welfare.

While Hanetay represents an honourable masculine figure, mamet depicts a symbol of purity, beauty, and elegance in the community. Unlike hanetay, who must achieve exceptional feats, mamet acquires her totemic feminine figure through the effect of her body and meekness of wisdom on the perception of the community towards her. In the oral traditions and tales, there are no faults in mamet's beauty and elegance and no limits to her wisdom and intelligence. For generations, people have sung about mamet's beauty and celebrated her virtue. Even in contemporary Tigrigna songs and comedies, mamet features as an enchanted idol of romance, attractiveness, and wisdom. In the specified contexts and times, the epithet mamet carried a sense of respect and a symbol of righteousness.

Many older generations of Eritreans, like Medhin, have lived through the norms and traditions of the community, actively participated in the struggle for their country's independence, and witnessed the profound transformation that Eritrea has undergone. In present day Eritrea, both hanetay and mamet have not only suffered a loss of their social status but have also been forcibly displaced from their homes and communities, as discussed in the subsequent chapters. They find themselves in a realm of damnation, prompting Medhin's question.

The story of Alex

Alex's story is long and mired in war and detention. He was wounded in a battle, captured by enemy soldiers, and taken to a hospital. Fearing further detainment, he escaped to a transit country, only to be arrested by border security and indefinitely imprisoned in an underground cell. For nearly 15 years, he endured the darkest of prisons, devoid of light or any sense of time. Chained to the walls, his body bore fresh wounds from torture, yet he never ceased to cry, pray, and sing. As he told us, these were his only signs of life and (de)existence.

Alex did not know anybody in the country where he was detained. After discovering his story, we traced his family in his home country through friends who themselves were survivors of detention and trafficking. His father died of old age, and his only brother died while crossing the border to a neighbouring country. At the time we discovered Alex's story, his mother was the only person left. When we told her the news of her son, Alex, his mother informed us that Alex was martyred and that 'he is not Christ to resurrect himself'. The government had notified her that Alex died in the war, and she was receiving compensation. We found it incredibly difficult to convince Alex's mother that her son was still alive.

In the end, Alex's ceaseless dreaming and praying to see the light of day became a reality. After his release, Alex visited a neighbouring country to meet his mother. He later told us that the reunion was a 'clash of mixed emotions': grief and happiness. Alex's mother was elated to find her son after all those years of isolation and being told he had died. Alex admitted that he was shocked to hear about the deaths of both his father and only brother. For Alex, not being able to bury his father, mourn his brother's death, and support his mother during these years of grief were, in his words, 'devouring of life'. He lamented,

> All the years
> I wasted in prison,
> I did not exist;
> I (de)existed'.

Are such forms of death mournable anyway? What does it mean to (de) exist?

The story of 23 refugees

This story recounts the experience of a group of 23 refugees who endured unimaginable suffering on their journey from Sudan to Libya, en route to Europe. Among the 23 people were 5 children and 18 adults, including a pregnant mother with a five-year-old boy. One of the children, a teenage girl named Ariam, recounted the group's story to us during our fieldwork.

The refugees were kidnapped by traffickers shortly after crossing the Libyan border. While being driven towards a place called Ajdabiya in Libya, the kidnappers were involved in a car accident. Tragically, the pregnant mother lost her life in the accident, leaving her five-year-old son behind. In her final moments, the mother entrusted Ariam with the responsibility of looking after her young child. Ariam shared with us her immediate reaction,

> First, I cried
> and didn't know what to say.
> I was only 16 myself,
> but I am a human being.
> How could I leave
> a five-year-old child
> alone in the middle of a desert?

Tears dropped down Ariam's face as she answered her own question, stating,

> I would rather die with him
> than leave him in the desert.

Two other men, one of whom was a trafficker, also lost their lives in the incident.

After the injured survivors were transported to a local hospital by local herdsmen, only ten refugees were able to continue their journey, this time with the assistance of different intermediaries. As they continued their journey to Tripoli, the intermediaries' facilitation turned into trafficking, resulting in rape and subsequent killing of Frehiwet by the smugglers. Ariam recounted to us,

> During the journey,
> two smugglers took my 14-year-old friend
> at night and raped her....
> One of our group members attempted to intervene,
> but he was shot in the leg
> by one of the smugglers.

Ariam continued,

> Then, they brought back Frehiwet,
> dragging her along,
> her steps unsteady,
> her body shaking.
> She tried to warn me,
> 'you would rather die
> here, before the group,
> than be taken alone
> into the darkness
> by the traffickers'.

The traffickers, having understood her plea, slapped Frehiwet across the face and threw her to the ground. They then dug a small hole, placed her in it with her head down, and, as Ariam recalled,

> Buried her alive
> with the desert dust.

What kind of life do these refugees contain if it can be stripped of dignity and ultimately 'buried alive'? Does it even possess any essence of human life?

The Lampedusa tragedy

The island of Lampedusa, where nearly 400 people, primarily Eritreans, perished within minutes on 3 October 2013, is a symbol of the unprecedented loss of refugee lives in the Mediterranean Sea (Ambrosini, 2018, p. 104). These refugees had to navigate routes regulated by rogue powers such as powerful militias, human traffickers, and border guards before reaching the sea. Many thousands die at the hands of these rogue powers. Those who have witnessed the horrors of trafficking report that the obscenities and violence they endure are even more commonplace and brutal in lifeless deserts, infamous torture camps, detention facilities, and at borders. These are carceral coordinates where vulnerable refugees not only suffer visceral pain but also face effective annihilation. Their reality is one of unrelenting exposure to unconditional death.

The Mediterranean Sea becomes a new calamity for trafficking survivors. Those who manage to reach the western shores of the Mediterranean Sea risk their lives in a perilous maritime journey in pursuit of a glimmer of hope—what one participant termed 'freedom in view'. They struggle for survival against the tides of the Mediterranean Sea and the maritime borders of 'Fortress Europe' (see Smith, 2017; Ambrosini, 2018; Mainwaring 2019; Anderson, 2020). To cross the sea, refugees once again rely on intermediaries and traffickers, who transport them through irregular means in tightly packed, fragile, inflatable boats. Frequently, the traffickers abandon the refugees in the middle of the sea, leaving them to find their way to Europe or vanish in the vast expanse. For instance, Wulud described the experience of being abandoned in the middle of the sea on an overcrowded inflatable ship as akin to 'the end of the world'. Once adrift in the sea on inflatable boats, the refugees have only the stars for guidance, or they submit to the natural forces of the sea when the sun shines bright. The other option for refugees is to prepare for the possibility of dying at any moment. Wulud recalled,

> You pray
> for the high tides
> not to come your way,
> and if they come,
> you are defenceless;
> the tides turn the boat upside-down.

The apocalyptic image of drowning at sea and the untold stories of those who disappeared without a trace continue to haunt the families and relatives of the deceased, and the survivors who witnessed the tragedy. The story of a young Eritrean woman, Yohanna, who drowned off the coast of Lampedusa with her new-born baby still attached by its umbilical cord, continues to shock many Eritrean refugees in the diaspora. While Yohanna's death epitomises the perpetual threat of death that refugees face, her new-born baby was born into death. Alongside Yohanna was our childhood friend, Héluf, who was 'Born rightless, die[d] rightless'. These phrases come from the last text message we received from Héluf a few days before he passed away. He was trafficked to Libya, and we attempted to reach him on his phone to no avail. A week later, we learned that he had perished off the Italian island of Lampedusa.

The victims of the Lampedusa tragedy, their bodies laden with rightlessness, on fragile and overcrowded boats, are not treated as a loss or something mournable, but rather as disposable bodies. Recently, reports from relatives of the victims indicate that the bodies of their loved ones are being exhumed for re-examination and to make room for the burials of COVID-19 victims (see also Olivieri et al., 2018). Ironically, these disposable bodies were granted posthumous Italian citizenship, while the survivors of the tragedy had to wander Europe in search of a safe place to seek asylum. Their posthumously granted citizenship now seems as meaningless as their disposable bodies. The central question is: What kind of existence is afforded to these refugees if they can be born without rights and die without rights? Why is this so?

The story of Farés

Farés is a young Eritrean man whose destiny was shared with us by his elder brother. Born and raised in the lowlands of Eritrea, Farés' journey took a new turn in 2010. He deserted indefinite national service in Eritrea, fled the country, and sought refuge in Sudan, only to be abducted by traffickers and transported to Libya. After seven months of torturous captivity, Farés eventually escaped from the traffickers. His subsequent journey led him to toil in exploitative labour for a Libyan family for several months. Despite the hardships, he resolved to board an inflatable boat, joining numerous Eritrean refugees in the perilous hope of crossing the Mediterranean to reach Europe. Tragically, Farés' brother, Sada, told us:

> Farés perished
> without a trace,
> forever lost.
> We have heard
> nothing of him since.

The last trace of Farés dates back to the beginning of 2011.

A married young man and a father of two, Farés left behind a shattered family—his young wife, two children, and wider kin, including parents and siblings, consumed in the darkness of grief for their loved one who perished without a trace. Although it is almost certain that Farés is no longer alive, the absence of any trace sustains his vicarious presence in the hearts of his family. Left to grapple with the challenge of tracing a loved one who vanished without a trace, Sada expressed a poignant lament:

> We know he is no longer alive,
> yet we refuse to accept it.
> We will carry the burden of
> trying to trace the lost
> until our last breath.

This theme of tracing the untraceable recurs each time we remember friends, relatives, and strangers who vanished into the abyss of the sea, desert, or unknown. How does one live with these memories?

The story of Hatem

Hatem, one of the stateless refugees we encountered, was born to Eritrean parents in Sudan and raised in Sudan by a Sudanese family. At the age of five, his parents entrusted him to the care of a Sudanese family while they joined the Eritrean People's Liberation Front. However, they never returned, and Hatem can only vaguely remember any details about them or their background. He was raised by the Sudanese family until his early thirties, but after their passing, he was trafficked to Egypt. Hatem has no ties to Eritrea, his parents' country of origin, and has also lost any connection to Sudan, where he was born. The Sudanese family knew little about his parents' background beyond being their landlord when the parents lived in Sudan. Hatem remembers that even his current name is not his 'real name': 'As a child, my name was Habtom'.

The Sudanese family renamed him Hatem after their own son who died in a car accident. Before their death, the Sudanese family told Hatem that his parents had died in the liberation war fighting against Ethiopian colonisation.

Hatem described his trafficking experience as 'hell on earth'. Unlike other victims who have family and connections to assist them in gathering the ransom demanded by traffickers, Hatem had no one to turn to for help when he was held captive in Sinai. He explained,

> It wasn't just me;
> there were five of us
> in that torture room
> who had no family
> or relatives to contact.

Tragically, all four of the others were killed by the traffickers because they had no means to pay the ransom. Hatem was grateful to his fellow Eritrean survivors who raised funds for his release after they themselves were freed following the payment of their ransoms by their relatives. However, Hatem's ordeal continued when he was apprehended by Egyptian border security while attempting to leave Sinai. After spending several years in prison, he was deported to Sudan. Upon his deportation, he was once again detained by Sudanese authorities due to a lack of proper documentation to prove his nationality and residence status in Sudan. Hatem revealed, 'I bribed a Sudanese prison guard with the little money I had and managed to smuggle myself into Egypt'. In Egypt, he sought asylum, but his application was rejected due to his inability to prove his identity and present a 'credible' testimony of a well-founded fear of persecution from a specific state, despite being stateless. Hatem noted,

> The rejection
> from the UNHCR
> was the final blow
> in my already
> unbearable situation.

Three years after our initial conversation, we finally located Hatem again, this time in Italy. We began by asking him how he managed to reach Italy, and he replied,

> I sold one of my kidneys
> to fiancé the sea journey to Italy.

For a decade, Hatem has been trapped between trafficking, detention, and deportation, with no trace of his origins, no knowledge of how his parents died, and no sense of his own identity or home. 'My life', Hatem lamented, 'has been a journey through hell on earth'. In a world where human existence is intertwined with familial and national relations, the question arises as to how people like Hatem, who have had their sense of self and identity stripped away due to circumstances beyond their control, can find a sense of identity, home, and belonging.

The stories of Yonas, Zenawi, and Harnet

Yonas and Zenawi arrived in the UK over a decade and a half apart. Yonas crossed the sea, reaching Italy in the summer of 2002, while Zenawi arrived almost 16 years later. Yonas had a sister already living in the UK and continued his journey to join her after surviving the perilous journey through the Sahara and the Mediterranean. Upon arrival, he sought asylum in the UK, but his claim was rejected. His fingerprints had been taken in Italy, disqualifying him from seeking asylum in the UK under EU Dublin Regulation rules.

Eventually, immigration authorities arrested Yonas and deported him to Italy after a year in hiding with his sister. Unable to find work in Italy for nearly a year, he decided to try his luck in Switzerland. Aware that his fingerprints remained on record in Italy, Yonas changed his name and date of birth to avoid detection by Swiss immigration officials. As he recounted:

> My fingerprints
> were not identified
> by the Swiss authorities,
> and I got my papers.

Similarly, Zenawi had his fingerprints taken in Italy but was able to secure residence in Sweden after being deported to Italy from the UK. He revealed that the Swedish immigration authorities were unable to identify his fingerprints because he had slightly burned his fingertips and rubbed them against a rough surface. He added that this was a common strategy used by refugees to avoid identification and deportation. By obscuring his identity, Zenawi evaded another deportation to Italy, where he might have been trapped in limbo. Today, he runs a thriving small business in Sweden.

Harnet's journey was different but no less poignant. Harnet arrived in the UK as a child with her mother in late 2003. Tragedy struck two years later when her mother died of a chronic illness while they were still navigating the asylum process. After her mother's death, Harnet was left without legal status for nearly 16 years. Her mother's asylum claim was withdrawn upon her passing, and Harnet had to reapply on her own. Without documentation to prove her identity, having left her home country at such a young age, her application remained in limbo for years. Harnet tearfully lamented:

> I have no status,
> no home,
> no life.

For her, being trapped in the asylum system felt like 'being in a grave'.

These three stories illustrate a paradoxical relationship between transparency and obscurity in the lives of people seeking asylum. For Yonas and Zenawi, biometric identification through fingerprints aimed to fix them to Italy while stripping them of the possibility of seeking refuge elsewhere. This severed vital ties, including the chance to live with family members in other countries. Conversely, for Harnet, the lack of identification documents has immobilised her within a system that neither granted her asylum nor allowed her to move elsewhere. She remained stuck in a realm of perpetual vulnerability, dehumanisation, and illegality.

The open wounds and scars inflicted by asylum regimes haunt the very core of their human existence. Their names are erased, their bodies disfigured, their movement restricted, and the possibility of a dignified life made unattainable. What future can one imagine with no name, no status, no home, no life? What kind of (de)existence is theirs, where their bodies are identified only to be immobilised, illegalised, and deported—or kept in perpetual limbo, outside the protection of laws and rights?

From the Middle Passage to the refugee abyss

In his *Poetics of Relation (2009)*, Glissant offers a profound theorisation of what he calls the 'open boat' as an opening to an even deeper philosophical treatise: *Poetics of Relation*. 'The open boat', according to Glissant (2009, p. 6), is a 'womb abyss' that bears the abyss slaves have suffered, giving birth to life and death, existence and de-existence. In Glissant's philosophy, the abyss represents the catastrophe, the (un)known, the (un)graspable, and the opaque. It also serves as a conceptual space where new possibilities, opportunities, knowledge, and ways of relating emerge. The abyss challenges rigid identities, specific forms of relationships, fixed ways of being, and singular modes of thinking. It symbolises the entirety of depth and breadth within Relation. Relation, according to Glissant (2009), is 'totality in evolution, whose order is continually in flux and whose disorder one can imagine forever' (p. 133). Glissant theorises Relation as the philosophical *arché* of being in the 'Whole-World', preceding ontology (see Glissant 2020). According to Glissant, Relation is made possible through irreducible, unpredictable, and rhizomatic processes of 'creolization' (2009, p. 34).

In the journey through the abyss, the slaves suffered multiple abyssal calamities. In the first instance, they were forcibly removed from their place of habitation and community. This abyssal condition, to use Mbembe's terms, 'results from a triple loss: loss of a "home," loss of rights over his or her body, and loss of political status' (2003, p. 21). 'This triple loss', Mbembe further articulates, 'is identical to absolute domination, natal alienation, and social death (expulsion from humanity altogether)' (2003, p. 21). In the second instance, they were chained, loaded onto the boat, and transported across the sea like mere breathing bodies. Glissant poetically describes the open boat as being 'pregnant with as many dead as living under sentence of death' (2009, p. 6). In the final instance, the open boat arrived in the new world, where the slaves disembarked in an unfamiliar place, still bound in chains, alongside dead bodies, with many already having sunk to the seabed or become sustenance for fish. Following the abyss of the open boat, the slaves found themselves bound to a centuries-old abyss in the plantation or 'the belly of the world', as Hartman (2016) maintains.

The enslaved people's abyssal condition marks the original wounds endured by forcibly displaced people. Following slavery, colonialism emerged with its deadly forces, ravaging and exploiting bodies, cultures, nature, and knowledge. History and archival records demonstrate that centuries of colonial rule consigned the enslaved, their descendants, and the colonised alike to what Fanon (1963) referred to as the 'Wretched of the Earth'. As succinctly stated by Maldonado-Torres (2016), 'Time, for the colonized, is less the time of production, and more the time of surveillance and of waiting for denigration, violation, and murder to take place' (p. 17). For the colonised, Maldonado-Torres (2016) further asserts, 'Life is lived as in a torture chamber making life acquire the overwhelming feeling of it being worse than death… being colonised means that life is lived waiting for the permanent possibility of one's body to be violated by another' (p. 17). Even after formal independence, former colonies continue to suffer from forced displacement, socio-economic exploitation, and ongoing conflicts. Furthermore, some countries are still entangled in the shackles of occupation and settler violence, as is blatantly evident in the situation concerning Palestine. The open wound persists, bleeding and spreading everywhere, infecting as it spreads.

These abyssal conditions left a profound injury not only to the dignity of the enslaved and colonised but also to their descendants, of which Glissant is one. In a documentary film, *One World in Relation*, directed by Manthia Diawara, Glissant himself admits, 'We lost everything. All we had left were traces' (*Édouard Glissant: One World in Relation* 2010). Glissant's philosophy of Relation is founded on the 'traces' of the profound wounds and ruins experienced by the slaves in the abyss. The concept of trace signifies the enduring residue, mark, or scar left by a human or non-human event, (de) existence, or experience, forming the foundation of the theory of Relation. Glissant clarifies that the idea of the trace, unlike systemic thinking, serves as a wandering guide: 'the trace is what puts us, all of us, wherever we are from, in Relation' (2020, p. 9). It is a thread that connects the past and present, the non-existent and the existing, the same and the Other. The trace, as Glissant insists, 'opens onto these diffracted times that human communities today are multiplying among themselves, through conflicts and miracles' (2020, p. 10).

We repurpose Glissant's concepts to understand the realities of forced displacement today. The objective is not to draw direct parallels between the open boat or the Middle Passage and the contemporary migrant boat experiences in the Mediterranean Sea or elsewhere. Instead, Glissant's concepts of the abyss, Relation, and trace are repurposed in this work to explore new possibilities and ways of understanding and existing in the world. The analysis employs some of Glissant's concepts to envision a journey from open wounds to scars and beyond. While the open wound is conceptualised as a profound injury to human dignity, the scar represents a permanent marker of a healed wound and a tainted past. This transition from open wounds to scars necessitates an exploration of the underlying matrices of power and their implications in the present. It involves tracing the physical and metaphysical imprints, mutations, memories, logics, and matrices of power from the past within the present—to examine whether the abyss of the open boat underpins the emergence of the migrant boat.

Analogously, the apocalyptic scenes of forced migrants in inflatable 'migrant boats' crossing the Mediterranean Sea, or the 'small boats' in the English Channel, and other treacherous waters are reminiscent of the experiences of slaves sailing in 'open boats' across the Atlantic Ocean to unfamiliar lands. From the natal alienation experienced by slaves to the damning oppression faced by colonised subjects and forcibly displaced people, they all embody the enduring pain of open wounds that transcends time, space, and history. In the grip of relentless tides, hunger, and the cruel lashings of their tormentors, these displaced people are plunged into the refugee abyss, where the depths reach the ocean floor, the tides resemble towering mountains, and the journeys to inhospitable destinations continue, bereft of safety (see Chapters 4 and 5). Faced by these relentless forces of (b)ordering, inflicting upon them modes of (de)existence, they bear the burden of enduring open wounds whose depths are yet to be fully understood.

The spectacle of violent (b)ordering and the proliferation of (b)order zones have extended to every corner of the planet, 'deepening the space and time asymmetries between different categories of humanity while leading to the progressive ghettoization of entire regions of the world' (Mbembe, 2019, p. 11). In the past two decades, the Mediterranean Sea has transformed into an abyssal sea-camp, much like the desolate deserts and impoverished camps spanning Africa, the Middle East, East Asia, and Europe. In these carceral spaces, thousands of forcibly displaced people endure unimaginable brutality on both sides of the Mediterranean, in Myanmar, Libya, Yemen, Ethiopia, Sudan, the US-Mexico border, Palestine, and various other countries. Once forcibly displaced from their homes and places of familiarity, a perilous journey awaits these displaced people, where thousands meet death as their fate, year after year. Like the experience of the enslaved people, some bodies may have found the shallow seafloor's grounds in treacherous waters, while others drift on, decompose in pieces or as sustenance to fish. So many others have perished in lifeless deserts, impoverished refugee camps, violent borders, or war zones.

These abyssal realities represent just the beginning of the abyss that forced migrants endure during their unending, merciless, and tumultuous journeys towards and within imagined destination lands. Those who manage to survive the perilous journeys and sneak into the polity, often in urban areas in metropoles, find themselves entangled in bureaucratic and dehumanising asylum systems, all while grappling with perpetual 'racial trauma' in Fanonian terms. Stripped of legal and political protection, they face abyssal challenges, compelled to wear masks to fit into inherently colonial logics and structures that govern social organisation. Placed in a state of spatio-temporal dislocation against the supposedly linear history of established national societies, as portrayed by mainstream media discourses and migration scholarship, their existence remains on the fringes. Yet, their silenced voices resonate as displaced voices, as Glissant would argue. The emergence of a displaced voice, one that can be spoken but not truly heard, leads to the creation of alternative agency outside the structures of the abyss. These displaced forms of poetics of relation and resistance find more prominent expression in 'underground understandings' (Glissant 2009, p. 39). As we have argued elsewhere, the signs of displaced voices are abundantly found in the fertile traces of 'ruderal spaces', namely, 'the spaces in which appear the phenomenologies of crying, prayer, music, poetry, and encounters with people living in near-life conditions' (Yohannes, 2024, p. 324). We return to the poetics of refuge in Chapter 6.

After all, the stories of open wounds and scars from the refugee abyss haunt us with the reminder that the story of the Middle Passage is not a distant lament or a mere chapter of history. It is a living, ongoing abyss with no end, only layers of timeless suffering.

From the Middle Passage,

the womb of the 'open boat',
pregnant with death and traces of life,
bodies chained together,
hands bound to broken legs,
floating and drowning
in the salt of the sea and
in the plantation of the lands.

To the Refugee Abyss,

the ordeals at borders and deserts,
the destitution of camps and shantytowns,
the agony of trafficking and detentions,
the belly of the sea-camps,
and the violence of asylum—
the abyss deepens with every passing tide,
covering distances, times, histories and memories
of bodies buried in the abyss of past and present.

Through the Poetics of the Abyss,

we trace a new relation,
where suffering births new worlds,
where the wound becomes the path,
and the abyss opens wide
for those who are lost and forgotten,
or those who wait, still waiting, to be traced.

Conclusion

The stories with which this chapter opened are *traces* of the open wounds and scars of the abyss of our times: the refugee abyss. The state of being an abandoned creature, the obsolescence of norms, the state of (de)existence, forced disappearances, rape and torture, the tears of a child in front of their dying mother, the condition of being buried alive, the circumstance of being born and dying without rights, the obliteration of life with absolute impunity, the unheard cries of a new-born baby struggling while still connected to their mother by the umbilical cord, and the unearthing of bodies represent the refugee abyss of our times. In this abyss, the refugees have not only lost their human dignity, but they also live haunted by the fates of those who have perished without a trace and their own (de)existence—'I (de)existed', 'buried her alive', 'born rightless, die rightless', 'no status, no home, no life', and so forth. These open wounds persist in the depths of their memories and their wounded and scared bodies.

Almost every year, we witness, through our TV screens and reports from humanitarian organisations like the United Nations High Commissioner for Refugees (UNHCR) and International Organization for Migration (IOM), the deaths of hundreds, if not thousands, of people who drown in the Mediterranean and other seas. Many more die in deserts, prisons, camps, through trafficking, and at borders before they even reach the coast. Yet, these deaths rarely evoke grief or generate any political or moral outrage. When the body of a drowned migrant is discovered, the most common response is to assign a number to the unidentified remains and bury them without ceremony, as was done with the victims of the Lampedusa tragedy. As long as their lives remain killable and disposable, their deaths are not counted as human casualties, because these bodies—and the territories from which they come—are inherently marked by violability and disposability (see Darling, 2009; Mbembe, 2019).

The survivors of these perilous journeys remain trapped in dehumanising asylum systems, enduring conditions where they fear life more than death. The clamours of victims, the prayers from deep prison cells below the surface, and the unattended cries of children may have been the only language the refugees could express. Yet, even in death, their cries persist when exhumed from their graves. The essence of these displaced voices transcends existing systematic and measurement-heavy modes of understanding. They demand an approach that goes beyond Eurocentric onto-epistemic traditions. Tracing these displaced voices can help us connect the experiences of refugees in the abyss of our time with the potential for a decolonial existence. Through careful tracing, we can envision a scar by interweaving decolonial possibilities that the abyssal (de)existence has rendered unknowable, disposable, or (de) existent. This requires reassembling the displaced voices, bodies, and beings that have been deemed unknowable, killable, and disposable, so they can become decolonial bodies and beings. Yet, beneath the lacquered surface of the scar, their wounds remain fresh and fragile, for one cannot erase lived experiences, blot out memories, or heal existential wounds.

In this chapter, we have raised the questions that haunt both us and this book, woven through stories of open wounds and enduring scars. As we journey onward, we delve deeper into the ordeals and poetics of the refugee abyss in the chapters to come, starting with the rights of the rightless in the next chapter.

References

Ambrosini, M. (2018) 'Becoming a Borderland: The "Refugee Crisis" in Italy and Beyond', in *Irregular Immigration in Southern Europe. Migration, Diasporas and Citizenship*. Cham: Palgrave Macmillan. https://doi.org/10.1007/978-3-319-70518-7_4

Anderson, B. (2020) 'Imagined Communities: Reflections on the Origin and Spread of Nationalism', in S. Seidman and J. C. Alexander (Eds) *The New Social Theory Reader*, pp. 282–288. London: Routledge.

Bourdieu, P. (1989) Social Space and Symbolic Power. *Sociological Theory*, 7(1), 14.
Darling, J. (2009) Becoming Bare Life: Asylum, Hospitality, and the Politics of Encampment. *Environment and Planning D: Society and Space*, 27(4), 649–665.
Édouard Glissant: One World in Relation (2010) K'a Yéléma Productions.
Fanon, F. (1963) *The Wretched of the Earth*. New York, New York: Grove Press New York.
Glissant, É. (2009) *Poetics of Relation*. Ann Arbor, Michigan: University of Michigan Press.
Glissant, É. (2020) *Treatise on the Whole-World*. Liverpool: Liverpool University Press.
Hartman, S. (2016) The Belly of the World: A Note on Black Women's Labors. *Souls*, 18(1), 166–173.
Mainwaring, Ċ. (2019) *At Europe's Edge: Migration and Crisis in the Mediterranean*. 1st ed. Oxford: Oxford University Press.
Maldonado-Torres, N. (2016) *Outline of Ten Theses on Coloniality and Decoloniality*. Paris: Frantz Fanon Foundation Paris.
Mbembe, A. (2003) Necropolitics. *Public Culture*, 15(1), 11–40.
Mbembe, A. (2019) Bodies as Borders. *From the European South*, 4, 5–18.
Olivieri, L., Mazzarelli, D., Bertoglio, B., De Angelis, D., Previderè, C., Grignani, P., Cappella, A., Presciuttini, S., Bertuglia, C., Di Simone, P., Polizzi, N., Iadicicco, A., Piscitelli, V., and Cattaneo, C. (2018) Challenges in the Identification of Dead Migrants in the Mediterranean: The Case Study of the Lampedusa Shipwreck of October 3rd 2013. *Forensic Science International*, 285, 121–128.
Smith, A. (2017) *The Million-Dollar Boat Ride Across the Mediterranean*. London: MEMO Publishers
Yohannes, H.T. (2024) 'Autobiographic Reflections on Loss, Longing, and Recovery', in M. Bosworth, K. Franko, M. Lee, and R. Mehta (Eds) *Handbook on Border Criminology*, pp. 311–327. Northampton: Edward Elgar Publishing.

2 The Right of the Rightless

Introduction

The rights-based order, as the prevailing mode of organising human relations, has a complex and intricate history, deeply rooted in colonial foundations. Traces of rights-based administrative practices can be found as far back as ancient Persia, where Cyrus the Great is described by Kuhrt (1983) as having implemented a form of rights-based governance centuries before the advent of Christianity. Some historians regard this as the earliest attempt by a ruler to employ governance and administrative methods akin to modern human rights frameworks. Similarly, the gradual emergence of democracy, with its attendant rights and duties, can be traced to the civilisations of ancient Greece, as well as the Roman and Ottoman empires. The renowned Greek philosophers Plato and Socrates advanced progressive notions of rights-based governance and classical democracy. Plato's seminal work, *The Republic,* has profoundly influenced Western discourse on rights, duties, ethics, and morality, continuing to shape the evolving concept of democracy (see Santas, 2006). These classical ideas were framed within distinct realms of the private (pertaining to the individual and the domestic) and the public (encompassed the shared and communal).

In the second millennium, the rights-based system underwent significant transformations. In the second millennium, the *Magna Carta* of 1215 marked a pivotal moment, curbing the absolute authority of monarchs and embedding the principle that rulers too were subject to the law (see Carpenter, 2018). This development was further advanced by the *Petition of Right* in 1628, which strengthened civil and political liberties. The Treaty of Westphalia, concluded in 1648, ended a protracted European war and heralded a new era of peace for the Roman Empire. This treaty is historically significant for laying the groundwork for the modern nation-state, enshrining principles such as state sovereignty and non-interference (Croxton, 1999). Although the consolidation of the nation-state took shape in the 19th and 20th centuries, many historians argue that the concept of Westphalian sovereignty played a crucial role in uniting diverse ethnic, linguistic, and cultural groups within bordered states.

DOI: 10.4324/9781003437192-3

The 18th century witnessed further profound developments in the understanding of rights. The United States Declaration of Independence, issued in 1776, articulated the bold proclamation: 'We hold these truths to be self-evident, that all men are created equal, that they are endowed by their Creator with certain unalienable Rights, that among these are Life, Liberty, and the pursuit of Happiness' (Congress, 1776). The United States Constitution, adopted in 1787, strengthened these principles within a legal framework, embodying the division of powers and the architecture of governance. Although it has been amended multiple times, the Constitution remains a 'cornerstone' of American political philosophy and practice (Stephens, 1861).

In 1789, the French *Declaration of the Rights of Man and of the Citizen* marked a significant moment in the evolution of rights. It represented a fundamental break from natural rights tied to hierarchical traditions, elevating the sovereignty of humankind. As Arendt (2017) observes, this declaration sought to universalise the notion of rights, severing ties with the stratified societies of the past. This historic milestone ushered in a wave of what Ignatieff (2000) refers to as an 'international rights revolution'. Among the most notable achievements of this era was the drafting of the Universal Declaration of Human Rights (UDHR) in 1948. Like its French predecessor, the UDHR aspires to extend rights universally, transcending borders. Its preamble proclaims: 'The recognition of the inherent dignity and of the equal and inalienable rights of all members of the human family is the foundation of freedom, justice, and peace in the world' (United Nations, 2015, p. I). By reframing the relationship between states and their citizens, the UDHR shifts the discourse from the national to the international stage, laying the groundwork for states to intervene in the affairs of other sovereign nation-states.

As these brief sketches suggest, the history and genealogy of the rights-based system have been neither 'linear' nor 'predictable' (Alston, 2013, p. 2081). This system has been shaped and reshaped by the currents of civilisation, the dictates of religious belief, the chains of slavery, the open wounds and scars of colonisation, and, more recently, the sweeping tide of globalisation and forced displacement. Each of these transformative forces continues to cast profound and far-reaching influences on the foundations of contemporary history and the global frameworks that mould national and human relations. Most significantly, while the UDHR endeavours to safeguard and promote fundamental rights, its claim to 'inalienability' has left many excluded from its protection framework. Refugees, for instance, find no place within the Declaration; their status remains unclarified within its Charter. This omission gave rise to the 1951 Geneva Convention, developed specifically to address the involuntary displacement of refugees in Europe in the aftermath of World War II. The Refugee Convention provided a framework to confront the structural challenges stemming from the exclusion of refugees from the realm of rights.

As refugees from across the globe began to seek sanctuary in Europe and beyond, the Convention's geographic limitations were lifted through the adoption of a 1967 protocol. Yet, despite its laudable aims, the Geneva Convention remains incomplete and ill-suited to the myriad contexts it sought to address. For example, it does not encompass the plight of internally displaced persons and other refugees that do not fall within its formulae of well-founded persecution. In response, various regional instruments have emerged to address more specific challenges. The Organisation of African Unity adopted a modified convention in 1969 to meet the particular needs of African refugees (OAU, 1974), while Latin America adopted the Cartagena Declaration on Refugees in 1984, a non-binding instrument reflecting the region's unique experiences (Organization of American States, 1984).

Despite these frameworks, the refugee's position within the rights-based order is deeply perplexing. Mackinnon (2018) observes, 'One approach, one historical legacy, is disavowed in favour of another; some legacies are passed down while others are made to appear discontinuous, part of some other genre or history' (p. 6). In this fraught evolution of rights, riddled with systemic and epistemic violence, what is lost in the sedimentation of rights? Which rights have we inherited? Most poignantly, who are the true bearers of these rights? Where does the refugee stand within this selective and fragmentary regime? Amidst the intricacies and shifting politics of the rights-based order, our aim here is to illuminate the refugee's status within the political sphere.

This chapter does not attempt to provide an exhaustive review of the contested history of rights. Rather, it seeks to spotlight key moments in the evolution of the rights-based order to understand the place of the refugee. To this end, we begin by exploring the transformation from the rights of man to human rights, drawing heavily on Arendt's insights on totalitarianism to examine the decline of the rights of man and the ascendancy of human rights. We then seek to locate the refugee within this evolving framework, demonstrating how the refugee is frequently reduced to a surplus figure whose rights and dignity are sacrificed in the relentless domestication of human rights by nation-states. The refugee occupies a realm of indiscernibility, suspended between life and death, a subject of coloniality whose existence is trapped in the liminal spaces of (de)existence and (de)humanity. Finally, we turn to what we describe as the right of the rightless. On the one hand, the absence of rights signifies a stark limitation; on the other, it evokes an awareness of new possibilities that lie beyond those limits.

From the Rights of Man to Human Rights

The Declaration of the Rights of Man emerged as a monumental achievement in the realm of human rights during the 18th century. Arendt (2017) demonstrates how this declaration marked a profound shift, liberating the concept of 'Man' from the confines of traditional natural rights and the hierarchical structures of society. In this transformative moment, 'Man' ascended to the status of sovereign over his own destiny. Yet, despite its revolutionary promise, the Declaration stood vulnerably exposed, as Arendt (2017, p. 380) explains:

> Man himself was their source as well as their ultimate goal. No special law, moreover, was deemed necessary to protect them because all laws were supposed to rest upon them. Man appeared as the only sovereign in matters of law as the people was proclaimed the only sovereign in matters of government.

This abstract formulation of the Rights of Man leaves two fundamental questions unanswered. First, it fails to clarify who the 'Man' of the Rights of Man truly is. Second, as Arendt points out, if Man is meant to signify an individual member of the human community, how inclusive are these rights? In addressing the first question, Arendt (2017) persuasively explores the intersection of the Rights of Man with 'an "abstract" human being who seems to exist nowhere, for even savages lived in some kind of a social order' (p. 381). According to Arendt, 'Man' has never been free from the larger social order of which he has been proclaimed the ruler. She argues that the Man of the Rights of Man is merely a member of a community organised within a system of nation-states. She further explains that the disappearance of Man in this new social order has led to the identification of 'the rights of man with the rights of peoples in the European nation-state system' (Arendt, 2017, p. 381).

Essentially, the Rights of Man emerge as a quixotic rhetorical project that only safeguards the rights of a select portion of humanity. The futility of this project becomes evident in the subordination of women's rights and the rightlessness of colonised, stateless, and involuntarily displaced people. For instance, Rancière (2004) highlights that although women are born with equal dignity and seek equal political participation, they are still not recognised as 'equal citizens' (p. 303). Marginalised groups, such as the colonised, stateless, and involuntarily displaced, have similarly suffered, stripped of their rights and relegated to a state of perpetual exceptionality and violability. Arendt (2017) notes, 'It turned out that the moment human beings lacked their own government and had to fall back upon their minimum rights, no authority was left to protect them and no institution was willing to guarantee them' (p. 381). The plight of marginalised people manifests starkly in the subjugation of Jews and other minorities in the concentration camps of 20th-century Europe, as well as in the genocidal crimes committed against colonised peoples in Africa and beyond.

From this perspective, Arendt asserts that the erosion of the Rights of Man gave rise to the concept of minority rights, now overseen by supranational organisations. In the aftermath of World War I, the League of Nations was established with the primary aim of 'maintaining peace' while also addressing the needs of displaced people (Easton-Calabria, 2015, p. 416). The formation of a new body tasked with safeguarding minorities seemed a triumph for the sovereign state, effectively separating the rights of citizens from the rights of the rest of humanity. This division marked a radical departure from the original promises of inalienable rights inherent in the Rights of Man. It signalled an irreparable existential damage embedded within the abstract formulation of these rights. Thus, as both Arendt and Rancière conclude, the Man in the Rights of Man, along with its claims of inalienability and universality within the rights-based system, reveals itself as a fictitious construct. Ultimately, the Rights of Man faced an abrupt and paradoxical decline; its logic and rhetorical significance have dissipated relatively quickly.

With the decline of the Rights of Man, the concept of Man evolved into that of Human, as Rancière (2004) notes: 'The actual subject of these Rights of Man became Human Rights' (p. 298). In the post-World War II era, a broader international consensus emerged around the imperative to prevent the atrocities that had led to devastating wars. During this time, the terms 'natural rights' and 'Rights of Man' began to fade, giving way to the more encompassing framework of 'human rights'. In 1945, the United Nations was officially established, with over 50 countries signing the United Nations Charter. Three years later, the General Assembly established standard human rights norms through the adoption of the UDHR, which member states have committed to uphold. The UDHR comprises 30 articles that proclaim and extend fundamental freedoms, rights, and protections to all people. Its Preamble recognises 'the inherent dignity and [...] the equal and inalienable rights of all members of the human family', and notes that these rights should be 'protected by the rule of law' (United Nations, 2015, p. 1). The UDHR explicitly opposes any form of discrimination (Articles 2 and 7), prohibits slavery in all its forms (Article 4), protects everyone against torture (Article 5), and forbids arbitrary detention (Article 9). Article 3 declares that 'everyone has the right to life, liberty and security of person' (United Nations, 2015, pp. 6–8).

The UDHR was swiftly succeeded by the drafting of the International Covenant on Civil and Political Rights (ICCPR) and the International Covenant on Economic, Social and Cultural Rights (ICESCR). The ICCPR highlights fundamental freedoms, including the rights to life, speech, and religion, while the ICESCR addresses essential needs such as food, health, shelter, and education. Together, these three documents form the cornerstone of the International Bill of Rights.

A growing consensus emerged that the UDHR, alongside these covenants, embodied the foundational principles of the post-war human rights framework. Yet, these principles remained largely unenforced until the 1990s, when 'Western organisations – the International Commission of Jurists, Amnesty International, and Human Rights Watch – roamed the globe looking for infractions' (Cmiel, 2004, p. 117). These groups, in tandem with grassroots activism and human rights movements, played a pivotal role in advancing the establishment of international human rights law. At the same time, the United Nations expanded its structures, creating new branches to support these efforts. Notably, the establishment of the International Criminal Court (ICC) and the UN Commissions of Inquiry (COI) marked a significant evolution, granting the human rights regime international jurisdiction and the capacity to undertake fact-finding missions. Even earlier, in 1945, the International Court of Justice (ICJ) had been founded to adjudicate disputes between nations and provide advisory opinions on matters of international law. The ICJ, together with the subsequent development of human rights laws, enabled the United Nations to strengthen its jurisdiction and enhance its executive authority.

Nevertheless, the proliferation of human rights organisations has given rise to tense and fragile relationships between sovereign states, many of which staunchly resist intervention or the involvement of such bodies. A poignant example lies in the strained interactions between the Organisation of African Unity (OAU) and the International Criminal Court (ICC) (see Murithi, 2013). At the same time, the dawn of a new human rights regime has enabled Western supranational entities such as NATO to cast themselves as guardians of the so-called inalienable rights proclaimed by this framework. Masked in the mantle of human rights, these organisations have intervened in the internal affairs of nation-states whenever they discern rights violations. The lineage of such actions can be traced to the Nuremberg trials and NATO's efforts in prosecuting war crimes (Cmiel, 2004).

In recent years, the ICC has drawn global attention with its convictions of Congolese warlords and rebel leaders (Human Rights Watch, 2019). Most notably, it issued an arrest warrant for Russian President Vladimir Putin, citing crimes committed amid the ongoing Russia-Ukraine conflict (ICC, 2023). Similarly, warrants were issued for Israeli Prime Minister Netanyahu and former Defence Minister Gallant in relation to the unfolding war in the Gaza Strip (ICC, 2024). South Africa has brought a genocide case before the ICJ, addressing Israel's actions in Gaza and the enduring dehumanisation of Palestinians. Across the world, countless crimes remain unanswered: the devastating wars in Iraq, Afghanistan, Syria, Yemen, Ethiopia, Sudan, Libya, and beyond, where efforts to establish accountability are often conspicuously absent. Outside the West, such selective warrants are frequently perceived as glaring symbols of double standards (Ibhawoh, 2008; Labuda, 2023).

Moreover, the universalisation of the human rights agenda stirs profound questions about its socio-cultural resonance in Africa, South America, and Asia. Many nations across these regions draw upon traditional practices of communal justice and customary laws to shape their human rights frameworks, rather than conforming rigidly to international norms. Grovogui (2006) offers a compelling analysis of Haitian human rights discourses, observing that 'ennobling existence through authoritative ethical categories is not foreign to other regions and cultures' (p. 5). The notion of Asian values, for instance, presents alternative narratives, entangled with Orientalist discourses and varied human rights practices in the Middle East and Southeast Asia (Mauzy, 1997; Said, 2003). Such differing traditions and discourses challenge the supposed 'Western origination of the concept and the ontological primacy of related Western institutions' (Grovogui, 2006, p. 4).

Yet human rights regimes bear the peril of infringing upon the sovereignty of states in their domestic spheres. The proliferation and coalition of human rights organisations deliver a sharp critique of how states wield their sovereign powers. In recent decades, international human rights organisations, often supported by global superpowers, have formed a formidable presence, intervening in sovereign affairs under the banner of addressing human rights abuses. These non-governmental organisations have not only established mechanisms to investigate and expose such violations but also demand justifications from sovereign states, taking action against violent practices. While such interventions may curtail a state's control over domestic matters, they do not abolish the sovereign powers (whether protective or repressive) that states exercise over their citizens. Instead, these actions have fostered 'a reconceptualized sovereignty in which a state accepts that gross violations of human rights will no longer be an issue solely within its domestic jurisdictions' (Sikkink, 1993, p. 415). Nonetheless, the nation-state remains both a primary source of threat and a supposed provider of protection for its citizens.

Within this framework, states retain considerable authority over the rights of their citizens and even greater control over the rights of non-citizens. It can be argued that human rights have increasingly become centred on, if not administered by, sovereign states. This dominance permits states to exclude unwanted groups from their polity, relegating them to spheres of constitutive exception. In effect, the state has succeeded in domesticating human rights into a paradigm of citizens' rights, reducing the Rights of Man to the realm of those denied their rights. 'Those rights that appear to be useless in their place', Rancière (2004, p. 307) observes, 'are sent abroad, along with medicine and clothes, to people deprived of medicine, clothes, and rights'. He continues: 'It is in this way, as the result of this process, that the Rights of Man become the rights of those who have no rights, the rights of bare human beings subjected to inhuman repression and inhuman conditions of existence' (Rancière, 2004, p. 307).

Who, then, are these bare human beings, stripped of the fundamental rights of medicine, clothing, and food? What role do they occupy within the framework of the nation-state, characterised by an unequal distribution of rights and power? Who, indeed, is the 'human' in human rights? Most crucially, as Mignolo (2011) provocatively asks, 'who speaks for the human' in the discourse of human rights? And where does the figure of the refugee find its place within this order of rights?

The emergence of the refugee

In contemporary history, the concept of a refugee emerged when 'the link between state, citizen, and territory [was] broken' (Betts et al., 2011, p. 89). Most refugees were once citizens living in their homelands, unless they were born stateless, in camps, or within the diaspora. Arendt (2017) compellingly argues that the loss of one's home and community, compounded by the absence of state protection, forms the essential preconditions for becoming a refugee. She explains that a refugee emerges when a state imposes a 'condition of complete rightlessness' to strip its citizens of their nationality (Arendt, 2017, p. 387). Once displaced and severed from the nation-state, the refugee becomes a figure of political exception, suffering also from the denial of socio-economic provisions. In essence, the refugee exists simultaneously as a subject of necropolitics and of humanitarian intervention.

Within the matrices of rights, the refugee has been recast as an inherently excluded figure in a rights-based world order. During the interwar years, refugees were classified as a category of migrants and their 'exile and destitution could be solved through continued movement' (Long, 2013, p. 9). In this context, the League of Nations issued refugee passports, known as Nansen Passports, which allowed refugees 'to travel and settle in other countries' (Chetail, 2003, p. 4). Ostensibly a means for freedom of movement, employment, and settlement, this initiative operated as a mechanism of sharing burden and responsibility, where refugees were expected not only to sustain themselves but to aid in addressing broader unemployment concerns. Thus, refugee resettlement during this era was intrinsically tied to the creation of surplus labour for national and international development programmes. 'Refugee exile', Long (2013, p. 10) clarifies, 'was thus one part of a broader concern to tackle the much greater project of global unemployment through targeted migration'.

Despite an emphasis on resilience and self-reliance during the interwar period, refugees were often exploited and politically marginalised. This became particularly evident after the World War II, as war-torn host states demonstrated scant regard for the safety and dignity of refugees. While refugee labour was deemed vital for national development during the Great Depression, their political agency remained largely disregarded. Economic exploitation and political marginalisation spanned continents, encompassing regions such as the Indian Subcontinent, South America, and Africa. Over time, refugees in these and other areas have been systematically depoliticised, their rights eroded, and their dignity diminished.

Interestingly, before the adoption of the 1951 Refugee Convention, the term refugee lacked a universally recognised legal definition. Nevertheless, regional and national frameworks offered protection to displaced persons, including initiatives by the United Nations Relief and Rehabilitation Administration (UNRRA) and, subsequently, the International Refugee Organisation (IRO). Established during the World War II, the UNRRA provided vital relief and rehabilitation to nations devastated by the conflict, with a focus on Europe and Asia. Its efforts were pivotal in aiding displaced persons, including concentration camp survivors, forced labourers, and prisoners of war, seeking to return home or resettle elsewhere. In 1946, the IRO was created as a specialised United Nations agency to succeed the UNRRA, with a refined mandate centred on resettlement and protection for refugees unable or unwilling to repatriate due to persecution.

Since the signing of the 1951 Refugee Convention, refugees have progressively been stripped of their migrant status and, with it, their rights to movement and employment. The Refugee Convention, forged in the aftermath of Europe's wartime displacement, delineates a refugee as distinct from other migrants (Article 1) and enshrines the principle of non-refoulement, prohibiting their return to danger (Article 33). Under Article 1(A)(2), a refugee is defined as an individual who has fled their country due to a well-founded fear of persecution, grounded in circumstances preceding January 1951. To qualify as a refugee, one must cross an international border and substantiate fears of persecution based on nationality, ethnicity, religion, political opinion, or membership in a particular social group (Article 1(A)(2)). Refugee Status Determination (RSD) processes, conducted by national governments, the UNHCR, or hybrid models, ascertain eligibility under international, regional, or national legal frameworks, as established by the 1951 Refugee Convention.

The Refugee Convention has long been the subject of considerable critique, its initial focus confined to a specific geographic region (Europe) and a limited temporal frame (pre-1951). Though its spatial and temporal reach was later expanded with the adoption of the 1967 Protocol, its scope remains fundamentally constrained. At its core, the Refugee Convention was not developed to comprehensively address or forestall the 'fear of persecution' it so definitively describes. Rather, its chief purpose has been to establish bureaucratic and confessional systems of asylum. The Refugee Convention itself, in its preamble, acknowledges the significant burdens asylum may impose on certain nation-states, underlining the indispensable role of international cooperation in confronting this shared global challenge. Yet it offers little in the way of directly resolving the root causes of forced displacement. Even with the advent of regional agreements, tailored to specific contexts in Africa and South America, the pressing issue of displacement and the pursuit of durable solutions remain largely unmet. Despite its waning relevance amidst the tightening of border controls and the hardening of immigration policies by nation-states, the 1951 Refugee Convention endures as the most widely invoked international legal framework for the protection of refugees.

While regional and international legal frameworks establish the rights and entitlements of refugees, the UNHCR is the institution entrusted with overseeing the implementation of these rights and entitlements. The organisation not only determines who qualifies as a refugee but also claims a leading role in addressing refugee issues. Its core responsibilities include monitoring the protection of those seeking asylum and refugees, providing humanitarian assistance, and offering limited long-term solutions. Broadly speaking, the UNHCR's mandate encompasses the protection of refugees' needs in both emergency and non-emergency situations, both within and outside refugee camps during their involuntary displacement (see Betts et al., 2011). Moreover, the UNHCR has expanded its humanitarian efforts by coordinating the responses of both state and non-state actors to refugee issues. For example, it works closely with the International Organisation for Migration (IOM) on a macro level and with local organisations on a micro level. Over the years, the UNHCR has evolved into a prominent humanitarian organisation, gaining legal, humanitarian, reputational, and expert credibility to support its involvement in global migration management, with a particular focus on asylum and refugee protection (Betts and Loescher, 2010; Betts et al., 2011).

Paradoxically, the state and humanitarian organisations function in tandem, as if they are two manifestations of the same power structure and (b)ordering spectacle. Wielded by the sovereign power of the nation-state and its institutions, the (b)ordering spectacle subjects forcibly displaced people to a necropolitical exercise of power through the use of sophisticated micro- and macro-level (b)ordering regimes. This mode of power, directed against vulnerable bodies whose existence is reduced to a realm of (de)humanity, underpins the refugee abyss. In this regard, the Refugee Convention and the UNHCR have played crucial roles in expanding 'carceral humanitarianism' (Oliver, 2017), while states fortify their borders through violent and necropolitical bordering practices. This hidden paradox of carceral humanitarianism begins with humanitarianism vacating 'its ethical sanctuary for the world of politics and power' (Betts et al., 2011, p. 106). This power operates, Betts et al. (2011, p. 108) affirm, 'by pointing a gun and forcibly repatriating refugees over the border and back to a place that remains a threat to their safety, or by assuming that a "refugee" is not only vulnerable but also probably does not have enough education, experience, or knowledge to make good decisions'. Betts et al. (2011) further clarify that both 'compassion and care exist alongside command and control' (p. 105). This is evident in the fact that refugees are thrust into realms of abjection at borders, in refugee camps, and in hotspots; they are dehumanised in torture camps run by human traffickers, drowned in treacherous waters, and trapped in bureaucratic asylum regimes. These apocalyptic realities have become symbols of humanitarianism in the 21st century.

The function of the state-humanitarian alliance is, at its core, one of assimilation, destitution, and containment. This alliance seeks to integrate lives into an expansive carceral regime, within which the refugee condition is perpetually regarded as a transient state—one that must either be absorbed into the nation-state's project or extinguished through the relentless application of (b)ordering and necropolitical forces, exemplified by the denial of asylum. As Behrman (2018) illustrates, there is no inherent right to asylum; rather, people seeking refuge possess the right to claim asylum. It is clear that the very act of claiming asylum has become increasingly difficult, not merely because of heavily fortified borders equipped with advanced surveillance technology, but also due to the denial of asylum by nation-states whose primary interest is to govern the forcibly displaced people outside the polity.

The establishment of a distinct regime of asylum, alongside its legal frameworks and humanitarian efforts, has stripped refugees of the very rights and dignity that are supposedly inalienable. Wielding its power over violent bordering, the nation-state dominates and regulates 'the entire conception of the political' (Nyers, 2013, p. xi). The nation-state, which ought to function within the confines of the law, also defines and creates the conditions for constitutive exception of the refugee, asserting the legitimate use of force to administer violence or permitting its institutions and allies to act on its behalf. The consequences of such state-sanctioned violence are glaringly evident in the name of national security, the war on terror, and self-defence (see Mbembe, 2019a). Here, sovereignty emerges as a paradox: to achieve 'perfection', violence is deemed necessary; to attain 'internal harmony', 'external chaos' must prevail (Nyers, 2013, p. xi). This paradox intricately weaves violence into the very fabric of asylum recognition and political intelligibility, establishing a hierarchy where the further one is from these constellations, the less their life is valued within the frameworks of asylum, subjectivity, hospitality, and humanity. Effectively othered and banned, the refugee is exiled to a realm of illegality, disorder, and deprivation of rights. Beyond the borders, the notion of asylum disappears; what remains is the stark reality of 'no-asylum', amid the violent spectacle of bordering that serves as a mechanism of dehumanisation.

In fact, even crossing a border and claiming asylum does not guarantee its grant. Those in need of refuge are subjected to what Mountz (2020) terms the 'death of asylum'. Mountz (2020) explains that the death of asylum manifests in three forms: 'physical death' resulting from offshore (b)ordering and enforcement measures; 'ontological death' caused by the prevention of crossing (b)orders and arrivals; and 'political death', where this necropolitical spectacle goes unnoticed or unaddressed (pp. 12–13). These forms of death collectively signify the denial of the right to asylum, placing the lives of those seeking refuge in jeopardy. At its core, however, the death of asylum signifies not only the absence of refuge but also the deliberate dehumanisation of those in need of protection, manifesting through a necropolitical spectacle. It represents a paradigm of no-asylum, where the suspension of asylum is systematically enforced. While some advocate for increased humanitarian intervention to offer relief to those whose asylum claims are deemed inadmissible, this perspective is ultimately untenable. Humanitarianism itself is marred by its inherent inhumanity, colonial legacy, and carceral nature, as argued. This approach perpetuates a cycle in which people seeking refuge become ever more dependent on external rescue, sustenance, and shelter, thereby entrenching them in a state of perpetual poverty and destitution. Such dependency underscores the pervasive structure of seemingly mundane coloniality that underpins humanitarianism.

Let us pause here and immediately ask: what, then, might the marker 'refugee' imply within the grammar of coloniality perpetuated by the rights-based order? As argued, it has become evident that the marker 'refugee' manifests as an exceptional void within this order. The refugee is caught in a relation of perfect vulnerability and exception and refugees' existence makes no sense outside of their absolute nakedness, through which the nation-state evokes the image of the citizen as a supposedly fully human being. If the state successfully subjects those seeking refuge to the marker 'refugee', it effectively simplifies and reduces their many identities and multiplicities into a clearly defined category. The refugee can then be quantified and marginalised, named or unnamed, violated and discarded, as the nation-state asserts decisive power over their bodies and movements. This naked violence, in its most blatant and unrestricted form, is administered at the level of the subject (necropolitical) and the body (biological). The idea of the refugee, when internalised as the Other of the nation-state, can only be naturalised as part of the state-sanctioned bordering regime of migration as a masked Other. The mask functions as an onto-epistemic descriptor through which the state delineates its exceptions. The bodies of those seeking refuge emerge as masked void, mere breathing bodies devoid of onto-epistemic significance, required to bear the marker 'refugee' in order to aspire to recognition as human beings, namely naturalised citizens.

For refugees themselves, the designation of 'refugee' is not merely a label but a scar, a mark of stigma wielded to strip them of their humanity. This stigma, a subtle yet pervasive violence, infiltrates the banalities of everyday life. The open wounds and enduring scars discussed in Chapter 1 bear witness to an ordeal of unimaginable brutality and chaos, an erratic and bestial reality that defies comprehension. Under such harrowing conditions, refugees are violated for the pleasure of others, buried alive, or cast aside without a moment's thought. Within the framework of rights, their voices and aspirations remain untranslatable into meaningful political action, caught within the capricious whims of sovereign power. Their lived experience becomes a relentless pursuit, a quest to forge a bond with the nation-state, first by seeking asylum and, if granted, through the eventual acquisition of citizenship. Their role is reduced to that of proving their eligibility for membership in a sovereign polity.

The asylum system, in turn, permits their presence only through exclusion from political life, offering a narrowly defined identity as victims of a well-founded fear of persecution beyond the borders of the receiving state. It extends to them basic entitlements such as the right to return, education, and food, but only in the most limited terms. To claim these necessities, those seeking refuge are compelled to offer their own bodies as evidence. The scars they bear and the memories of suffering etched into their flesh serve as irrefutable proof of persecution. They must demonstrate, unequivocally, that return to their homeland is impossible. Should these criteria be met, they are admitted, but only as masked Others who are bound to be moulded into useful, naturalised citizens. Ironically, in their striving for citizenship, refugees are endlessly reconstituted as bodies that are both usable and disposable, 'objects' within the machinery of sovereign power.

Their relation to the nation-state remains fundamentally economic and humanitarian, not political (Long, 2013). As recognised refugees, their right to work is granted at the discretion of the state, while education and skills crucial for their labour to benefit the host society must often be acquired at their own expense. Yet the nation-state assigns a diminished value to the labour of refugees compared to that of its citizens. Refugee labour is absent from political discourse, dismissed in legal frameworks that focus exclusively on their status. They are seen as bodies of utility, valued solely for their capacity to labour, stripped of participation in the political sphere. Their identities are crushed into their physical usefulness while they strive to meet the standards of a politically qualified body. Even further, should the nation-state deem it necessary, it reserves the right to exercise its self-legitimised violence, detaining, deporting, or expelling refugees with impunity. These acts of exclusion reaffirm the state's sovereign authority to define exceptions and to decide who must be cast into them.

Thus, the fictive narrative of refugee protection, entwined with its seemingly benign projects of humanitarianism and human rights, constitutes a grammar of coloniality whose central purpose is to articulate the containment of refugees. Cast as both a logical and metaphysical imperative around which all other discourses must orbit, this grammar of coloniality becomes an arsenal that perpetuates the racialisation and mortality of marginalised bodies, such as those seeking refuge. Humanitarianism aligns its transfigured forces with the state-centric project of human rights, weaving a narrative of rescue and rehabilitation. Yet the nation-state traps refugees within a realm of perpetual necropolitical existence. The refugee's capacity for political agency is frequently immobilised, confined to a perpetual state of potentiality through a violent bordering spectacle and a grammar of coloniality that thrives on sophisticated metrics, spurious threats, and lethal violence. Refugees are often vilified and their humanity eroded by racialised rhetoric, labelled as invaders, infiltrators, or bogus asylum seekers. Even those granted declaratory status are reduced to symbols of failed multiculturalism, caught within the tangled discourse of incomplete assimilation and failed integration. There is no need to further list or echo these toxic narratives, reductive metrics, or fabricated threats, for their mere signposting suffices to remind the reader already acquainted with them.

These matrices and metrics coloniality emerge as measurable schematics, quantifiable statistics, polished graphics, reductive racialised categories, and increasingly discredited figures. They are produced through regimes of data generation, regulated by a tripartite alliance of state, corporate, and humanitarian forces. This coalition encompasses governmental bodies such as Immigration and Visa Services, Ministries of Immigration, Home Affairs, local governments, border security, intelligence agencies, embassies, and consular services. It extends to local and international humanitarian organisations like UNHCR and IOM, as well as supranational entities such as Frontex that operate beyond the jurisdiction of any single nation. Private corporations, including airlines and security contractors, are implicated in bordering practices, particularly in forced removals and deportations. Even individuals such as landlords and doctors, compelled by state legislation, perform acts of (b)ordering, as is the case in the UK (Yohannes et al., 2024).

This concerted mechanism seeks to surveil and control refugees across locations and temporalities, aiming ultimately to confine, manage, and expel them. Invasive regimes of oversight and policing categorise and track forced migrants based on their arrivals and departures, legal status, criminality, lack of documentation, or instances of disappearance. Through the exclusive process of 'datafication' (Mbembe, 2019b, p. 7), the state-humanitarian-corporate nexus produces reports across multiple levels, whether global, regional, national, or specific to targeted services. Drawing upon measurable schematics, quantifiable statistics, and polished visuals, this alliance establishes and legitimises the narrative of a humanitarian crisis and national security threat. Within the grammar of coloniality, the enduring presence of crisis and threat becomes the sanctioned narrative, demanding urgent attention and justifying immediate action.

The more urgent question concerning the emergence of the refugee as a category of (de)humanity, fractured and diminished, lies in the deadly violence of the nation-states that first created the abyss of exile and continues to enforce their (b)orders with brute force. In essence, the refugee has become a new locus of subjugation to the colonial matrices of nation-state and the violent dominance it embodies. For the refugee, the search for safety and political agency demands a renunciation of this abyss and the systematic structures that perpetuate it, such as the rights-based frameworks that enshroud it. True agency for the refugee cannot be found by invoking human rights alone but emerges through a radical departure from any system of rights, towards a new mode of existence, a poetics of refuge, an untamed life in its Glissantian sense. The refugee must transform into a decolonial force, one whose struggle transcends mere survival to forge a new relational co-existence, a dynamic and ever-evolving totality of relations, interwoven with the delicate yet resilient thread of traces. Being a refugee is born of the fugitive, unthought, and unknown and as the Ethiopian philosopher Zara Yacob wisely reminds us, its poetics must be conceived at the confluence of freedom, relation, and imagination (Kiros, 2005).

The right of the rightless

The emergence of the refugee as a figure devoid of rights within the colonial framework of a rights-based order calls for further exploration of its links to the foundations of the nation-state. Tracing the juridico-political evolution of Western politics through the archives of Roman and Greek civilisations, Agamben presents a compelling argument: the foundation of the nation-state and its rights-based order lies in the inherent exclusion of what he terms 'bare life' (Agamben, 1998). Drawing on the classical Greek distinction between *zoe* (biological life) and *bios* (political life), Agamben establishes that *zoe* represents a basic existence as a living organism—merely a fact of life, or bare life. Bare life thus lives a general condition of violability, killability, and disposability without committing crime or sacrilege. In contrast, *bios* signifies a qualified life embodying political rights and responsibilities. It denotes a rights-bearing subject whose rights are contingent upon the rightlessness and naked existence of the *zoe*.

Agamben then employs the concept of *homo sacer* to elaborate on his theory of the 'state of exception', wherein sovereign power inclusively excludes certain categories of people from the juridico-political order as its primary function, relegating them to a condition of bare life (Agamben, 2015). In this political theory, *homo sacer* is a legal figure existing both outside the law and at the mercy of that same law. This duality means that while such lives are not afforded legal protection, they remain perpetually exposed to its violence. Agamben maintains that the primary task of sovereign power is to create a biopolitical life, wherein the distinction between bare life (biological existence) and qualified life (political existence) becomes increasingly blurred and indistinguishable. Within this realm of indistinguishability, it becomes impossible to ascertain whether one exists inside or outside the juridico-political order. According to Agamben, the tension between bare existence and political life within a realm of indistinction forms the very essence of politics. Politics exists because the human is 'the living being who, in language, separates and opposes himself to his own bare life and, at the same time, maintains himself in relation to that bare life in an inclusive exclusion' (Agamben, 1998, p. 12). This blurring between naked existence and political life means that bare life has permeated politics as a defining figure, while political life, in turn, may readily dissolve into the nakedness of bare existence.

In this juridico-political order, the law sustains its authority through simultaneous application and withdrawal, inclusion and constitutive exclusion. To affirm the existence of *bios* (the sphere of politics), the law establishes the realm of indistinguishability as a zone wherein the rights of the rightless emerge as no-rights. Here, no-rights are paradoxically constituted as the rights of the dispossessed. Agamben demonstrates that the foundation of the nation-state, including its concepts of rights and democracy, is rooted in the primordial violence of creating and perpetuating naked bodies relegated to a constitutive outside of the realm of rights. He asserts, 'The inclusion of bare life in the political realm constitutes the original – if concealed – nucleus of sovereign power' (Agamben, 1998, p. 11). This configuration of the juridico-political reduces the application of human rights to the narrow purview of citizens' rights: 'the only real rights [are] the rights of citizens, the rights attached to a national community as such' (Rancière, 2004, p. 298).

The nation-state's domestication of human rights transforms them into the exclusive prerogative of citizens, leaving marginalised people surplus and undesirable. In this process, their rights and human dignity are forfeited as human rights are confined within the borders of the nation-state.

Agamben, however, seems to overlook that the law, when applied to racialised, enslaved, colonised, and forcibly displaced peoples, functions solely as an instrument of violence. Within the plantations of slavery and the segregated ghettos of colonisation, there was no ambiguity, no indistinction, between the presence of the law and its withdrawal. The law met these racialised people in the realm of objecthood, devoid entirely of any recourse to rights or protection. In these spaces, the law served two entwined purposes: to entrench the dehumanisation and exploitation of racialised peoples in a void bereft of rights, and to fortify the privileges of enslavers, plantation owners, and colonisers. In his later writings, Agamben concedes that juridico-political arrangements condemned the enslaved to a condition he terms 'being-in-use', with their bodies appropriated by the enslavers, who themselves existed in a state of 'being-at-work' (2015, p. 7). To have one's body consigned to the Other is to endure a state of absolute rightlessness, stripped entirely of the ability to claim sovereignty over oneself or one's actions. As a mechanism to legitimise colonial and racial violence, the law became the ultimate manifestation of the exception as a perpetual rule, animating a relation where some humans could wield absolute dominion over others. Even today, as Mbembe (2019a) reminds us, the law endures as a necropolitical instrument, confining racialised peoples within a perpetual state of exception and rightlessness. In its most harrowing expressions, it annihilates through calculated determinations of life and death. This necropolitical calibration of existence has, for centuries, been the *nomos*—the physical and metaphysical order—of slavery, colonisation, coloniality, and forced displacement.

Thus, within this racialised configuration of rights-based order, both the Man in the Rights of Man and the Human in Human Rights are enfolded into the law as its teleological field of power. In her analysis of colonial and post-colonial Egypt, Esmeir (2012) illustrates how the concept of the human is interwoven with legal frameworks, leading to the emergence of humanity as a 'juridical category' (p. 3). According to Esmeir (2012), the law's function is to bind 'the living to the state' (p. 3). This inscription of life into a singular framework of juridico-political humanism permits the nation-state to demand that its citizens relinquish their rights in exchange for supposedly greater protection and freedom under the rule of law, all the while denying such protection to the marginalised and forcibly displaced. This configuration traces its roots to Western theorists such as Thomas Hobbes, John Locke, and Jean-Jacques Rousseau, who conceptualised the social contract around the principle of the rule of law. Their ideas gained traction as the nation-state increasingly succeeded in consolidating its dominion.

The structures underpinning juridico-political humanity are deeply entangled with violent power dynamics, modes of knowledge, and ways of being collectively identified as 'coloniality'. Proposed by the Peruvian sociologist Quijano (2000) and later developed by influential decolonial thinkers such as Mignolo (2021), Maldonado-Torres (2016), and Ndlovu-Gatsheni (2013), the concept of coloniality represents the metaphysical logic of being, power, and knowledge that sustains the juridico-political order we inhabit after centuries of slavery, colonisation, and forced displacement. The coloniality of being human entails the classification and stratification of humanity based on race, gender, class, and other markers. These hierarchies of human value are institutionalised and maintained by power structures that engender 'death-worlds… in which vast populations are subjected to conditions of life conferring upon them the status of living dead' (Mbembe, 2003, p. 40). Colonial onto-epistemic logics ensure the continued domination of knowledge production, perpetuating these violent structures. Together, these matrices of differential human existence, the associated systems of knowledge, and the governing power regimes sustain the precarious condition of racialised and marginalised peoples as subjects of no-rights. The refugee, in particular, exists at the crossroads of these colonial abstractions, cast as a subject stripped entirely of rights.

The coloniality of rights forms the foundation of the suffering and unhealed wounds inflicted on forcibly displaced people. These conditions subject them to the rule of no-rights, the epistemologies and discourses that legitimise this subjection, and the bordering regimes that govern their existence. Confined to abyssal conditions of sub-humanity, they inhabit, as Anzaldúa (2012) observes, the 'borderlands' that demarcate the racialised divisions of juridico-political humanity. In their world, as evoked by the open wounds described in the Introduction, nothing is secure; all remains suspended in a state of perpetual fragility and flux, dissolving the boundaries between being fully human and not. The conditions of raciality, violability, and disposability create the conditions of (de)humanity, a perpetual oscillation between existence and negation, where one's human status is both present and absent. Amidst this liminal state, (de)humanity emerges as the sole mode of being, defined by immobility, violability, killability, and a ceaseless struggle for safety.

As demonstrated, the human rights framework, which centres on nation-states organised by principles of territory, sovereign power, and population, ultimately reveals the (de)humanisation inflicted upon forcibly displaced people through the violent spectacle of racialised (b)ordering regimes. The nation-state, with its legal, political, and territorial structures, systematically excludes refugees from the realms of law, justice, and politics. As Agamben (1995) articulates, the refugee embodies 'the original fiction of sovereignty' (p. 117), often depicted as a disposable body, emblematic of destitution and poverty within carceral spaces, as well as a victim of human trafficking during perilous journeys. Paradoxically, however, refugees are also perceived as threats when crossing borders, seen in metropolitan areas as disturbances to the very foundations of the nation-state and the welfare of its citizens. For this reason, as Agamben (1995) argues, the refugee stands as an exceptional figure whose existence challenges the violent foundations of the nation-state and its juridico-political humanism. The refugee condition is one of despair and resistance, a profound abyss of damnation and rage.

Ultimately, the human rights system, which rhetorically claims to uphold the rights of all people, reveals itself to be a colonial project of 'pseudo-humanism', in which 'its concept of those rights has been – and still is – narrow and fragmentary, incomplete and biased and, all things considered, sordidly racist' (Césaire, 2023, p. 3). The pursuit of rights often entails acquiescence to the matrices of coloniality, perpetuating a ban on the political life of racialised and forcibly displaced people. Stripped of their subjecthood, refugees find themselves in a state of (de)humanity, not even constituted as subjects but perceived instead as vulnerable, dehumanised, and bereft of political existence. Their identity is affirmed through the relinquishment of their status as state subjects or citizens, and their humanity is only acknowledged in relation to a life that can be extinguished with absolute impunity—simply for existing and moving, even as victims. The feelings of abandonment and entrapment stemming from being born without rights and dying without rights, buried alive and perishing without a trace, for example, signify both the physical and metaphysical calamities of the refugee abyss.

Conclusion

The primary aim of briefly tracing the long and intricate evolution of rights-based ordering of human relations is to interrogate the onto-epistemic significance of 'Man' and 'Human' as presumably foundational constituents of the rights-based order. As Mignolo (2011) observes, 'Man' and 'Human' embody 'the bottom line of racial classification' (pp. 162–163). He further suggests that these terms signify and articulate 'the Western ideal of being Christian, being man and being human' (Mignolo, 2011, p. 160). The declarations of 'Man' and 'Human', deeply rooted in colonial, masculine, and racialised origins, underpin the profound wounds inflicted on the dignity and onto-epistemic significance of human relations. As Maldonado-Torres (2017) explains, the 'declaration' is 'more like a way of saying, or perhaps shouting, depending on the case, as if one is the bearer of absolute truths' (p. 125). The project of human rights, along with its declarations, which position the Human as the bearer of absolute truth for all humanity, projects an absolutist, totalitarian, and colonial vision of the world. Its conception of pseudo-humanism embodies the inherently exclusive telos of the Western Westphalian nation-state. The ultimate function of the rights-based order, as Agamben (2000) writes, revolves around 'the inscription of natural naked life in the political-juridical order of the nation-state' (p. 19).

Outside the West, the notion of human rights can no longer sustain its fictitious rhetoric or continued existence; it has lost both legal authority and intellectual substance. It is, if anything, a relic of the European colonial project 'responding to imperial necessity' (Mignolo, 2011, p. 161). As Fanon (1986) reminds us, affirming the relevance of these quixotic claims to rights requires wearing a white mask. The human rights project represents the final guise of the colonial saga of the civilising mission. It professes to ennoble humanity, elevate humankind, and humanise the entire world, starting with those deemed uncivilised savages. Yet its mask of benevolence, once passionately upheld in the metropoles of empire, and its rhetoric, which once inspired both activists and pacifists, now stand exposed as hollow and subdued. Stripped of its pretence, its brutal essence is starkly revealed as a foundation of violent force (and of a grammar of coloniality), continuing to fuel genocides as it teeters on the brink of collapse. The façade that once appeared benevolent is now exposed as superficial, sustaining only a relationship with the violence of raciality and coloniality. After all, the human rights project has reached a deadlock from which there appears to be no return. In his latest work, Agamben evokes this impasse through the image of a house ablaze, symbolising the juridico-political catastrophe unfolding across the world, whether in Europe or beyond, as an overwhelming fire we have chosen to ignore or pretend not to witness in all its consuming wrath (see Agamben, 2023).

In our poetic forethought, the essence of human relations, our presence in the world and our understanding of ourselves in relation to other beings and things, transcends the Western colonial project of a rights-based system or its associated conception of juridico-political humanity. As demonstrated, the limited and fragmented perspective of human rights, along with the juridico-political framework it upholds, has given rise to a hierarchical and racialised organisation of humanity, where certain groups are deemed less human than others, stripped of any rights whatsoever. This inherently colonial organisation, as described by Maldonado-Torres (2016), has inflicted upon human relations a 'metaphysical catastrophe', whose function is to create 'zones of being human and not being human or not being human enough' (p. 13). Being human entails the recognition and affirmation of one's full humanity amidst this metaphysical catastrophe, while sub-humanity encompasses not only a lack of access to the basic necessities of life but also the constant questioning of one's humanity by oneself and others (Maldonado-Torres, 2016). This racially hierarchised conception of humanity seeks to erase the possibility of unpredictability, incalculability, opacity, and emergence by reducing the complexities of existence to measurable metrics, transparency, and rigid classifications.

What is often overlooked in the grand claims of human rights is the metaphysical and physical catastrophe they impose on racialised people, including the forcibly displaced. The open wounds inflicted by the nation-state on those seeking refuge demand profound questioning of the nation-state itself, its laws, politics, and powers, along with the associated modes of being and knowing. It has become imperative to argue that, even in abstract contemplation, the nation-state, our era's dominant political entity, and its domesticated system of rights have had their limitations radically exposed in moments of genocidal wars across multiple regions. As we write this book, the international foundational principles of sovereignty, law, rationality, and nationality tremble before our eyes amidst ongoing genocidal conflicts in the Middle East, particularly in the Gaza Strip in Palestine (see Albanese, 2024). As Arendt (2017) famously argued, the nation-state's expansion of power, imperialist ambitions beyond its borders, bureaucratisation of political life, and racialised (b)ordering epitomise its decline and the erosion of its protective institutions.

The figure of the refugee stands at the centre of self-inflicted disruptions, exposing the futility of the rights-based order and the violence of sovereign power of the nation-state, widening the cracks within. As Agamben (1995, p. 117) articulates, 'If in the system of the nation-state the refugee represents such a disquieting element, it is above all because by breaking up the identity between man and citizen, between nativity and nationality, the refugee throws into crisis the original fiction of sovereignty'. 'For this reason', Agamben (1995) adds, 'this apparently marginal figure deserves rather to be considered the central figure of our political history' (p. 117). The refugee, compelled to inhabit these fissures and endure open wounds, calls for an urgent reimagining of life amidst the ruins of coloniality and raciality. The rightless possess a right to demand 'human behavior from the other' (Fanon, 1986, p. 179). To demand humanity from the other requires not only confronting the inhumanity projected onto them but also the humanity expected of the other. While the inhumanity is evident, the humanity demanded of the other is not grounded in human rights discourse, as it is the source of colonial violence and the structure of coloniality. This is an invitation to challenge Eurocentric modes of existence, human relations, and ways of knowing, while envisioning a new seed of life.

The right of those who are deprived of rights cannot be reduced to mere recognition within a system built upon their rightlessness; instead, their focus must be on imagining a new world. The non-experience of rights is not merely a void, but an opening to new possibilities yet to be explored. The refugee embodies this concept of limits, veering into a new world beyond them. The question, then, becomes: how can this non-experience of rights give rise to new experiences, and under what circumstances? The refugee stands as a foundational *arché*, at least in understanding the open wounds and scars from which we can begin to reimagine the world anew. The refugee offers a lament for existing at the edge of life and death, and an announcement of the new openings that lie beyond the current juridico-political landscape. These openings call for respect for opacity, urging us to move beyond ideas of transparency and predictability. Hold onto these thoughts, as we return to them in the chapters that follow. For now, let us proceed to the next chapter to examine the structure and anatomy of the womb-abyss that gives rise to the refugee abyss.

References

Agamben, G. (1995) We Refugees. *Symposium: A Quarterly Journal in Modern Literatures*, 49, 114–119. https://doi.org/10.1080/00397709.1995.10733798

Agamben, G. (1998) *Sovereign Power and Bare Life, Homo Sacer*. Stanford, California: Stanford University Press.

Agamben, G. (2000) *Means Without End: Notes on Politics, Theory Out of Bounds*. Minneapolis, Minnesota: University of Minnesota Press.
Agamben, G. (2015) *The Use of Bodies, Homo Sacer*. Stanford, California: Stanford University Press.
Agamben, G. (2023) *When the House Burns Down: From the Dialect of Thought, The Italian List*. London–New York: Seagull Books.
Albanese, F. (2024) Anatomy of a Genocide. Available from: https://reliefweb.int/report/occupied-palestinian-territory/anatomy-genocide-report-special-rapporteur-situation-human-rights-palestinian-territories-occupied-1967-francesca-albanese-ahrc5573-advance-unedited-version (accessed 23.4.24)
Alston, P. (2013) Does The Past Matter? On the Origins of Human Rights. *Harvard Law Review*, 126, 2043–2081.
Anzaldúa, G. (2012) *Borderlands: la frontera: The New Mestiza*, 4th ed. San Francisco, California: Aunt Lute Books.
Arendt, H. (2017) *The Origins of Totalitarianism*. London: Penguin Classics.
Behrman, S. (2018) Refugee Law as a Means of Control. *Journal of Refugee Studies*. https://doi.org/10.1093/jrs/fey016
Betts, A., and Loescher, G. (2010) *Refugees in International Relations*. Oxford: Oxford University Press.
Betts, A., Loescher, G., and Books, D. (2011) *Refugees in International Relations*. Oxford: Oxford University Press.
Carpenter, D. (2018) 'Magna Carta 1215: Its Social and Political Context', in L. Goldman (Ed) *Magna Carta: History, Context and Influence*. London: School of Advanced Study, University of London, pp. 17–24.
Césaire, A. (2023) 'Discourse on Colonialism', in D. Brydon (ed.) *Postcolonism*, pp. 310–339. London: Routledge.
Chetail, V. (2003) Fridtjof Nansen and the International Protection of Refugees: An Introduction. *Refugee Survey Quarterly*, 22, 1–6. https://doi.org/10.1093/rsq/22.1.1
Cmiel, K. (2004) The Recent History of Human Rights. *American Historical Review*, 109(1), 117–135.
Congress, U.S. (1776) Declaration of Independence (1776) [WWW Document]. Bill of Rights Institute. Available from: https://billofrightsinstitute.org/primary-sources/declaration-of-independence/ (accessed 12.2.21).
Croxton, D. (1999) The Peace of Westphalia of 1648 and the Origins of Sovereignty. *The International History Review*, 21, 569–591. https://doi.org/10.1080/07075332.1999.9640869
Easton-Calabria, E.E. (2015) From Bottom-Up to Top-Down: The 'Pre-History' of Refugee Livelihoods Assistance from 1919 to 1979. *Journal of Refugee Studies*, 28, 412–436. https://doi.org/10.1093/jrs/fev004
Esmeir, S. (2012) *Juridical Humanity: A Colonial History*. Redwood City, California: Stanford University Press.
Fanon, F. (1986) *Black Skin, White Masks*, Repr. ed, Pluto classics. London: Pluto Press.
Grovogui, S.N. (2006) 'Mind, body, and gut! Elements of a postcolonial human rights discourse', *Decolonizing International Relations*, pp. 1–30. https://digitalcommons.law.umaryland.edu/cgi/viewcontent.cgi?article=1002&context=iclc_papers.
Human Rights Watch (2019) ICC: Congo Warlord Guilty of Crimes Against Humanity [WWW Document]. Human Rights Watch. Available from: https://www.hrw.org/news/2019/07/08/icc-congo-warlord-guilty-crimes-against-humanity (accessed 14.2.21).
Ibhawoh, B. (2008) *Imperialism and Human Rights: Colonial Discourses of Rights and Liberties in African History*. Albany, New York: State University of New York Press.

ICC (2023) Situation in Ukraine: ICC Judges Issue Arrest Warrants Against Vladimir Vladimirovich Putin and Maria Alekseyevna Lvova-Belova | International Criminal Court [WWW Document]. Available from: https://www.icc-cpi.int/news/situation-ukraine-icc-judges-issue-arrest-warrants-against-vladimir-vladimirovich-putin-and (accessed 8.1.25).
ICC (2024) Situation in the State of Palestine: ICC Pre-Trial Chamber I Rejects the State of Israel's Challenges to Jurisdiction and Issues Warrants of Arrest for Benjamin Netanyahu and Yoav Gallant | International Criminal Court [WWW Document]. Available from: https://www.icc-cpi.int/news/situation-state-palestine-icc-pre-trial-chamber-i-rejects-state-israels-challenges (accessed 8.1.25).
Ignatieff, M. (2000) I. Human Rights as Politics II. Human Rights as Idolatry. The Tanner Lectures on Human Values, Delivered at Princeton University (April).
Kiros, T. (2005) *Zara Yacob: Rationality of the Human Heart*. Trenton, New Jersey: Red Sea Press.
Kuhrt, A. (1983) The Cyrus Cylinder and Achaemenid Imperial Policy. *Journal for the Study of the Old Testament*, 8, 83–97. https://doi.org/10.1177/030908928300802507
Labuda, P.I. (2023) Beyond Rhetoric: Interrogating the Eurocentric Critique of International Criminal law's Selectivity in the Wake of the 2022 Ukraine Invasion. *Leiden Journal of International Law*, 36, 1095–1116.
Long, K. (2013) When Refugees Stopped Being Migrants: Movement, Labour and Humanitarian Protection. *Migration Studies*, 1, 4–26. https://doi.org/10.1093/migration/mns001
Mackinnon, E.S. (2018) Declaration as Disavowal: The Politics of Race and Empire in the Universal Declaration of Human Rights. *Political Theory*. https://doi.org/10.1177/0090591718780697
Maldonado-Torres, N. (2016) *Outline of Ten Theses on Coloniality and Decoloniality*. Paris: Frantz Fanon Foundation.
Maldonado-Torres, N. (2017) On the Coloniality of Human Rights. *rccs*, pp. 117–136. https://doi.org/10.4000/rccs.6793
Mauzy, D.K. (1997) The Human Rights and "Asian Values" Debate in Southeast Asia: Trying to Clarify the Key Issues. *The Pacific Review*, 10, 210–236. https://doi.org/10.1080/09512749708719218
Mbembe, A. (2003) Necropolitics. *Public Culture*, 15, 11–40.
Mbembe, A. (2019a) *Necropolitics, Theory in Forms*. Durham: Duke University Press.
Mbembe, A. (2019b). Bodies as Borders. *From the European South*, 4, 5–18.
Mignolo, W. (2021) *The Politics of Decolonial Investigations, On Decoloniality*. Durham: Duke University Press.
Mignolo, W.D. (2011) Who Speaks for the "Human" in Human Rights? *Cadernos de Estudos Culturais*, 3.
Mountz, A. (2020) *The Death of Asylum: Hidden Geographies of the Enforcement Archipelago*. Minneapolis, Minnesota: University of Minnesota Press.
Murithi, T. (2013) *The African Union and the International Criminal Court: An Embattled Relationship*. Institute for Justice and Reconciliation.
Ndlovu-Gatsheni, S.J. and Chambati, W. (2013) *Coloniality of Power in Postcolonial Africa: Myths of Decolonization*. Dakar: Codesria.
Nyers, P. (2013) *Rethinking Refugees: Beyond State of Emergency*, 1st ed. London: Routledge.
OAU (1974) OAU Convention. African Union. Available from: https://au.int/sites/default/files/treaties/36400-treaty-36400-treaty-oau_convention_1963.pdf
Oliver, K. (2017) *Carceral Humanitarianism: Logics of Refugee Detention, Forerunners*. Minneapolis, Minnesota: University of Minnesota Press.
Organization of American States (1984) Cartagena Declaration on Refugees. Colloquium on the International Protection of Refugees in Central America, Mexico and Panama. Available from: https://www.oas.org/dil/1984_cartagena_declaration_on_refugees.pdf

Quijano, A. (2000) Coloniality of Power and Eurocentrism in Latin America. *International Sociology*, 15, 215–232.
Rancière, J. (2004) Who is the Subject of the Rights of Man? *The South Atlantic Quarterly*, 103(2), 297–310.
Said, E.W. (2003) *Orientalism, Reprinted With a New Preface. Ed.* London: Penguin Books.
Santas, G. (Ed.) (2006) *The Blackwell Guide to Plato's Republic*, 1st ed. Wiley. https://doi.org/10.1002/9780470776414
Sikkink, K. (1993) Human Rights, Principled Issue-Networks, and Sovereignty in Latin America. *International Organization*, 47, 411–441. https://doi.org/10.1017/S0020818300028010
Stephens, A.H. (1861) Cornerstone speech. March 21, 226.
United Nations (2015) Universal Declaration of Human Rights. Available from: http://www.un.org/en/udhrbook/pdf/udhr_booklet_en_web.pdf
Yohannes, H.T., Yemane, T.H., and Wangari-Jones, P. (2024) 'Chapter 1: The Hostile Environment, Covid-19, and the Creation of Asylum Colonies in the UK', in G. K. Bhambra, L. Mayblin, K. Medien, and M. Viveros (Eds.) *The Sage Handbook of Global Sociology*. London: SAGE.

3 The Nation-State as a Womb-Abyss

Introduction

This chapter has two primary objectives. The first is to propose an underlying proposition and theoretical orientation: the nation-state is a womb-abyss in Glissantian sense of the concept. The womb-abyss underpins the nation-state both as a system of juridico-political organisation and as a condition of life that shapes human experience within and beyond its physical borders. We examine the structures of sovereignty and governmentality within the womb-abyss, focusing on what Simon (2007) describes as a 'carceral state'. Simon defines the carceral state as one that prioritises the creation and expansion of prisons, as well as the regulation and supervision of prisoners. He argues that 'the carceral state is both more and less than a state that builds and fills prisons' (Simon, 2007, p. 476). While Simon's analysis primarily focuses on the prison system in the United States, the concept of the carceral state challenges the idea of the nation-state, including the welfare state, as the dominant political entity. Understood from Foucauldian perspective, it offers critical insights into the gradual transformation of the nation-state into a womb-abyss.

The second objective is to explore Eritrea as a quintessential example of the postcolonial womb-abyss. Eritrea is one of the few countries to have achieved independence in the final decade of the 20th century, in 1991. Despite the initial euphoria, the country descended into a self-colonising state, where its primary function became the protection of its hard-won sovereignty at any cost, including the lives of its people. For more than three decades, the country has remained trapped in a precarious relationship with its people, its neighbours, and the international community. Obviously, the precariousness in Eritrea is not solely of its own making, but is part of a global coloniality and its colonial world order, one driven by geopolitical interests, resource exploitation, and the associated modalities of governance through dominant power structures. The country is a typical example of a postcolony yet to grow into 'mature adulthood'. Understanding the country that Eritrea has become is essential for contextualising the experiences of Eritrean refugees, both within and beyond the womb-abyss. We explore the experiences of Eritreans in their homeland before delving

DOI: 10.4324/9781003437192-4

into their experiences as refugees, outside the womb-abyss that gave birth to them, in the following chapter.

Together, these objectives offer insight into the refugee abyss, both within and beyond the belly of the womb-abyss. The central question explored here concerns how state power is formed, administered, and projected within the womb-abyss, regulating the (im)mobilities of populations in an era of global (b)ordering.

The nation-state as a womb-abyss

On 13 May 1881, William Westgarth[1] published a proposal titled *Trade Relations of the Colonies and the Mother Country* in the *Journal of the Society of Arts*. The proposal begins by praising the contributions of the 'colonial family' or 'British Dominions' to the 'mother country', Britain. He then outlines what he describes as his 'mode of treating the subject' through four steps, which can be summarised as follows: a) measuring the profit, b) examining the key 'features' and 'items' of the trade, c) understanding the complexities of tariffs in trading relations, and d) offering 'some general reflections on the whole case' (Westgarth, 1880, p. 536). He concludes the proposal by emphasising that these 'subjects' must be fully understood by his audience, namely the colonial administrations he advised at the time.

Our focus, however, is neither on these colonial remarks nor the history of the British Empire. Instead, we are drawn to the evocative pairing of 'mother' and 'country', a socio-linguistic and ideological construct deeply embedded in the grammar of empire and colonialism. In this grammar, the 'mother country' is portrayed as a benevolent protector and provider. The mother country, as Mbembe (2001) writes, 'portrays itself as a *free gift*, proposing to relieve its object of poverty and free it from debased condition by raising it to the level of a human being' (pp. 34–35, emphasis in original). In exchange for its 'free gift' and humanisation, the mother country demanded unwavering loyalty and reverence from its colonies and subjects. The mother country not only claims to provide and civilise but also disciplines and punishes, much like a parent chastising a wayward child. It exerts and maintains its authority over its colonies and subjects through what Mbembe (2001, p. 24) describes as '*commandement*'. The colonies and the empire's subjects are depicted as perpetual children, bound to obedience regardless of their dissatisfaction. Their existence is entirely devoted to serving the interests of the mother country, often at the expense of their own malnourishment, destitution, and exploitation. Most significantly, the children (colonies and subjects) are never permitted to mature. The mother country dictates their growth and death, and any attempt to challenge this imposed childhood is met with devastating retribution. At the same time, the mother country resists ageing. It strives to remain an eternal and commanding adult, its strength intended to inspire fear even in the gods and ghosts of its children.

This mother-child dynamic is not a mere exploitative analogy between the mother country and its colonies; rather, it unfolds as an omnipresent and omnipotent projection of racial and colonial power, consciously and unconsciously woven into the fabric of the relationship between coloniser and colonised. It is projected as the sole framework for forming human relations or the civilised humanism that the mother country proclaims to promote. Within this fraught and asymmetrical relation, Fanon (1986) argues, the colonised are coerced into a forced marriage with 'white culture, white beauty, white whiteness' as the only avenue to 'civilisation and dignity' (p. 45). Yet, within this paradigm, civilisation and dignity, however they may be understood, remain unattainable for the colonised, who are confronted by an unrelenting impasse: '*turn white or disappear*' (Fanon, 1986, p. 75, emphasis in original). For Fanon, the reclamation of dignity must transcend this colonial impasse, breaking free from the suffocating binaries of the colonial condition and the rigid hierarchies of race. This reclamation, he insists, can only be achieved through the transformative struggle for radical decolonisation, or a struggle to reimagine human relations beyond the violent confines of the colonial framework.

As history reads, after centuries of unchallenged dominance, the mother country began to falter, and the colonies dared to yearn for growth. In the 20th century, nationalist movements, independence struggles, and the pursuit of self-determination emerged as a collective quest for 'adulthood' and 'motherhood'. The colonies aspired to become 'mothers' to their own citizens, a vision achievable only through independence from their former oppressors. Ultimately, the mother country retreated to its metropole, and the former colonies mutated to what Mbembe (2001) terms the 'postcolony'. However, as Fanon (1986) poignantly observes, the children (the colonies) face a profound challenge: they do not know how to become adults, having never been allowed to be. Fanon warns against these children (the colonies) imitating their mothers in an effort to become 'white' (1986, p. 4). Unfortunately, many of the structures and institutions of colonial power still remain intact in these postcolonial states. As Fanon feared, independence resulted in little more than territorial sovereignty, with the most compliant children replacing the colonisers in positions of authority.

This meant, in effect, that the mother country still retains its structures of power, with its commandement not only mimicked but still deployed in the postcolony. '*Commandement*', Mbembe (2001, p. 25, emphasis in original) writes, 'rested on a very specific *imaginary* of state sovereignty', or an entanglement of rightlessness and violence, in which the former is both underpinned and maintained through the latter. This constitution of 'colonial sovereignty', he further clarifies, was sustained by 'founding violence', 'the sole power to judge', and the 'maintenance, spread, and permanence' of this colonial relation of violence (Mbembe, 2001, p. 25). According to Mbembe (2001), while the first two ensured conquest and absolute rule in the colony, the latter 'ended up constituting the central cultural *imaginary* that the state shared with society' (p. 25, emphasis in original). Today, the chains and tentacles of this colonial constitution of sovereignty and governance can be found everywhere in the postcolony, within power structures, institutional frameworks, physical infrastructure, governance, as well as in the socio-cultural fabric, education, and language. The postcolony remains endlessly entangled with the mother country, which has since rebranded itself as the nation-state. In fact, whether in the postcolony or the mother country, the nation-state has become the universal principle of sovereignty, territoriality, and identity.

Born of colonial violence, the nation-state is a 'womb-abyss', a matrix that both gives birth to and devours life. It emerges as a mutation of Glissant's theorisation of the womb-abyss, akin to a slave ship adrift in the vast expanses of time, space, and reason. While the womb symbolises fertility, potentiality, and possibility, the abyss evokes violence, the unknown, and existential uncertainty. From Glissant's poetic vision, three key features of the womb-abyss can be identified. First, the womb-abyss is 'pregnant with as many dead as living under the sentence of death' (Glissant, 2009, p. 6). It both gives birth and consumes, including and excluding life in its belly. Second, the womb-abyss is a 'tautology' (Glissant, 2009, p. 6), which, by its very logic and structure, manifests as a necessity that is redundant and circular, constituting violence and devoid of emergence. Third, as Glissant eloquently writes, 'The experience of the abyss lies inside and outside the [womb-abyss]' (2009, p. 7). Within and outside the womb-abyss, life is perpetually experienced as an abyss of open wounds and elusive dreams and memories.

These three features of the womb-abyss are tantamount to the archetypal foundations and principles of the modern nation-state. Agamben, in his extensive exploration of sovereignty, biopolitics, and governance, demonstrates that the nation-state's foundation lies in the three-fold relationship between the state, nation, and territory (see Agamben, 1995, 1998, 2005, 2015). For Agamben, the state functions as the apparatus of sovereignty: the entity that holds the exclusive authority to decide on the 'state of exception' and enacts political authority and juridical order (1998, p. 83). Territory refers to the defined physical space, a geographic domain and a site for control, surveillance, and regulation, where the apparatus of the state operates. 'Space', Mbembe (2003, p. 23) writes, is 'the raw material of sovereignty'. The concept of the nation introduces 'distinct' cultural, ethnic, or historical identities into the framework of governance of the population that reside in a given territory. It creates a mirage of collective identity, or what Anderson (2020) describes as an 'imagined community', often associated with existence of shared language, traditions, or myths of origin. This imagined identity underpins and reinforces operations of inclusion and exclusion, distinguishing between insiders and outsiders.

Agamben demonstrates that, in this articulation of the 'trinity of state/nation/territory', the nation-state asserts its monopoly over law, life, and power by integrating the elements of state (legal authority), nation (identity/nativity), and territory (spatial domain) (Agamben, 1995, p. 117, 1998).

This tripartite structure enables the governance of life itself, creating zones of indistinction between inclusion and exclusion, life and death. At its core, the nation-state both includes and excludes, determining who belongs and who does not, as it 'decides on the value or the nonvalue of life as such' (Agamben, 1998, p. 83). It suspends the law to uphold its inherently exclusive order, merging sovereign power, national identity, and territorial control. According to Agamben, this creates a 'state of exception' in which the law is suspended, reducing life to bare existence (Agamben, 1998, 2005). Central to this state of exception is the biopolitical management and necropolitical experimentation of populations, carried out through the implementation of (b)orders, camps, detention centres, and similar constructs on a 'global scale' (Mbembe, 2019a, p. 11).

Wielding a monopoly over legitimate violence, the nation-state enforces its will by deploying and withdrawing laws and rights, legislating the very processes of life and death, waging wars, and committing monstrous crimes such as genocide, war crimes, and crimes against humanity. It reduces its citizens to mere naked corporealities, existing in a state of perpetual docility, utility, and violability. They oscillate between mobility and immobility, existence and de-existence, all through the calculated manipulation, abuse, and exploitation of their physical and human potential. These actions are often justified under the banners of self-determination, self-preservation, or military domination. Underpinned by the matrices of coloniality and raciality, state violence becomes indefinitely normalised. The immediate site of the projection and experimentation of the matrices of coloniality and raciality is the postcolony.

Simultaneously, as Foucault (1998) asserts, the nation-state feigns a commitment to fostering life through a biopolitical calibration of existence, employing sophisticated social, economic, medical, and genetic mechanisms to nurture life. Foucault's optimism is rooted in the hopeful belief that the application of power at the societal level is gradually supplanted by what he terms 'bio-power' or 'productive power', a power that optimises, multiplies, and positively impacts life (1998, p. 140). This power, according to Foucault, operates by regulating and disciplining bodies to maximise their utility. Unlike sovereign power, bio-power 'does not celebrate death' (Ojakangas, 2005, p. 7). However, this ostensibly life-enhancing role of the state is inherently paradoxical: while it seeks to promote vitality, it simultaneously undermines it through necropolitical deployments, exposing a violent interplay between the fostering of life (biopower) and its destruction, or the exercise of 'necropower' (Mbembe, 2003, p. 25). Contrary to Foucault's optimism, biopower and necropower function as mechanisms of necropolitics that distinguish between lives qualified as liveable and those deemed disposable (Mbembe, 2003, 2019b).

The qualification of liveable and disposable lives is regulated through the arrogated distribution of rights, enacted by laws, as outlined in Chapter 2.

Anything or anyone positioned beyond the confines of territorial boundaries and outside the realm of rights-bearing bodies is cast into a state of exception, existing in a condition of constitutive exteriority to the borders and order of the womb-abyss. The rights-based system depends on the confinement of the Other (including othered faces and places) in a constitutive outside of its metropoles and matrices of power. Within the structure and grammar of coloniality, as Mbembe demonstrates in his examination of the *Aesthetics of Superfluity*, the Other appears as a mere 'surface', 'quantity', or 'graphics' (Mbembe, 2008), while the Other's place is condemned to what he calls '*death-worlds*' (Mbembe, 2003, p. 40, emphasis in original). Undoubtedly, most postcolonial countries in Africa find themselves caught between the euphoria of gaining independence from colonisation and the lingering effects of the dark underbelly of the structure and grammar of coloniality.

In his influential book *On the Postcolony* (2001), Mbembe explores the commandments of the death-world, offering a comprehensive analysis of the pervasive portrayal of Africa as a continent defined by extreme brutality, bestiality, death, and destruction. He argues that this portrayal adopts an animistic and necropolitical perspective, projecting Africa as 'a bottomless abyss where everything is noise, a yawning gap, and primordial chaos' (Mbembe, 2001, p. 3). However, Mbembe maintains that this sordidly racist and colonial representation of the expansive and intricate continent fails to acknowledge the profound anguish stemming from its historical and contemporary challenges. Mbembe summarises the challenges faced by the continent in general, and the postcolonial state of Africa in particular, as follows:

> Terrible movements, laws that underpin and organize tragedy and genocide, gods that present themselves in the guise of death and destitution, monsters lying in wait, corpses coming and going on the tide, infernal powers, threats of all sorts, abandonments, events without responses, monstrous couplings, blind waves, impossible paths, terrible forces that everyday tears human beings, animals, plants, and things from their sphere of life and condemn them to death.
>
> (Mbembe, 2001, p. 8)

This imbrication of the shackles of coloniality and postcolonial letdowns highlight the main characteristics of the underlying womb-abyss in the postcolonial state. Historically, the condition of the postcolonial state is characterised by the unequal determination of human worth through various mechanisms of exposure to 'necropolitics' or 'the capacity to define who matters and who does not, who is *disposable* and who is not' (Mbembe, 2003, p. 27, emphasis in original). This fundamental distinction between human experiences, underpinned by the physical and metaphysical operations of coloniality of power, knowledge, and being, has emerged as the prevailing paradigm in the postcolonial trajectory (see Ndlovu-Gatsheni, 2013).

In an age of global 'borderization' (Mbembe, 2019a, p. 8), however, the reality of necropolitics—the violability, disposability, and perishability of life—is no longer confined to specific times and places. Instead, these experiences of necropolitical experimentation are now projected on a global level as fundamental forces that underpin nation-states, which have been transformed into womb-abysses. Whether in a postcolonial setting or in the metropole, the determination and administration of the necropolitical forces to regulate who lives and who dies has given rise to death-worlds or 'forms of social existence in which vast populations are subjected to conditions of life that confer upon them the status of *living dead*' (Mbembe, 2003, p. 40, emphasis in original). Within these realms of necropolitical experimentation in the death-worlds, Mbembe further explains that 'the calculus of life passes through the death of the Other' (2003, p. 18). This passage of death through the Other, with its titrations and calculations of life and death, embodies the defining characteristics of the womb-abyss.

The Foucauldian concept of the 'carceral system' offers valuable insights into how sovereignty and governmentality operate within the womb-abyss, both in tshe metropole and the postcolony. The concept of the 'carceral system' is derived from his influential work, *Discipline and Punish* (2012), and refers to a network of institutionalised practices that go beyond the limits of law and rights, forming what can be described as modalities of punishment and control. Foucault (2012) clarifies:

> The "carceral" with its many diffuse or compact forms, its institutions of supervision or constraint, of discreet surveillance and insistent coercion, assured the communication of punishments according to quality and quantity; it connected in series or disposed according to subtle divisions the minor and the serious penalties, the mild and the strict forms of treatment, bad marks and light sentences. (p. 299)

Foucault argues that the techniques and institutions of punishment and control deployed by the carceral system extend beyond the prison itself. These techniques permeate society through various disciplinary and punitive measures. For instance, the prison complex, along with its institutions and technologies for incarceration, surveillance, supervision, and rehabilitation, as well as the advanced borders equipped with electronic passports, biometrics, entry/exit points, and checkpoints, and the bureaucratisation of life through systems of control and punishment, which are deeply intertwined in everyday life, present evidence of the manifestation of the carceral system in everyday life. These practices of the carceral system and biopolitical supervision exist in many countries, whether they are liberal or authoritarian.

In her book *Precarious Life: The Powers of Mourning and Violence* (2006), Butler explains that these exercises of power are deeply rooted in the practices of 'governmentality' and 'sovereignty'. According to Butler, governmentality is commonly understood as a form of power that maintains, controls, and regulates the movement and administration of people, goods, and entities within a specific country or beyond. Meanwhile, sovereignty refers to the governing power of the state, encompassing both the body that holds authority and the people within a defined space who make up the womb-abyss. Historically, the power to determine and act outside the bounds of normal legal order (the exception) has shifted from monarchs to authoritarian leaders, and more recently, from states to legal institutions and constitutions. This shift has resulted in new techniques for exercising control and governance. This transfer of power to womb-abyss and its institutions has given rise to biopolitical regulation, where power is exerted over 'life itself' (Foucault, 1998, p. 143).

The application of sovereign power in ways that directly inscribe life into power has created a situation where sovereignty not only overpowers human communities, but also poses a threat to life itself and its conditions of liveability, durability, and perishability. In Foucault's terms, sovereign power is armed with the 'right to take life or let live', symbolised by 'the sword' (1998, p. 136). This characterisation by Foucault highlights how the principles of sovereignty of the womb-abyss have become a mysterious aspect of modern political life. Foucault argues that in modern societies the sovereign state exercising power in the name of its entire population has exposed to death 'the biological existence of a population... because power is situated and exercised at the level of life, the species, the race, and the large-scale phenomena of population' (1998, p. 137). Sovereignty, as explained by Foucault, poses the greatest threat to the organised human life, as seen in state-sanctioned genocides, mass murders, and massacres.

As stated, for the colonised, sovereignty only served to condemn them to a necropolitical realm of exception, a space 'between subjecthood and objecthood' (Mbembe, 2003, p. 26). In this realm of necropolitical operation, sovereignty and governmentality assume a new dimension, where their purpose is to exert control over life by subjecting it to a differentiated and calculated death, including death within life. Butler (2006) explains, 'sovereignty is exercised in the act of suspension, but also in the self-allocation of legal prerogative; governmentality denotes an operation of administration power that is extra-legal, even as it can and does return to law as a field of tactical operations' (p. 55). In other words, sovereignty diffuses itself throughout bureaucratic institutions and structures of governmentality, wielding lawless and violent power. Human life is subjected to the possibility of being killed without conditions or limits in the name of sovereignty. The womb-abyss becomes a necropolitical matrix, where life is perpetually lived under the shadow of death, an imminent threat of perishability. It generates and expels life without end.

Eritrea as a womb-abyss

Eritrea is a striking embodiment of this womb-abyss, where the possibility of a dignified life is inextricably entwined with the omnipresent violence of the sovereign projected into an indefinite future. The result is a disquieting reality in which death, including a death that resides within life itself, becomes the prevailing norm, rendering the very essence of life an elusive possibility. Within this womb-abyss, existence unfolds only within the confines of carcerality, violability, and pervasive perishability, leaving a profound, open wound upon its people. The structure and condition of the womb-abyss that defines the state of Eritrea is shaped by three interconnected forms of violence: *colonial violence, gedli or 'the struggle', and state violence*. Our focus lies on state violence, the principal force behind forced displacement in the post-independence era, while also tracing a brief outline of the historical evolution that preceded it.

Colonial violence

Colonial violence, pervasive in many former and present-day colonies, can be traced back to the brutal conquest of what is now Eritrea. This violence stemmed from the exploitation of its resources, the racialisation and dehumanisation of its people, and the subsequent erasure and transformation of their cultural and historical identities. Eritrea's current borders were established during Italy's colonial expansion into the Horn of Africa. These borders were shaped through a series of agreements between the Italian colonial government and King Menelik of Ethiopia during the first two decades of Italian colonisation, culminating in three key treaties (De Guttry et al., 2021). The first treaty, known as the Mereb-Belesa-Muna line, was signed in 1900 and defined part of the Eritrean-Ethiopian border. The second treaty, signed in 1902, outlined the western section of the border, creating a tri-point where Eritrea, Ethiopia, and Sudan converge. The final treaty, signed in 1908, completed the border by establishing another tri-point between Eritrea, Ethiopia, and Djibouti. The entire Eritrean-Ethiopian border stretches between these two tri-points, from Djibouti in the southeast to Sudan in the west.

Italian colonisation not only delineated Eritrea as a territorial entity but also integrated it into what Woldemikael (2013) calls 'a hierarchically organized global system of nation-states' (p. ix). This inclusion profoundly affected the local population, disrupting their way of life, socio-political structures, and cultural identities. For example, significant numbers of Italian settlers migrated to Eritrea, imposing exploitative and discriminatory policies. Local Eritreans were barred from certain streets in major cities and granted only limited access to education. This period marked a significant disruption in historical continuity, sense of belonging, socio-cultural identity, and connection to their lands for the local population (see Woldemikael, 2013). Italian rule in Eritrea came to an end with Italy's defeat by the Allies in World War II.

After the Italians, Eritrea came under the British Military Administration (BMA) for a decade. During this period, the BMA plundered Eritrea's infrastructure and resources while fostering divisions along ethnic and religious lines. As Kibreab (2009a) notes, the British approach denied Eritrea's sovereignty and the Eritrean people's right to self-determination. To advance its political interests in the region, the BMA proposed partitioning Eritrea between Ethiopia and Sudan. This policy, however, faced strong opposition from both Eritreans and the international community. Ultimately, the BMA relinquished control, leaving Eritrea's fate to be decided by the international community and Ethiopia.

In 1950, the United Nations resolved to federate Eritrea with Ethiopia. Despite being denied the right to self-determination, Eritrea officially became a federated independent state in 1952. However, this federation was short-lived. In 1962, Ethiopia invaded Eritrea, dissolved the federation, and annexed the territory into its own domain.

As in many African colonies, the colonisers determined who could live under what conditions in pre-independent Eritrea. In their pursuit of total domination, they subjected the local population to relentless systemic colonial violence for centuries. This violence infiltrated every facet of existence, seizing lands, depleting resources, and dismantling ways of life, while casting an enduring shadow over the destiny of the oppressed. It scarred bodies and minds, fractured cultures and languages, and tore histories asunder, leaving open wounds that persist across generations. It was not confined to conquest, but also stained being, knowledge, and relationships, embedding profound scars in the essence of life itself. Colonial violence became the foundation for perpetual violence, their ripples extending through time. We briefly return to some of the impacts at the beginning of the next chapter.

Gedli or the struggle

Ethiopia's annexation of Eritrea and its treatment of the Eritrean people gave rise to a liberation movement, known as Gedli or 'the struggle'. The primary goal of this struggle was to achieve independence by bringing an end to colonisation. Even before Ethiopia dissolved the federation and annexed Eritrea, Eritreans opposing Ethiopia's colonial ambitions had already initiated armed resistance against the occupation. In 1961, a liberation war began in the western and northern regions of the country, gradually gaining momentum. Initially led by a small group of Eritrean lowlanders, the armed struggle eventually attracted thousands of Eritrean youths from all parts of the country. Eritrean men and women joined the fight for independence and self-determination in significant numbers.

For three decades, successive Ethiopian regimes sought to crush the Eritrean people's demand and struggle for self-determination. In their attempts to suppress the resistance, the colonial authorities normalised extreme violence, including mass murder, massacres, arbitrary detentions, and torture.

Ordinary Eritreans were relentlessly terrorised and killed in their homeland. The escalating bloodshed turned Eritrea into a vast crime scene marked by unimaginable human suffering. As the guerrilla war intensified, Ethiopian colonial forces targeted the physical environment and infrastructure of Eritrea. Forests, farms, villages, and towns were burned, while roads and bridges were destroyed or blocked. Mountains became deadly minefields, and hospitals and schools were repurposed as detention centres and military camps. 'Even the stones are burning', declared Zeinab Yassin, the celebrated Eritrean poet and mother, capturing the devastating impact of these acts (Grey and Pateman, 1991). The Ethiopian regime sought to reinforce Eritrea's inherited status as a no-man's-land, reducing its people to what Woldemikael (2013) describes as 'bare existence, merely bodies that have no rights and protections' (p. ix).

In May 1991, after three decades of relentless struggle and sacrifice, Eritrea achieved its long-awaited independence with the defeat of Ethiopian forces. Two years later, in April 1993, Eritrea was internationally recognised as a sovereign state through a referendum. During the first five years of independence, the one-party transitional government focused on consolidating its power, establishing a centralised administration, and organising a military apparatus. Ironically, the provisional government also drafted a constitution, which was ratified and published in May 1997. The constitution was highly symbolic, with its ratification celebrated as a pivotal moment in Eritrea's post-independence history.

Despite the symbolic relief that independence brings, it is worth noting that the combination of colonial violence and the struggle against it has systematically deprived the local population of political and socio-economic opportunities, leaving them without meaningful avenues for political participation or protection. In fact, the enduring chains of colonial violence, reinforced by colonial matrices of power, still persist in Eritrea, as they do in many postcolonial states. Even after the formal process of decolonisation, the legacy of the colonial violence continues to pervade the country, often perpetuated by Western colonial powers through their imperial and geopolitical dominance. In Eritrea, this ongoing violence takes both overt and subtle forms, including unilateral sanctions and the use of a fictitious human rights narrative to delegitimise, exceptionalise, and suppress the country on the international stage (Müller, 2016; Hirt, 2019).

Unfortunately, despite initial optimism, independence did not lead to the peaceful self-governing state many had aspired to. In May 1998, tensions escalated into a war between Eritrea and Ethiopia. This conflict had devastating consequences for the people of both nations, who share a common ancestry and history. The toll was catastrophic: over 70,000 soldiers lost their lives, more than a million people were forcibly displaced, and numerous opportunities for peaceful coexistence were squandered (Woldemikael, 2013, p. x; Plaut, 2016, pp. 38–40). The two-year border conflict inflicted profound human suffering. Many children lost their parents, young brides became widows, and countless young people perished, leaving families shattered in grief and despair. Trenches, artillery, and landmines physically divided neighbouring communities that had intermarried for generations and shared common cultural, linguistic, and ancestral ties. The war left the people of both nations traumatised and mired in socio-economic stagnation.

In 2000, both countries signed a peace agreement, and a Boundary Commission was established to demarcate the disputed border. By April 2002, the Commission issued a 'binding decision on the border' (Plaut, 2016, p. 42). Although both governments initially accepted the decision and agreed to implement it unconditionally, they have since remained deadlocked. Since then, the border dispute remains unresolved.

The already troubled relationship between Eritrea and Ethiopia became further strained in November 2020 when a war broke out between Ethiopia's regional government in Tigray and its federal government, with Eritrea playing a significant role in the conflict. While the full consequences of this devastating war are still unfolding, reports from the UN and human rights organisations have documented numerous atrocities. These include the killing of thousands, the rape of women and young girls, the forced separation and disappearance of children, the displacement of tens of thousands of civilians, and large-scale massacres (UN News, 2020; Abai, 2021; Human Rights Watch, 2021). Although an independent assessment of the damage is pending, the war has been described as involving war crimes and crimes against humanity targeting the Ethiopian people (see Abai, 2021).

Eritrea's involvement in this Tigray war has not only exacerbated its strained relations with the neighbouring Ethiopian people but also deepened the suffering of its own population, leaving them in a state of perpetual war, imprisonment, and forced servitude. Even after the recent conflict, the unresolved Eritrean-Ethiopian border dispute and the resulting tensions between the two countries continue to raise significant concerns among Eritreans. In an era where defined borders are central to sovereignty, the ambiguity surrounding the border poses a constitutional and national security crisis for Eritrea. For many Eritreans, particularly those who fought in wars to defend the nation's independence, any threat to sovereignty undermines the sacrifices made by the country's martyrs. These national security concerns represent one of the few areas of alignment between the Eritrean government and its people.

The legacy of successive wars and ongoing tensions with Ethiopia has profoundly shaped Eritrea's trajectory since the post-independence conflict with Ethiopia. This situation has effectively triggered an undeclared state of emergency, granting the government unchecked authority to punish, discipline, and control its citizens. National security has been elevated to the government's top priority, especially in the aftermath of the war with Ethiopia. The government uses the border war and related external pressures to frame its narrative of existential threats that must be countered at all costs. National security is consistently portrayed as the supreme and non-negotiable principle; measures to defend against perceived threats are pursued relentlessly, irrespective of their human toll. Thus, the perpetual wars, widespread oppression, and dire socio-economic conditions have rendered Eritrea nearly unliveable for its predominantly young population, with many subjected to indefinite national service. As a result, Eritreans remain trapped in a cycle of servitude with little hope for reprieve.

State violence

This situation has given rise to a third form of violence: state violence. The state violence is characterised by the exertion of absolute control over the entire population, institutions and resources within the framework of state sovereignty and governmentality. In Eritrea, this type of violence manifests arbitrarily and indiscriminately, subjecting the population, authorities, and resources to its disciplinary power without adherence to national or international laws or rights. Simultaneously, sovereign violence shapes the country's authority, national identity, and moral framework, deeming anything outside its parameters as treasonous or unlawful. Since gaining independence, Eritrea has lacked a functioning constitution, a sovereign parliament, or an elected government. In fact, the country has never conducted a single election. To this day, all official and legal processes required to establish a constitutional government, and the rule of law remain indefinitely suspended.

The country has devolved into a carceral state for its violent form of governance and the precarious existence it imposes on its people. It stands as an anomaly within the rights-based international system, exemplifying a womb-abyss where the exercise of sovereign rule poses significant practical challenges for its citizens. The state employs three key carceral modalities to establish and perpetuate its system of violence: *the rule of no law nor rights, indefinite national service, and arbitrary detention and forced disappearance.* These modalities are enforced through a centralised system of control and punishment, overseen by a regime of arbitrary rule under the country's sole President.

The rule of no law nor rights

The state's relationship with its people has become paradoxically precarious. The country, to use Agamben's (2015) terms, 'does not found itself on a social link but on the prohibition of its dissolution' (p. 237). Agamben clarifies that the absence of a social link does not simply involve severing an existing relationship with the state; rather, the bond itself lacks substance beyond the tenuous threads created by the threat of dissolution. He explains: 'Since there is originally neither bond nor relation, this absence of relation is captured in state power in the form of the ban and of prohibition' (Agamben, 2015, p. 237). From this perspective, the relationship between the Eritrean state and its people is not based on a direct relation but on paradoxical interplay between the state's dissolution and its people.

The state's primary purpose appears to be mobilising its people to guard against its own dissolution. This relation of exception, sustained through the prohibition of dissolution, exposes the Eritrean people to a perpetual risk of unsanctioned death. Practices such as the government's successful recruitment of people across age groups and backgrounds for the border war with Ethiopia, along with subsequent conflicts, illustrate this violent relation (Kibreab, 2017). However, in the Eritrean context, the decision of exception does not entail a suspension of the law. Instead, the exception manifests as a state entirely devoid of law or rights—a condition characterised by the complete absence of legal and rights-based framework. This rule of no law nor rights has emerged as the prevailing state violence in post-independence Eritrea.

The government maintains this precarious relationship between its dissolution and the necropolitical existence of its people by projecting a rule of no law and no rights throughout its institutions and hierarchical governance. The ruling party controls all political, organisational, economic, and cultural aspects of the state, extending its influence over every dimension of individual and communal life. These government functions, often described in national media as the country's 'pillars', serve as instruments to compel submission to the state's overwhelming power, generating a precarious life perpetually overshadowed by unrestricted death, even if its death in life.

Once people are transformed into manageable bodies, they are compelled to obey the authority of the state as directed by the government. Ordinary citizens are subjected to coercive controls over their movements, employment, education, housing, food purchases, and communication with others. Whether concerning national or international issues, local or regional interactions, or private or communal life, the state's control is pervasive. Ultimately, the fate of the country, its people, and its future rests in the hands of a single president, a single political party, and a single ideology. Any decision, whether to end life or protect it, originates from the central authority, and the people are forced to comply. These decisions come not from the law but from decrees issued by the president and his inner circle. Since gaining independence, this has become the new normal in the country.

The pervasive nature of state violence, emanating from the bureaucratic structure of the state, ensures that administrators in every institution visibly and consistently affirm their allegiance to a higher authority that seems both invisible and unreachable. Within the chain of command, administrative bureaucrats validate the state's authority through encounters that occur in the absence of law and rights, where the state's violent gaze dominates citizens. As Arendt (1970, p. 81) famously reminds us, 'In a fully developed bureaucracy there is nobody left with whom one can argue, to whom one can present grievance, on whom the pressures of power can be exerted'. Essentially, Arendt argues that 'the rule by Nobody is not no-rule, and where all are equally powerless we have a tyranny without a tyrant' (1970, p. 81). The government officials' roles are solely to administer the violent sovereign power, and in doing so, they feel superior to the ordinary citizens who continue to struggle for their basic needs.

This integration of sovereignty and governmentality in a unified apparatus of violent state power is embodied in the rule of no law nor rights in the relatively young Eritrean state. While Agamben's notion of the suspension of the law (the exception) might be remedied, at least conceptually, by a return to the law, there is no possibility of returning from the rule of no law nor rights. In this absolute absence of law and rights, such a return simply does not exist. The stories recounted at the beginning of the book highlight the pervasive control strategies that stem from the absence of rights, a condition that persists from birth to death. Confronted with various losses, such as the loss of traditional embodiments of social organisation, cultural identity, and sociality, Eritreans are reduced to being born rightless and dying rightless. There are no limits to the dominion of the sovereign over its oppressed population. The government is accountable neither to natural law nor human law, but only to its obnoxious decrees.

Indefinite national service

During the early years of independence, the transitional government of Eritrea introduced mandatory national service for all Eritreans aged between 18 and 50. According to the government, the main objective of this policy was to safeguard and advance the nation. Article 5 of the National Service Proclamation 82/1995 outlines six specific 'objectives' (UNHCR, 1995):

- to establish people-based strong defence force to assure the existence of free and sovereign Eritrea.
- to preserve the courage and culture of heroism… and pass them to the next generation.
- to create hard-working, disciplined and an ever-ready new generation that participate in reconstruction.
- to enhance the economic development of the country… in a trained and organised manner
- to provide regular and continuous military training and vocational training… promote physical fitness.
- to cement the unity of our people by promoting unity and nationalism and eradicating sub-national attitudes.

These objectives prioritise protecting national sovereignty over the welfare of the Eritrean people. The national service is a coercive process through which all physically capable Eritreans are organised, trained, disciplined, and transformed to achieve these specific goals. Its objective is to produce personnel who are physically fit, hardworking, disciplined, and compliant, capable of serving both as a workforce and as soldiers. As Kibreab (2009b) argues, the country violently utilises its labour and military force to promote a distinct national identity, facilitate nation-building, and enhance national unity, while also addressing national security threats. Beyond these initial objectives, it is important to understand the nature of national service by examining how compliant bodies are produced, transformed, lived in, and even destroyed. This requires a closer look at the recruitment, training, assignment, and retirement processes. Each of these processes involves the state deploying the rule of no law nor rights to produce compliant and submissive bodies.

Recruitment into national service first began in 1991 but did not become operational until July 1994, when the first group of trainees was recruited. In its initial years, the recruitment process was organised by local governments in coordination with the Ministry of Defense and involved what is referred to as the 'registration' process. According to Article 11(1) of Proclamation 82/1995, 'When the Ministry of Defense makes a call [for] registration, an Eritrean national between the age of 18 and 40 who has a duty to take part in Active National Service shall register at the nearest Registration center in accordance with the programme of the Ministry of Local Governments' (UNHCR, 1995). Kibreab (2013) notes that for the first four years at least, until the border war with Ethiopia (1998–2000), the government complied with the proclamations and requirements of the law, and the duration of national service was 18 months. Since the beginning of the border conflict with Ethiopia, however, the recruitment process has undergone a significant change. It has evolved from a partially voluntary registration process to a mandatory and coercive method of forced recruitment. Tronvoll and Mekonnen (2017, p. 170) describe this shift as 'one of the most draconian government policies in Eritrea, causing immense suffering and vulnerability to a large number of Eritreans'. To this day, the government continues to use an undisclosed state of emergency as a pretext for compelling people to join the military.

The forced recruitment process in Eritrea, commonly known as gifas, involves the rounding up of people from various aspects of daily life, including schools, civilian society, and detention centres. Particularly, schools and education have been the primary sources of potential draftees for national service. Since the 2002/2003 academic year, the government has mandated that students who have completed Grade 11 attend military training in Sawa before taking the national exam for secondary education completion. For the past two decades, thousands of students have joined the military service in Sawa each year, as part of the government's initiative to instil 'discipline and patriotic commitment among the student community' (Müller, 2008, p. 123). Education has become synonymous with military training, leading to the renaming of Sawa as Warsai Yikealo Secondary School. Students are now required to undergo strict military training, attend political lessons, and simultaneously prepare for their matriculation exams.

After spending a year in Sawa, students have the option to pursue higher education if they receive passing grades. However, those who fail the matriculation exam are required to join the national service indefinitely. Since the closure of Asmara University in 2004, students who pass the national exam are directed to specialised colleges that operate under strict state supervision. Furthermore, teachers who have already completed their national service are also obligated to participate in regional military training. This is done to ensure discipline and physical fitness are instilled at all levels of education. The recruitment of students, the military oversight of colleges, and the training of teachers collectively contribute to what is referred to as a complete 'militarisation of education' (see Tronvoll and Mekonnen, 2017).

In addition to militarising education, the government also enforces compulsory national service by conscripting individuals from civilian society using coercive methods. These methods include roundups (gifas), distribution of order letters, and issuing fines to those who refuse to comply. With the exception of young children and married women, the government expects all able-bodied civilians, regardless of age, to undergo locally organised military training and join the national service. As pointed out by Tronvoll and Mekonnen (2017, p. 181), even senior civilians, including elderly men, are drafted into what is commonly referred to as the '*Hizbawi Serawit* or people's army'. The government also recruits detainees into the national service. These detainees belong to various groups, including individuals who have committed minor crimes, deserters, draft evaders, border crossers, and youths who have dropped out of school. Unfortunately, the national service has become a vast necropolitical experimentation, aimed at encompassing everything and everyone within its grasp.

Training involves subjecting bodies and minds to specific techniques, followed by assignment to military units. To achieve this goal, the government has established training centres at national and regional levels, including Sawa, Kiloma, Hishferay, Mi'ether, Gahtelay, and Kormena'e, among others. Additionally, there are training centres in almost all subzones to train local people, including senior citizens. The nature and type of training at these local and regional levels differ from those conducted at the national level. While local and regional training primarily focuses on educating draftees, particularly senior citizens, about Eritrea's history, the liberation struggle, and nationalism, national military training combines these lessons with intensive physical activities, weapons training, and military simulations.

The local and national training programmes aim to equally impact both the body and the mind. In Foucauldian terms, recruits' bodies and minds are transformed into objects of disciplinary power, which functions to train, regulate, shape, and ultimately create submissive subjectivities. According to Foucault (2020), as the body becomes the object of operation of disciplinary power, the mind is subjected to 'new forms of knowledge' (p. 155). Foucault argues that this is not a body focused solely on physical fitness, but rather one directed by authority, a body shaped by 'useful training' rather than 'rational mechanics' (2020, p. 155). In this process of subjection and subjugation, various mundane training requirements and operational strategies are deployed alongside strict instructions and orders. These activities such as waking up early and quarrying stones, as well as more complex, pre-scheduled physical, technical, and mental exercises. The training of the body begins by maximising its fitness levels, or at least reaching the required capacity. This is achieved through physical training which includes various exercises such as running, marching, interval sprints, push-ups, sit-ups, military expeditions, mountain climbing, labouring, and sporting activities.

Once the body has reached the necessary level of fitness, another layer of training is added: the acquisition of military skills and techniques. This involves organising the draftees into manageable units such as regiments and squadrons, and also meticulously training different body parts (e.g. limbs, head, and chest) to perform specific actions. For example, hands are trained to handle and throw grenades, as well as to clean, assemble, disassemble, and effectively use various types of weapons. Eyes are trained for accurate shooting and aiming at distant targets. Head, legs, hands, and chest are trained to march uniformly, in an organised and steady manner. Every part of the body is fine-tuned to perform predefined exercises with precision. The fittest and most talented recruits are praised and selected to participate in well-designed, colourful parades on occasions like Independence Day.

The mind is trained alongside the body, routinely exposed to military strategies and war tactics. It is required to idolise the liberation struggle and its values, ideology, and nationalist project, while also accepting and enduring pain, stress, sleep deprivation, and exhaustion. Moreover, the mind becomes accustomed to performing routine disciplinary procedures, such as waking up early in the morning, staying late for active duty, queuing up for attendance, and obeying disciplinary rules. Developing a warrior mindset includes instilling traits such as selfishness, altruism, heroism, and strict adherence to secrecy. This comprehensive approach to training the mind is an essential part of national and military service in the country.

The coordinated efforts to train organs, limbs, muscles, and the mind ultimately aim to transform trainees into compliant servants. The government's nationalist project and its fictitious principle of 'self-reliance' require the transformation of trainees into obedient subjects. The government's National Charter, adopted in 1994, outlines 'The six basic principles which can serve as guidelines for our activities are national unity, active public participation, the human element, linkage between national and social struggles, self-reliance, and finally, a strong relationship between people and leadership' (Congress of the EPLF/PFDJ, 1994). Since the National Charter was written, these principles have either been disavowed or perpetuated in the form of unfounded rhetoric. The relationship between the government and its people has become one of subjection, rather than participation.

The government's promises of comprehensive civic engagement have become empty slogans. Among these empty slogans, self-reliance is the most frequently and loudly proclaimed. The project of self-reliance is defined in the National Charter as follows: 'Politically, it means to follow an independent line and give priority to internal conditions; economically, to rely on internal capabilities and develop internal capacities; and culturally, to have self-confidence and develop one's own cultural heritage' (Congress of the EPLF/PFDJ, 1994). The enforced indoctrination of draftees confirms that the six basic principles, in general, and self-reliance, in particular, are integral elements of national service. The government pursues these indoctrination strategies through workshops, seminars, youth programmes, festivals, cadre courses, and local government initiatives. The government presents these mobilisation and indoctrination programmes as the foundations of its nationalist projects and efforts to forge national identity.

The training, mobilisation, and indoctrination programmes imposed on trainees consist of control and punishment methods enforced by military personnel known as trainers. These trainers are given unrestricted power to train, punish, discipline, and exploit the trainees. During discussions for this book, many of us—the participants—highlighted various examples of punishments inflicted by trainers, including press-ups, stone quarrying during rest periods, severe beatings, cleaning toilets for commanders, facing the sun with hands tied and legs bound, and deprivation of food and water. These punitive measures and forms of control are implemented at both the individual and group levels. We also recounted instances of sexual exploitation of women by trainers and their commanders. For instance, one former student and trainee in Sawa shared a story of her friend who attempted suicide after becoming pregnant due to repeated incidents of rape by her unit leader. Although the victim was eventually sent home after several suicide attempts, the trainer who assaulted her continued to perpetrate sexual abuse against other young female students. Tragically, the victim reportedly died at the age of 17 from an unsafe abortion procedure performed at home. Kibreab (2017) notes that trainers and their commanders keep these violent practices shrouded in secrecy, despite the widespread prevalence of stories about women falling prey to sexual exploitation.

Sawa is a prime example of how Eritreans are subjected to training regimes, disciplinary procedures, and various forms of exploitation. Since the introduction of national service in the early 1990s, the camp has undergone significant changes. It has evolved into a multifunctional institution, serving as a military training centre, a school, an educational centre, and a cultural hub. In terms of military training, Sawa accommodates soldiers, war masters, military commanders, and military strategists. It also provides education and training for students, teachers, artists, musicians, carpenters, electricians, veterinarians, and paramedics. Furthermore, Sawa serves as a cultural hub, hosting annual military academy graduations, festivals, sporting events, and national holidays. As Müller (2008, p. 126) aptly notes, 'Sawa was meant to be the place where the defence of the country's sovereignty was passed on militarily and ideologically to a committed future generation'. Ironically, however, the symbolic importance of Sawa has gradually diminished among many young Eritreans. In present-day Eritrea, Sawa primarily represents the country's centre of violent power and control over its people, especially the youth, and is increasingly avoided and deserted. Eritrean youths leave the country simply because they do not want to attend Sawa. The infamy surrounding Sawa is attributed to its role in restricting the potential and aspirations of Eritrean youth within the confines of the country's military apparatus and indefinite national service.

Assignment is the stage that follows military training, where trained conscripts are systematically distributed to various state institutions. The assignment process varies based on the conscripts' status, age, gender, and health. For instance, students who pass the national exam are admitted to higher education, while those who fail undergo vocational training before being assigned to different civilian departments as part of the indefinite national service. Non-student conscripts, excluding those in education, are distributed to different branches and units of the state military complex. The government's implicit agenda of internal immobilisation and maximum utilisation of skills and capacities is reflected in the assignment of these conscripts. The government employs various factors to achieve this strategy, including distance from home and the border, age and gender, and fitness and skills. For example, youths who have attempted irregular border crossings are assigned to remote locations like the Dahlak Archipelago in the Red Sea region. Similarly, draft evaders and deserters are assigned to places far from their hometowns.

However, the intrusive training and exploitation of the bodies and labour of the conscripts do not end with their assignment. Instead, they are subjected to a dual regime of biopolitical control and servitude under the Warsay Yikealo Development Campaign (WYDC). Introduced after the border conflict, the WYDC is an open-ended national service project that requires all able-bodied people to participate in national defence and nation-building in exchange for a small amount of pocket money. Hirt (2010) points out, 'The WYDC is a new strategy of total mobilization. It means extreme interference in the private lives of people and has a strong impact on the fabric of society, rendering individuals unable to follow long-established role expectations' (p. 11). Although the training in the WYDC may differ slightly from military training, both aim to produce disciplined, regulated, and obedient bodies and minds. The primary objective of WYDC is, in Foucault's (2020) terms, 'to bind them together in such a way as to multiply and use them' (p. 170). Thus, the bodies and minds that have been trained, regulated, and transformed are subjected to 'a relation of docility-utility' (Foucault, 2020, p. 137). Avoiding this biopolitical system for necropolitical purposes is considered a betrayal of one's national duty by the government. Punishment for evading the draft includes several years of arbitrary imprisonment and torture without official charges.

As stated in Article 8 of the National Service Proclamation 82/95, the national service was initially designed as a temporary programme. It involved 6 months of intensive military training, followed by 12 months of active service in national development programmes overseen by the military. However, after the border war with Ethiopia from 1998 to 2000, the government not only reenlisted those who had been discharged but also retained those who had been conscripted since the war (see Kibreab, 2013). Moreover, it is worth noting that the distinction between the military and non-military aspects of the national service has disappeared. In recent years, approximately 50% of Eritrean people aged 18 and above are indefinitely stuck in the national service (Tronvoll and Mekonnen, 2017, p. 168). People with severe medical problems, married women, and disadvantaged individuals who are deemed unfit for service by the government, as well as former combatants with life-changing injuries, are the only exceptions to the indefinite national service (see Belloni, 2018). However, for the majority of Eritrean citizens, demobilisation from the military or retirement from the open-ended national service is not an option. This is a significant factor contributing to the forced migration from the country.

Detention and forced disappearance

Experiences of detention and forced disappearance are a grim reality in Eritrea. Within this study, we encountered young men and women whose fathers had vanished into the undergrounds cells of the country's prison system, young brides whose husbands were detained by security agents and have languished in captivity ever since, and stories of teenagers who endured years of torture in prison before managing to escape their homeland. Where are our missing loved ones, some lost for years, others for decades? What became of our brothers and sisters, taken from their homes in the dead of night? And where are our parents, whose only 'crime' was our decision to flee the country? Why are they detained without accountability? Thousands of Eritreans disappear within their country's prison system. Are they still alive?

These questions weigh heavily in the minds of Eritreans, yet they remain unanswered, shrouded in silence by a government that refuses to offer evidence or permit independent investigation. Politicians, journalists, draft evaders, and dissidents are held in solitary confinement without trial. While those who surrender their bodies and minds to the state's carceral regime endure exploitation within bureaucratic administration and interminable national service, those who defy the government's expectations find themselves trapped in its regime of imprisonment. The disappearance of 11 politicians, former members of the G-15 group who were once hailed as heroes of the liberation war and respected government officials, reveals the stark normalisation of arbitrary detention. As Hedru (2003) observes, 'Eritrea has become a place where comrades-in-arms of a lifetime have turned on each other, heroes of yesterday are the "traitors" of today, and brother dare not to trust brother' (p. 435). This blurring of lines between heroes and traitors exemplifies the carceral state's totalitarian grip and its power to punish indiscriminately.

The state's unaccountability and the harrowing absence of knowledge about prisoners' whereabouts lay bare at least two realities: the spectacle of the carceral complex and the existential plight of the detainees. The carceral complex is constructed from intertwined necropolitical operations of power and physical architectures of control. Its necropolitical methods include mass arrests, arbitrary imprisonment, and forced disappearances. Complementing these are monitoring programmes, which employ surveillance networks, routine attendance protocols, and mandatory self-reporting regimes. These mechanisms are enforced by secret intelligence, police forces, and the military. The physical architecture of the carceral complex encompasses military training centres, detention camps, and prisons. Within its reach lie dungeons, police stations, repurposed shipping containers, checkpoints, and barracks. It even infiltrates private homes, imposing house arrests and enforced solitude. These structures, as Mbembe (2003, p. 28) suggests, embody the 'panoptic fortification' of both public and private spaces, creating a landscape of omnipresent control and fear.

Together, mass surveillance, mass supervision, arbitrary incarceration, and physical architectures are the mechanisms through which the government exercises control over society. As Foucault reminds us, the panoptic state and its carceral architecture do not rely solely on prison institutions but also on dispersed surveillance and incarceration systems spread throughout society. By deploying these carceral institutions, the womb-abyss asserts its constant presence and its ability to respond swiftly to dissent, resistance, or disobedience. It operates by reinforcing exploitative and invasive forms of control and punishment, including mass supervision, mass militarisation, and mass imprisonment. Isolated from the rest of the international community, the government has effectively held its people hostage in a condition of carceral incommunicado. In its report, the UN Commission of Inquiry (COI) on Eritrea has accused the country's government officials of committing 'acts of enslavement, imprisonment, enforced disappearance, torture, reprisals as other inhumane acts, persecution, rape and murder' (COI, 2016, p. 46). The COI states:

> Because State officials have relied so extensively on the commission of the crimes to establish, consolidate and maintain total control over the Eritrean population, the Commission has determined that they have engaged in a widespread and systematic attack against the civilian population of Eritrea since May 1991 which remains ongoing.
>
> (2016, p. 46)

Although the COI report has been vehemently rejected by the Eritrean government and criticised by certain academics for its alleged politicisation and bias (Müller, 2016), it nonetheless provides valuable insight into the widespread abuses committed by the Eritrean regime against its own people. The government's unrestricted exercise of power, which results in violent repression and arbitrary incarceration, is indicative of its oppressive control over the population. This excessive use of power is evident in the lawlessness and lack of rights that have ensued after the betrayal of hopes for constitutional rule. This has led to the suppression of transition to elected government, widespread violations, destruction of private institutions, and the arbitrary detention of numerous citizens, including prominent politicians and leaders of the liberation movement (see Kibreab, 2009b). In post-liberation Eritrea, forced disappearance and indefinite incarceration pose a pervasive threat to people, regardless of their social and political standing. The state's oppressive machinery permeates all facets of society, leaving no one safe. This ominous menace extends to all segments of the population, including those within the government apparatus itself. Citizens are subjected to constant surveillance while also facing the peril of forced disappearance and arbitrary incarceration.

The second calamity arising from indefinite detention and forced disappearances pertains to the prisoners' ontological condition. The crime of forcibly disappearing thousands of people within the carceral system results in the indefinite suspension of their ontological state. Those who are subjected to forced disappearances are not only eradicated from the public and private domains, but also from the realm of imagination. The fact that they are confined to a realm of perpetual invisibility and unknowability suggests that their bodies are either transformed into spatially fixed, disposable corporealities or annihilated without a trace, with impunity. In either case, their ontological state is inherently tied to the condition of mortality, as denoted by their permanent disappearance and unknowability.

Similarly, for those detainees whose locations are known and who can receive visits from their families and relatives, there is little noticeable difference between their conditions and those of the missing people. The fact that they are held in detention indefinitely without a trial means that not only are they positioned outside the realm of legal recourse, but they are also rendered unrecognisable. For these captives of the carceral system, the prison functions as a site where the impersonal logic of exception perpetually enforces the annihilation and disfigurement of its inmates. The impersonal logic of exception, along with its institutions of mass incarceration, concretise the reduction of the captives' status to mere existence and its subsequent securitisation. The incarcerated are trapped within a sphere in which the distinction between law and its absence, as well as between life and death, becomes indistinguishable. These forms of state violence, as succinctly stated by Mbembe (2003, p. 14), 'are what constitute the nomos of the political space in which we still live'.

In short, Eritrea has become a womb-abyss where the primary role of the state is to prevent its own dissolution, even if it comes at the expense of a significant portion of its population. The rule of no law nor rights, as a set of arbitrary decrees and commands, the political domain devoid of rights and ethics, and the state as a governing authority, converge into a state of indistinction embodied in the sovereign power of the state. The state, simultaneously, assumes the roles of the legal order, the political principle, and the governing authority. The ruling authority commands, orders, and rules over the lawless territory inhabited by a population without rights. The state projects itself as an all-encompassing juridico-political *necessitas*. Hence, necessity becomes the decisive power that preserves the integrity of the state at the expense of its people.

Conclusion

The nation-state is a womb-abyss where the citizen belongs to sovereign power, and the Other is irrevocably cast out as a naked life upon which the machinery of violence is inscribed. Life and death are the twin dominions of the womb-abyss where existence itself, marked by its inevitable perishability, is subsumed under a sovereignty that wields dominion over both life and death, presence and absence. The very act of defining and delineating life and death demands the systematic exclusion of the Other and the disobedient. Within this abyss, sovereignty sustains itself not through the preservation of life but through its unlimited capacity to annihilate, dissolving the distinctions between life and death into an indistinguishability. The womb-abyss is a matrix in which law, life, and reason intertwine irrevocably with violence, both physical and metaphysical.

While the postcolony is often associated with chaos and unruliness, the metropole is typically characterised by legitimacy, democracy, and the rule of law. Yet, as demonstrated, both chaos and order are constitutively exclusive domains of sovereign power, which deploys law and exception as instruments of control and punishment (Agamben, 2005). Chaos frequently emerges as the consequence of the law's withdrawal, serving as the backdrop against which the law asserts its own order and structure. Thus, whether manifesting in the death-worlds of the postcolony or the apparatuses of the former coloniser (ex-mother country), with the metropole as the central seat of power, both are rooted in the violent and colonial construct of the womb-abyss, now the defining *nomos* of our time.

Eritrea exemplifies the abyss of the womb-abyss, where life is inseparably bound to perpetual violence, loss, and perishability. In this context, existence is constrained by the rule of no law nor rights, leaving its people scarred and burdened by an enduring despair rooted in colonial and state violence, as well as the ongoing struggle against both. The womb-abyss as a juridico-political *necessitas* gives rise to the inevitability and necessity of fleeing one's homeland in pursuit of a dignified life. In the next chapter, we explore the experiences of Eritrea's forcibly displaced people, who grapple with the precarity, violability, and perishability of life in the belly of the refugee abyss.

Note

1 William Westgarth, originally from Scotland, was a prominent figure in the Australian state during the 1850s. He was known for his roles as a merchant, politician, historian, and advisor to various colonial administrations. He also served as a legislator in the governing councils of what was then part of colonial Australia state.

References

Abai, M. (2021) War in Tigray and Crimes of International Law. *Canadian Centre for Victims of Torture*, 8(3), 16–22.

Agamben, G. (1995) We Refugees. *Symposium: A Quarterly Journal in Modern Literatures*, 49 (2), 114–119. https://doi.org/10.1080/00397709.1995.10733798

Agamben, G. (1998) *Sovereign Power and Bare Life*. Stanford, California: Stanford University Press (Homo sacer, 1).

Agamben, G. (2005) *State of Exception*. Chicago, Illinois: University of Chicago Press.

Agamben, G. (2015) *The Use of Bodies*. Translated by A. Kotsko. Stanford, California: Stanford University Press (Homo sacer, IV, 2).

Anderson, B. (2020) 'Imagined Communities: Reflections on the Origin and Spread of Nationalism', in *The New Social Theory Reader*. Routledge, pp. 282–288. https://www.taylorfrancis.com/chapters/edit/10.4324/9781003060963-46/imagined-communities-benedict-anderson (accessed 12.1.24).

Arendt, H. (1970) *On Violence*. New York, New York: Harcourt, Brace & World.

Belloni, M. (2018) 'Becoming Unaccustomed to Home: Young Eritreans' Narratives About Estrangement, Belonging and the Desire to Leave Home', in K. Davis, H. Ghorashi, and P. Smets (Eds) *Contested Belonging: Spaces, Practices, Biographies*, pp. 161–181. Emerald Publishing Limited.

Butler, J. (2006) *Precarious Life: The Powers of Mourning and Violence*. London–New York: Verso.

COI, H.R.C. (2016) UN Commission of Inquiry Report.pdf. Available from: https://www.ohchr.org/Documents/HRBodies/HRCouncil/CoIEritrea/A_HRC_32_CRP.1_read-only.pdf (accessed 10.5.25)

Congress of the EPLF/PFDJ (1994) 'PFDJ National Charter'. Congress of the EPLF/PFDJ (1994) 'PFDJ NATIONAL CHARTER'. https://snitna.com/PFDJCharter_Eng.pdf (accessed 10.05.25).

De Guttry, A., Post, H.H.G., and Venturini, G. (Eds) (2021) *The 1998–2000 Eritrea-Ethiopia War and Its Aftermath in International Legal Perspective: From the 2000 Algiers Agreements to the 2018 Peace Agreement*. The Hague: T.M.C. Asser Press. https://doi.org/10.1007/978-94-6265-439-6

Fanon, F. (1986) *Black Skin, White Masks*. Repr. Translated by C.L. Markmann. London: Pluto Press (Pluto classics).

Foucault, M. (1998) *The Will to Knowledge*. Amended reprint. Translated by R. Hurley. London: Penguin Books (The history of sexuality, v. 1).

Foucault, M. (2012) *Discipline & Punish: The Birth of the Prison*. Translated by A. Sheridan. New York, New York: Vintage.

Foucault, M. (2020) *Discipline and Punish: The Birth of the Prison*. Translated by A. Sheridan. London: Penguin Classics.

Glissant, É. (2009) *Poetics of Relation*. Ann Arbor, Michigan: University of Michigan Press.

Grey, R.D. and Pateman, R. (1991) Eritrea: Even the Stones Are Burning. *The International Journal of African Historical Studies*, 24 (3), 691. https://doi.org/10.2307/219131

Hedru, D. (2003) Eritrea: Transition to Dictatorship, 1991-2003. *Review of African Political Economy*, 30 (97), 435–444. https://doi.org/10.1080/03056244.2003.9659776

Hirt, N. (2010) "Dreams Don't Come True in Eritrea": Anomie and Family Disintegration Due to the Structural Militarization of Society, *SSRN Electronic Journal*. https://doi.org/10.2139/ssrn.1541908

Hirt, N. (2019) 'Commentary: UN Security Council Resolution 2444 (2018) and the Lifting of Sanctions Against Eritrea: A Commentary on Domestic and Regional Perspectives', in Z. Yihdego, M.G. Desta, and M.B. Hailu (Eds) *Ethiopian Yearbook of International Law 2018: In Pursuit of Peace and Prosperity*. Cham: Springer International Publishing, pp. 269–285. https://doi.org/10.1007/978-3-030-24078-3_13

Human Rights Watch (2021) *Ethiopia: Unlawful Shelling of Tigray Urban Areas*, Human Rights Watch. Available from: https://www.hrw.org/news/2021/02/11/ethiopia-unlawful-shelling-tigray-urban-areas (accessed 19.2.21).

Kibreab, G. (2009a) *Eritrea: a Dream Deferred*. Woodbridge, Suffolk, UK; Rochester, NY: [Uppsala, Sweden]: James Currey; Nordiska Afrikainstitutet (Eastern Africa series).

Kibreab, G. (2009b) Forced Labour in Eritrea. *The Journal of Modern African Studies*, 47 (1), 41–72. https://doi.org/10.1017/S0022278X08003650

Kibreab, G. (2013) The National service/Warsai-Yikealo Development Campaign and Forced Migration in Post-Independence Eritrea. *Journal of Eastern African Studies*, 7 (4), 630–649. https://doi.org/10.1080/17531055.2013.843965

Kibreab, G. (2017) *The Eritrean National Service: Servitude for 'the Common Good' and the Youth Exodus*. Martlesham, Suffolk: Boydell & Brewer.

Mbembe, A. (2001) *On the Postcolony*. Berkeley, California: University of California Press. (Studies on the history of society and culture, 41.)

Mbembe, A. (2003) Necropolitics. *Public Culture*. Translated by L. Meintjes, 15(1), 11–40.

Mbembe, A. (2008) '1. Aesthetics of Superfluity', in S. Nuttall and A. Mbembe (Eds) *Johannesburg*. Durham, North Carolina: Duke University Press, pp. 37–67. https://doi.org/10.1515/9780822381211-003

Mbembe, A. (2019a) Bodies as Borders. *From the European South*, 4, 5–18.

Mbembe, A. (2019b) *Necropolitics*. Translated by S. Corcoran. Durham, North Carolina: Duke University Press. (Theory in forms.)

Müller, T.R. (2008) Bare Life and the Developmental State: Implications of the Militarisation of Higher Education in Eritrea. *The Journal of Modern African Studies*, 46(1), 111–131.

Müller, T.R. (2016) Representing Eritrea: Geopolitics and Narratives of oppression. *Review of African Political Economy*, 43(150), 658–667. https://doi.org/10.1080/03056244.2015.1111201

Ndlovu-Gatsheni, S.J. (2013) *Coloniality of Power in Postcolonial Africa: Myths of Decolonization*. Dakar: Codesria.

Ojakangas, M. (2005) Impossible Dialogue on Bio-Power: Agamben and Foucault. *Foucault Studies*, 2, 5. https://doi.org/10.22439/fs.v0i2.856

Plaut, M. (2016) *Understanding Eritrea: Inside Africa's Most Repressive State*. Oxford: Oxford University Press.

Simon, J. (2007) Rise of the Carceral State. *Social Research: An International Quarterly*, 74 (2), 471–508. https://doi.org/10.1353/sor.2007.0000

Tronvoll, K. and Mekonnen, D.R. (2017) *The African Garrison State: Human Rights & Political Development in Eritrea*. Melton, Woodbridge, Suffolk: James Currey.

UN News (2020) *Tigray: Hundreds of Civilians Reported Killed in Artillery Strikes, Warns UN Rights Chief*, *UN News*. Available from: https://news.un.org/en/story/2020/12/1080622 (accessed 19.2.21).

UNHCR (1995) *Eritrea: Proclamation on National Service No. 82/1995 of 1995*, *Refworld*. Available from: https://www.refworld.org/legal/legislation/natlegbod/1995/en/32119 (accessed 4.1.25).

Westgarth, W. (1880) 5th Meeting: Trade Relations of the Colonies and the Mother Country. *RSA Journal*, 29, 536.

Woldemikael (2013) Introduction to Special Issue: Postliberation Eritrea. *Africa Today*, 60 (2), v–xix. https://doi.org/10.2979/africatoday.60.2.v

4 Realities Within the Refugee Abyss

Introduction

When it becomes a lived reality that an entire population is held hostage in a state of perpetual servitude and vulnerability as subjects of the state's self-preserving violence, what course of action is available to them? What are the conditions of possibility for a dignified life? As shown in the previous chapter, post-independence Eritrea is built upon the exercise of violence and control over its people, and the enforced obedience of its citizens to its authority, despite the extreme violence inflicted upon them. Although many Eritreans remain trapped within this cycle of state violence, thousands of men, women, and children choose to flee their country in order to escape the physical and existential threats posed by state violence. In essence, those who manage to flee the country and become forcibly displaced are cast into what we call the refugee abyss.

The refugee abyss is used here as a metaphor to illustrate the harrowing realities faced by refugees. It signifies the dehumanisation, trauma, and deep wounds inflicted by forced displacement, violent (b)orders, and the haunting experience of exile. This concept encompasses the immense suffering and loss endured by those who are forcibly displaced as they navigate a journey marked by extreme brutality, (im)mobility, and mortality. It also involves the loss of one's citizenship or identity in their country of origin. Being in the refugee abyss means being trapped in a constant state of (un)becoming, as one seeks safety in an unfamiliar place and time that is foreign to their upbringing and imagined future. The refugee abyss represents a journey through the fringes of humanity, an abyssal experience that includes the intertwined conditions of fleeing one's home country, enduring a perilous journey, and facing exile. These conditions are the focal points of exploration in this chapter; the conditions of exile are discussed further in the following chapter.

Becoming refugee

The first encounter with the refugee experience occurs when the conditions for leaving one's home country or place of origin are established. These conditions

DOI: 10.4324/9781003437192-5

often arise from the absence of human security and the subsequent loss of essential aspects of living with dignity. The resulting suffering places a constant burden on individuals, depriving them of their dignity in their country of origin, their homes within their own country, and their communities. Setting aside the legal definition of a refugee, the factors that lead to becoming a refugee can be caused by both state-sanctioned violence and human-made natural disasters. These include wars, civil unrest, organised crime, state violence, as well as human-made environmental catastrophes such as floods, droughts, and land degradation. This study focuses on the realities of refugees, and an exploration of the various causal factors is beyond the scope of this book.

Forced displacement in the context of Eritrea is not a recent phenomenon. Instead, it has persisted from the colonial era to the post-colonial period. As discussed, colonial violence transformed politics into necropolitics, or the politics of perpetual violence, death, and destruction. Within the colonial order, as Maldonado-Torres (2016, p. 17) writes, 'Life is lived as in a torture chamber making life acquire the overwhelming feeling of it being worse than death'. Maldonado-Torres further explains that the lives of colonised people are characterised by the constant anticipation of their bodies being violated by others. This necropolitical reality is perpetuated by the imposition of dehumanising and depoliticising structures and conditions, which the colonised have endured for centuries without any opportunity for a dignified life. Eritreans were born into and lived within these conditions of damnation during colonial times. Particularly since the 1890s, when the Italians first occupied and established Eritrea as a colony, the local population have been subjected to constant wars, racial segregation, and destitution by successive colonisers. Not only were their cultural traditions, religious rituals, legal norms, systems of knowledge production, and ways of life eroded, but they were also forcibly replaced by those of the colonisers. The erosion of the traditions, customs, and religious rituals of the local population has ultimately undermined the normative structure of communal life. This has instilled a loss of faith in their own knowledge systems, led to the fragmentation of identities and languages, weakened established values, and resulted in their assimilation into the dehumanising relations of colonisation.

During the struggle for independence, Eritreans were trapped in a state of constant violence, inflicted both by the colonising power (Ethiopia) and the violence inherent in the struggle itself. The only form of political expression was through popular resistance against colonial oppression, supported and led by guerrilla-style armed conflict. The Eritrean people were organised through clandestine methods, both within the country and in exile. Many men and women joined the armed struggle, while others supported it through covert operations, often at great personal risk. Their existence was essentially defined by the ongoing battle against death and destruction, imposed by colonial violence, with the hope of achieving liberation and self-determination. People from all backgrounds and demographics were subjected to brutal acts of torture, domination, exploitation, and indignity by the colonial government.

Although independence marked the end of colonial rule, it was insufficient to emancipate the Eritrean people from the shackles of dehumanising state violence. The compounding effects of successive conflicts and pervasive authoritarian rule have played a key role in transforming Eritrea into a womb-abyss. The post-independence transitional government established a centralised regime, where an unaccountable sovereign power ruled through centrally administered decrees. As Arendt (2017) argues, authoritarian governments often employ 'rule by decrees' to render traditional norms obsolete and impose their own repressive powers. She explains that this approach is effective in dismantling customary norms, bypassing the slow 'development of general law' (Arendt, 2017, p. 319). Furthermore, Arendt notes that 'rule by decrees' is particularly useful for establishing centralised administration of power, as it automatically supersedes 'local autonomy' (Arendt, 2017, p. 319). Like other authoritarian regimes, the Eritrean government employed decrees to replace traditional norms with a carceral system devoid of laws and rights. The possibility of transitioning to a civilian government remains indefinitely suspended, and the absence of laws and rights has become the new reality within a state caught in a no-war, no-peace conundrum.

Under this new carceral regime, communities no longer have fully functioning customary laws, and the state has become the ultimate authority. The departure from long-standing traditions and customary laws has caused significant shifts in the social fabric of communities. Those previously organised under patriarchal structures have now been brought together under a unified carceral system. This change has also eroded social divisions and exacerbated the gender-based hierarchies that define patriarchy. For instance, in the traditional community, the relationship between the community and its members was based on mutual respect, with both parties influencing one another. However, after gaining independence, this intricate relationship transformed into a more subordinate one between the people and the state. As a result, people gradually lost their private and collective sense of identity and instead adopted a national identity rooted in territorial claims (Sorenson, 1991; Bernal, 2004). As Bernal (2001) rightly points out, women's involvement in the struggle is often seen as a crucial turning point in challenging deeply rooted gender-based societal norms. However, achieving and maintaining gender equality in post-independence Eritrea has proven to be a difficult task.

The fragile relationship between the people and the state has had a profound impact on people's aspirations and life goals. Hirt (2010) examines the dismantling of the traditional 'hybrid system of norms and values' and links it to the concept of 'anomie' (p. 10). She argues that there is a disconnection between the socio-cultural norms and practices necessary to fulfil people's aspirations: 'culturally accepted goals cannot be accomplished using socially accepted means' (Hirt, 2010, p. 11). She further connects this 'normlessness' to the imposition of indefinite national service, a policy that has ensured perpetual servitude for all able-bodied Eritreans. Hirt (2010) suggests that by legitimising indefinite national service, the government has alienated 'a whole generation' from their 'customary values' and 'societal goals' (p. 11).

Politically, therefore, the period following independence is characterised by governance through decrees, amidst a constant spectacle of the rule of no law nor rights. This created a new regime of necropolitics in the country, which appears to fluctuate between three domains: *prohibition, training and indoctrination, and servitude.* In the domain of prohibition, as argued, the dissolution of the state or any form of dissent against the government is strictly forbidden. Any expression of dissent is met with terrifying menace, as the state solidifies its prohibition by imprisoning dissidents in carceral spaces, subjecting them to forced disappearances, or even systematically eliminating them. Indefinite detention and forced disappearance serve as typical modalities employed to systematically subject people to a state of fear and anxiety. This prohibition is justified through the notion of national security, establishing a precarious relationship between the state and its people. The prohibition of state dissolution entails people being constantly exposed to the imminent threat of death, as evidenced in the perpetual wars the country has been embroiled in.

The relentless subjugation of both the physical and mental faculties of its people through training and ideological conditioning has allowed the government to systematically subdue the entire population of the country as ostensibly obedient subjects within an oppressive regime, thereby suppressing any semblance of individual or communal autonomy or resistance. The state has effectively hindered the human potential and capabilities of its citizens through its apparatus of disciplinary control and indoctrination. The prevailing sentiment within the country seems to be one of widespread fear and uncertainty, as demonstrated by Bozzini (2015). The state's sovereign violence, with its apparent omnipresence and omnipotence, has quelled any internal resistance and sown fear and division among those living outside the country. The prevailing narrative of political activism now revolves around the suppression of resistance and the elimination of differences both within the country and among the diaspora communities. In fact, government supporters in the diaspora confidently reject dissidents their Eritrean identity, asserting with absolute conviction that they are 'not Eritreans'. The toxic discourses, entrenched divisions, and consequent confrontations among Eritreans living in exile have tragically resulted in loss of several lives and violent clashes with police (see Plaut, 2024). This form of violence and the polarised debates among Eritreans living abroad that contribute to it, have been present since the struggle and are often overshadowed by broader national losses (see Bernal, 2024).

Once the body and mind have been fully subjected to disciplinary power, Foucault (2020) explains that power becomes detached from the body and mind: 'on one hand, it turns it [power] into an "aptitude", a "capacity", which it seeks to increase; on the other hand, it reverses the course of the energy, the power that might result from it, and turns it into a relation of strict subjection' (p. 138). According to Foucault, the modern state's exploitative use of its human and non-human resources involves aligning human resources with capital and linking the management of people to the expansion and production of productive resources, all in the pursuit of maximising profit. In addition to producing a national army, indefinite national service achieves this purpose by ensuring the availability, fitness, and compliance of human resources, while optimising their value and productive capacity for maximum output. People are reduced to mere resources for the state's benefit, and if they express distress from the pain of endless servitude or seek relief from it, their dignity and existence are called into question. As Foucault (1998, p. 141) asserts, 'the investment of the body, its valorization, and the distributive management of its forces' are intimately tied to modes of production. The politics of self-reliance is a fictitious rationale for indefinite servitude.

These (necro)political domains, characterised by prohibition, servitude, and indoctrination, define the country's citizenship. The citizenship that emerges under these regimes is marked by uncertainty, confinement, immobility, and a lack of belonging. Essentially, it is a citizenship inseparably linked to an impersonal logic of sovereignty, or, as Foucault (1998) describes it, 'the right to *take* life or *let* live' (1998, p. 136, emphasis in original). Life itself becomes a sacrificial offering to sustain the prohibitions and self-reliance on one hand, and to serve as a means of indoctrination, servitude, and subjugation on the other. These realities are experienced by people trapped in indefinite national service, as well as those who are dehumanised and confined to carceral spaces.

Under the grip of the womb-abyss, Eritreans are either immobilised within the country or forced to flee in large numbers. Those with the means, resources, and social connections may escape the incessant incarceration, exploitation, and (im)mobilisation, but the entire population is outlawed, dispossessed, and forced to make life-or-death decisions to cross (b)orders. Among those who flee, young people and young adults make up a significant portion. This forced migration is driven not only by the state violence they currently face but also by the violence of uncertainty and despair about the future. In the past, during the colonial era, their futures were either racially envisioned or destroyed. Since independence, however, their prospects are buried under the oppressive stagnation imposed by their own government and the enduring shackles of coloniality. In other words, their involuntary displacement results from entangled power dynamics, violent spatial and temporal arrangements, and incarcerated subjectivity. This intermingling of spatialities and temporalities fundamentally undermines 'the self and its relation to the other in time and space' (Maldonado-Torres, 2016, p. 2). The womb-abyss has effectively eroded its citizens' imaginations and their expectations of sociality, civility, and dignity, leaving them trapped in a state of suspended animation. There are no hiding places from the clutches of the omnipresent sovereign, nor any glimmers of hope for a better future.

The suspension of spatial and temporal scales opens multiple prospects for control, exploitation, and incarceration by the carceral state. In an attempt to evade this necropolitical spectacle, people of all ages, including the elderly and children, continue to risk their lives in pursuit of safety elsewhere. The older generations of Eritreans, like Medhin, have lived under the norms and traditions of their community, actively participated in the struggle for independence, and witnessed the profound changes Eritrea has undergone since gaining independence. If we revisit Medhin's enquiry, 'Where are our mamets and hanetays?', it has become apparent that not only have they lost their social status, but they have also lost a dignified existence in their country of origin. Medhin's poetic lament reflects this reality.

> I was a Mamet, now, I am nothing, but
> an abandoned creature, surrounded by bones –
> the bones of my sons, my daughter, my husband,
> who have all gone. I have nothing left to wait for,
> except to join them.

Hanetay and mamet have lost their social standing and become ensnared in the carceral system, where life and death are inextricably linked. While both have been turned into indispensable servants of the state, mamet has also endured the most extreme forms of exploitation. This includes separation from family and community, sexual abuse within the military, and forced displacement under harsh conditions (see Kibreab, 2017). Younger generations have witnessed their country abandon their aspirations, descending into lawlessness and a state devoid of rights. Many see no choice but to flee in search of safety elsewhere.

Forced displacement

The process of becoming a refugee often begins with the wrenching force of forced displacement, born from the violence of oppression, exploitation, enforced disappearance, torture, and detention. These acts of brutality shape the painful calculus of whether to leave behind one's home, land, and the rhythms of a familiar life. When the spectre of violence strips people of the possibility of living with dignity in their own country, flight becomes the only option. Eritrea is a stark example, where escape has become an act of survival and a quest for dignity. For countless Eritreans, leaving their homeland is a desperate effort to break free from the inhuman bonds of systemic state violence, layered upon the enduring scars of colonial violence. Their departure bears witness to profound suffering even prior to their departure.

Yet forced migration is fraught with peril, its path obstructed by (b)ordering regimes and the spectres of danger. (B)orders, both visible and hidden, manifest through checkpoints, the demand for documents, surveillance, relentless patrols, and the ever-watchful eyes of those who seek to prevent flight.

Interrogations, forced detentions, and violent arrests cast shadows over every attempt to flee. To escape these barriers is to navigate a gauntlet of dangers such as militarised (b)orders, covert crossings, and the harsh endurance of long journeys through desolate landscapes, often with little food or water. It demands not only resilience but access to scarce resources and hidden networks of those willing to guide the way.

These (b)orders, marked by cruelty, blur the line between exit and entry, between life and its erasure. They form violent fortresses, yet paradoxically porous, allowing those with means and secret connections to slip through. For others, these (b)orders are spectacles of necropolitics, where death and survival are wielded as instruments of control. Thousands of Eritrean men, women, and children traverse these liminal spaces each year, driven by desperation to escape their torment. For them, displacement is haunted by a sense of endless (im)mobility, where vulnerability and disposability shadow every step. The abyss of forced displacement demands the ultimate gamble of risking life in pursuit of a dignified life elsewhere. For many Eritreans, movement is the last thread of hope, a chance at survival when remaining means succumbing to the slow death of a life denied. In their flight, they carry with them not only their pain but the unyielding belief that somewhere beyond the (b)orders, a life worth living may still be found.

The (b)order operates as a colonial apparatus, denying entry to, and even expelling, those who are racialised, illegalised, and immobilised. It is a site where multiple axes of exception and indifference converge, creating a violent stasis. For Eritrean refugees, this can be understood through the metaphor of living amidst perpetual (b)orders, a defining characteristic of life inscribed within the (b)order. Whether through state actors such as (b)order security, immigration authorities, and national security agents, or non-state actors like intermediaries, organised criminals, and other beneficiaries, these forces enforce overlapping states of exception to systematically exclude potential refugees from the realms of rights and political recognition. This exclusion aligns closely with the structure of the 'ban', as Agamben (1998) explains: 'the force of simultaneous attraction and repulsion that ties together the two poles of the sovereign exception: bare life and power, *homo sacer* and the sovereign' (p. 66). Just as the ban binds naked life to sovereign power, the (b)order is perpetuated as a continuous logic and regime of violence in which multiple states of exception intersect. To live at the (b)order is thus to exist at the junction where these states of exception converge.

The (b)order also functions as a filter, giving rise to three necropolitical mechanisms. First, it designates certain categories of people as 'rightless' and 'illegal', thereby barring their entry into the polity. Second, it confines these designated and racialised people to necropolitical spaces where the boundaries between life and death blur. Within these spaces, they are subjected to perpetual vulnerability, disposability, detainability, and deportability. Finally, the (b)order becomes inscribed on the bodies of these excluded people through technologies such as 'biometric' and 'e-borders' (Salter, 2004; Aas, 2006;

Amoore, 2006). While the first two mechanisms are prevalent in countries of origin and immediate transit, such as Eritrea, Sudan, and Egypt, the last mechanism is more commonly employed in the Global North and some parts of the Global South. Even those who manage to reach Europe and other destination countries find their bodies permanently marked by these (b)orders (see Chapter 5). Their lives are reduced to an existence akin to living with open wounds and scars, trapped within protracted (b)ordering and asylum regimes.

For those who do cross the (b)order, a new set of spatial, temporal, and structural arrangements emerges to contain them or remove their physical presence. Crossing the (b)order marks the beginning of a new (b)ordering spectacle, wherein refugees are criminalised, marginalised, and subjected to deportation or confinement in squalid camps. In the camps, they endure prolonged destitution and exploitation. Eritrean refugees seeking asylum in their first countries of refuge must submit to sovereign powers whose primary objective is to seal (b)orders against unauthorised crossings and apprehend those who succeed. For these refugees, leaving Eritrea is not a resolution but the start of a complex struggle within an expansive carceral network. They are faced with stark choices: remain in refugee camps, attempt to settle in urban areas such as Khartoum or Addis Ababa without access to basic necessities, or continue perilous clandestine journeys in search of safety. Each choice carries its own risks such as being trapped in abject poverty in desolate camps or heavily policed cities, intercepted and deported by (b)order authorities, recruited into human trafficking networks, or perishing in desolate deserts or treacherous waters. Wherever they find themselves, they frequently encounter impoverishment, imprisonment, deportation, and even death.

The belly of the refugee abyss

The forced migration, undertaken in pursuit of safety and a dignified life, unfailingly plunges refugees into the depths of damnation during their abyssal journey. Damnation, as theorised by Fanon (1963) in his seminal work *The Wretched of the Earth*, speaks to the existential condition of colonised and displaced bodies. It is the machinery of coloniality, confining the damned to spaces and times that render them 'fixable', excluded from what is deemed 'human space and time' (Maldonado-Torres, 2016, p. 21). This condition of (de)existence finds its starkest expression in the belly of the refugee abyss, a regime encompassing refugee camps, detention centres, torture camps, and cities policed into submission. The belly of this abyss stretches from forsaken homelands, stripped of rights and laws, to journeys hemmed in by fortified (b)orders. It includes squalid camps overcrowded with the wounded, underground prisons veiled in perpetual darkness, desolate deserts stripped of life, treacherous waters turned to graveyards, and the void of the unknown, where no traces remain. In the belly of the refugee abyss, refugees are reduced to mere bodies, commodified, discarded, and stripped of humanity. Existence becomes a constant confrontation with imminent death. These forms of dehumanisation and existential erasure suffocate refugees, their plight transformed into an experiment orchestrated on 'a planetary scale' (Mbembe, 2019, p. 15). Below, we cast light upon the harrowing realities endured by Eritrean refugees within the belly of the refugee abyss.

Refugee camp

Eritrean refugees constitute one of the largest and earliest groups to seek refuge in the refugee camps of Ethiopia and Sudan. According to the UNHCR Ethiopia Country Response Plan 2020–2021 (Ethiopia CRP), 139,281 Eritreans sought refuge in Ethiopia in 2019, with an estimated caseload of 137,182 in 2020 (UNHCR, 2020a, p. 7). The report also reveals that 70% of these arrivals remained in refugee camps across the Tigray region, with 44% of them being children, 27% of whom were unaccompanied (UNHCR, 2020a, p. 9). The Hitsats and Shimelba refugee camps, nestled within Tigray, were devastated in the conflict between the Tigray regional government and the Ethiopian federal forces, with Eritrea heavily involved. As a result, the whereabouts of approximately 20,000 refugees who fled these camps remain unknown (Miller, 2022, p. 3). Moreover, according to UNHCR's 2022 briefing notes, more than 25,000 refugees in the Mai Aini and Adi Harush camps face catastrophic conditions, deprived of basic necessities and protection (see UNHCR, 2022). Reports of forced abductions and returns to Eritrea have added to their suffering. These conditions highlight the precarious fate of over 149,000 Eritrean refugees in Ethiopia as of 2022 (Miller, 2022, p. 5).

Similarly, in eastern Sudan, refugee camps have long been home to tens of thousands of Eritrean refugees, even before the outbreak of hostilities between the Sudanese Armed Forces (SAF) and the Rapid Support Forces (RSF) in April 2023. East Sudan hosts one of the world's longest-standing refugee populations. The UNHCR Sudan Country Response Plan (Sudan CRP) notes that Eritrean refugees began arriving more than 50 years ago. Over 40% of the refugees in East Sudan have sought refuge for over two decades, with nearly half of those in the camps born there (UNHCR, 2020b, p. 39). Most remain confined to camps such as Kilo 26, Shagarab, Girba, and Um Gargour. Among these, Shagarab has become a significant hub, housing thousands of Eritrean refugees and earning the nickname 'Little Eritrea' (Smith, 2017, p. 11).

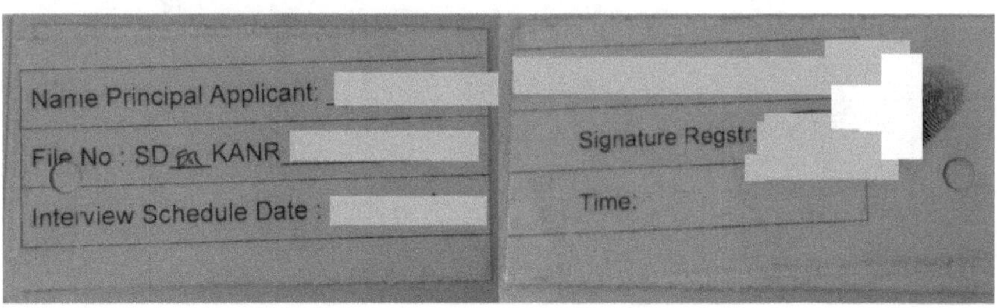
Name Principal Applicant:
File No : SD KANR
Interview Schedule Date :
Signature Regstr:
Time:

Figure 4.1 Registration document issued by the UNHCR at Shagarab Refugee Camp.

The process of seeking asylum within these camps is marked by bureaucracy, hardship, and lengthy delays. It unfolds in conditions of destitution, mismanagement, and corruption. Upon arrival, refugees must make their asylum claims, enduring long queues often under the relentless sun for registration, documentation, and biometric procedures. Once registered (Figure 4.1), claimants are provided with basic assistance such as food, shelter, tents, and clothing. Yet, due to the camps' under-resourced and impoverished nature, these essentials are frequently in short supply. Those whose identities are verified and whose claims are deemed credible are issued a 'yellow card' (Figure 4.2), while others, whose claims are rejected, flee the camp and embark on perilous journeys.

After a successful asylum claim, claimants may apply for refugee status determination (RSD), a process that often stretches over several years. Many refugees describe this ordeal as an arduous wait for a hollow affirmation of vulnerability, offering little more than a nominal refugee status at best, or a complete rejection at worst. Those whose asylum claims are denied find themselves caught in a cyclical state of limbo, repeatedly making fresh claims and appealing against decisions. For those who hold refugee status or 'blue cards', life does not differ significantly from those whose claims have been refused. While a very small number may find resettlement in third countries through UNHCR resettlement programmes, the vast majority remain trapped in camps, devoid of protection or any glimpse of a future, living in a state of destitution. This unyielding condition of perpetual poverty compels many to continue their journeys towards the 'police cities' and beyond. Yet, for those unable to proceed due to disability, injury, illness, or a lack of resources, the camps become an indefinite prison. Adiam poignantly described this condition:

> While our children are born as refugees,
> we [the parents] die as refugees,
> stripped of humanity and dignity.

Figure 4.2 Yellow card issued by the UNHCR at Shagarab Refugee Camp.

Life in the refugee camps remains a brutal struggle for most of these stranded refugees. Basic necessities like food, shelter, clean water, healthcare, and protection are scarce. The Sudan CRP estimates that around 20% of refugees in camps in Sudan live with disabilities or chronic illnesses, yet have no access to the medical care they urgently need (UNHCR, 2020b, p. 41). Furthermore, there is evidence suggesting that refugee camps have become fertile ground for trafficking, with both state and non-state actors involved, including UNHCR security guards (see Reisen et al., 2012; Reisen and Mawere, 2017; Yohannes, 2021). For instance, the Shagarab refugee camp has become notorious for hosting a complex network of human trafficking. Former residents, including those who have been trafficked, have described it as an 'open prison'. Sada, a former resident, was forcibly taken from the camp in 2010 by traffickers, and his sister endured a similar fate a few years later. Sada affirmed that UNHCR security guards were complicit in his abduction, stating, 'I was sold to Rashaida by a UNHCR security guard'. He portrayed the refugee camp as 'an open prison', adding, 'For some, the camp is a life sentence. For others, it serves as a market for human commodities'.

Sada's and his sister's experiences are tragically far from unique. More than a dozen survivors of trafficking have corroborated reports of collusion between traffickers and UNHCR security personnel. In fact, three survivors revealed they had been sexually assaulted by security guards at the Kilo 26 camp in Kassala, before being transported to the Sinai, where they witnessed their friends being raped and tortured to death. The testimonies of trafficking victims, documented in Reisen et al. (2012, pp. 32–41), further reveal that the Shagarab camp has been used as a source of human commodities by traffickers operating in the Sinai, Libya, and others. Refugees were transferred from intermediaries to traffickers upon crossing the border, taken forcibly during their journeys, or abducted in towns along the way. Reisen et al. (2013, p. 25) summarises:

> Many of the refugees held hostage in the Sinai were kidnapped while in a refugee camp or on their way to a family reunion in Sudan or Ethiopia. A significant proportion of refugees were kidnapped from within refugee camps or surrounding areas, especially in Sudan (from Shagarab refugee camp) or while working in Kassala (Sudan). A smaller number of interviewees were taken on their way to Khartoum (Sudan), from within Khartoum or from Cairo.

At refugee camps such as Shagarab, some UNHCR staff go beyond their humanitarian duties, engaging in the trafficking and blackmailing of refugees. This is not simply a matter of a few security staff reversing their roles; it is a system that allows rogue elements within humanitarian organisations to become entangled in lawlessness, ultimately fostering a disturbing trafficking alliance with forces that prey on refugees (Mekonnen and Estefanos, 2011;

Yohannes, 2021). However, the greatest harm is wrought by the collusion between state actors, including border security, the police, and the military, and organised criminal groups, notably the Rashaida, Bedouins, and others, as we shall explore further in relation to refugee trafficking.

Life in refugee camps is, in general, profoundly distressing. The camp is a place where people wait for hours to receive a meagre ration of food; where children suffer and even perish from malnutrition, malaria, and various other diseases; where unaccompanied children are abducted by traffickers, forced to endure torture, or left to die slowly in trafficking warehouses; where young girls are subjected to sexual abuse, including rape, and coerced into unwanted relationships with traffickers; where single mothers plead for food to feed their crying children; where hope is constantly deferred, and life is endured in a state of abject destitution, bureaucratic limbo, immobility, and violation. In the camp, the distinctions between right and wrong, ethical and immoral, disappear entirely. Within its confines, life is experienced as though in an open grave, where time and space expand and contract in ways that strip away any semblance of a dignified human existence. With its walls of containment, impoverishment, and suffering, the camp becomes an abyss that swallows lives, silences displaced voices, and transforms dreams into nightmares. As Agamben (1998) puts it, the camp is an 'impassable biopolitical space' (p. 72).

The police city

The police city is a carceral complex where refugees live in constant fear of detention and deportation. In this city, state power is wielded arbitrarily, fostering a sense of both real and perceived omnipresence and omnipotence. Those deemed unwanted inhabitants reside in a perpetual state of anxiety, acutely aware that they are under unceasing surveillance, relentlessly pursued by the police, who possess the means and authority to track them down, apprehend them, and subject them to criminalisation and deportation. Unlike the refugee camp, which exists in a liminal space between the inside and outside of the polity, the police city is an integral part of the carceral network at the heart of the postcolony. These police cities can be found in (b)order regions and transit hubs, from the shanty towns to the capital cities of transit countries. While some refugees settle in the hidden underbelly of these cities, others pass through them as a temporary stopover while they plan or attempt to reach a safer destination. The police cities also serve as sites for humanitarian operations and asylum regimes.

The scarcity of basic necessities and the widespread insecurity within refugee camps compel many to continue their journeys to the urban centres of neighbouring countries. As Andom (2018) and Kibreab (1996) perceptively note, cities like Khartoum, Kassala, and Addis Ababa have historically been sought-after destinations for refugees from both rural and urban Eritrea.

These cities have long offered better access to essential services and employment opportunities compared to the refugee camps. However, as Kok (1989) demonstrates, self-settled refugees in these cities face numerous challenges, including a lack of protection, limited prospects, and an uncertain future. The vulnerability of these refugees is starkly evident in the recurring incidents of violent arrests and exploitation they endure on the streets. Humanitarian organisations, journalists, activists, and members of the Eritrean diaspora have campaigned against the exploitation and deportation of self-settled refugees for years (Human Rights Watch, 2016; Siegfried, 2016; Yohannes, 2024). Yet, despite these efforts, the relentless violence and exploitation directed at refugees remain the greatest obstacles faced by those self-settling in neighbouring countries. Recent reports reveal not only an unwillingness to register and process new asylum claims but also the arrest of hundreds of Eritrean refugees in Addis Ababa, followed by their deportation to Eritrea (OHCHR, 2023).

Beyond the lack of safety, refugees in the police city face other profound challenges: the absence of opportunities, widespread exploitation, and an uncertain future. Forced into exploitative work, they take on informal jobs such as domestic, agricultural, and infrastructure work for meagre wages. These conditions leave them vulnerable to further abuse, with women, young girls, and unaccompanied children especially susceptible to domestic violence and sexual exploitation. For refugees, the workplace in these cities is a site of multiple forms of exploitation. In this study, we encountered several young girls who recounted their harrowing experiences: 'During my first week on the job, the son of the woman I worked for locked me in his bedroom and raped me'; 'The woman I worked for, her husband would come to my room at night'; 'I was often forced to sleep in a small room where I also did the family's ironing'; 'One night, a man attempted to rape me, so I quickly escaped into the darkness'; 'I never received payment for the five months I worked'; 'I was required to work day and night during Ramadan'. Caught between unemployment and exploitation, these self-settled refugees often rely on remittances from their relatives and friends in the diaspora, including those in the Gulf countries, Europe, and the Americas.

For those without connections abroad, survival often hinges on becoming intermediaries. Contrary to the prevailing discourse on smuggling, refugees frequently use the term *intermediary* to describe the act of facilitating movement across fortified (b)orders, crossing points, and between destinations. They view this work as a means to enable their own mobility, believing that through movement, they can create a safer, better future for themselves. Edris shared his experience: 'Initially, I worked at a restaurant owned by an intermediary. Later, I became an intermediary myself, as the salary was not enough to survive'. He explained: 'I had to sleep on the streets for several months, but helping refugees with their journeys allowed me to earn enough to support myself and continue my own journey'. In such dire circumstances, some were left with little choice but to accept any work that promised funds for their journey to safety, even if it involved actions akin to organised crime. Reflecting on their past, some refugees expressed ironic gratitude: ‘I consider myself fortunate not to have been kidnapped by the traffickers, though they forced me to watch their hostages during the journey’; ‘I paid friends to find people in Eritrea willing to go to Sudan, and used the money to cross the sea’; ‘I even started sending my own intermediaries to Eritrea to make more money for the journey to Libya’; and so on.

Paradoxically, the police city also serves as a hub for humanitarian operations, particularly the processing of asylum claims. In neighbouring countries, many self-settled refugees apply for asylum to obtain legal status. Gaining refugee status offers some protection against deportation and access to limited services such as healthcare, employment, and education. The process for assessing asylum claims may differ slightly depending on the country, but generally involves evaluating the vulnerability of applicants to establish a well-founded fear of persecution, as defined by the 1951 Refugee Convention. The UNHCR, the host country, and organisations like the IOM and legal aid providers assist with asylum seekers and the processing of their claims. However, it is crucial to note that obtaining refugee status does not necessarily guarantee meaningful protection for refugees.

Cairo is a major destination for Eritreans, especially as neighbouring Sudan and Ethiopia are plagued by internal conflicts. Once home to over a million refugees, Sudan now faces its own dire situation due to ongoing war. Reports from the UNHCR (2025) reveal that, since the war began in April 2024, nearly 3 million people, including Sudanese refugees, have sought refuge in neighbouring countries as of October 2024. Additionally, more than 8 million people have been displaced within Sudan (UNHCR, 2025). Tragically, the conflict has already claimed tens of thousands of lives, primarily among the civilian population. The Tigray war, internal conflicts, political instability, and famine in Ethiopia have led to devastating losses of life, livelihood, and hope for the future (Research and Evidence Facility, 2023). As a result, internal displacement within Ethiopia has surged, along with cross-border secondary displacement as refugees seek safety within the country.

Upon arriving in Cairo, people seeking asylum must endure a lengthy process of registration and Refugee Status Determination (RSD). Similar to the asylum procedures in refugee camps, the registration process requires hours of waiting in crowded queues to obtain a lengthy form, often written in English or Arabic. Applicants must complete the form to meet the UNHCR’s registration requirements and then wait for months for an interview and biometrics. Many people seeking asylum have described the registration process as ‘messy and corrupt’, with some alleging the existence of a clandestine black market where registration forms are bought and sold, and individuals are paid to complete them. Some have admitted to paying $150 to community members for a UNHCR registration form and assistance with filling it out. They have also expressed concern about the difficulties faced by people seeking asylum who lack

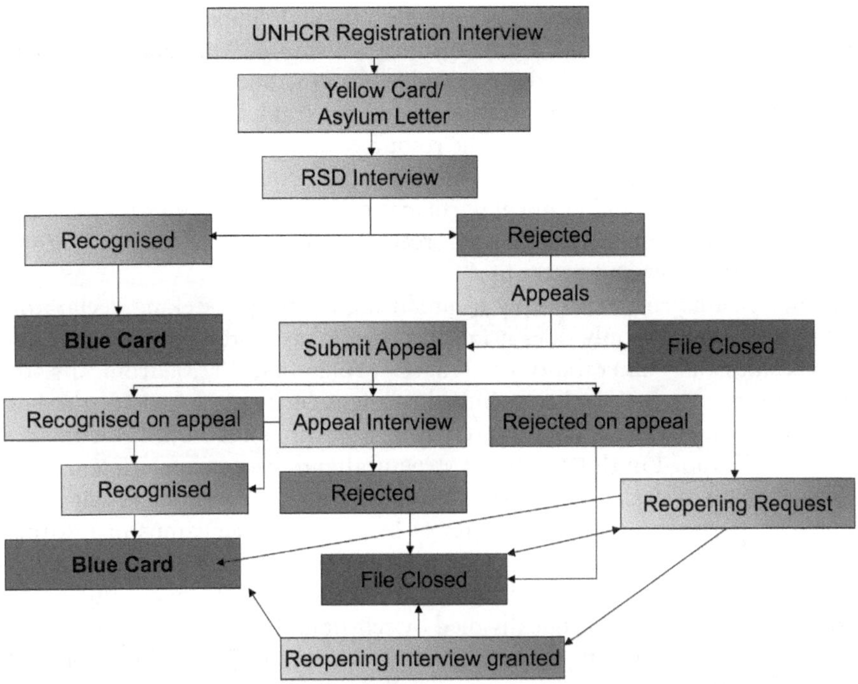

Figure 4.3 Stages of the UNHCR asylum process in Cairo, Egypt.

the necessary resources and skills to navigate the process. Figure 4.3 illustrates the various stages of the asylum process in Cairo, as implemented by UNHCR in Egypt.

Once successfully registered with the UNHCR, people seeking refuge are issued yellow cards or asylum papers, depending on the establishment of their identity and age. Following registration, most people endure a waiting period of one to several years for their RSD interviews, with an additional wait of six months to several years for their RSD results. Those who receive positive RSD results are granted refugee status, while those whose asylum claims are rejected must undergo a lengthy and arduous process of counselling and appeals, which may include the possibility of further rejections and file closures. Refugees have described the appeals process as both traumatic and excessively bureaucratic. In fact, some have suggested that people seeking asylum who have exhausted their right to appeal are left with no choice but to embark on perilous secondary movements in search of safety.

Each stage of the UNHCR asylum process takes several months to several years. The length of time depends on various factors, including the UNHCR's capacity to assess cases, the individual circumstances of the claimants, and access to legal advocacy and psycho-social support. Throughout the process, host countries and the UNHCR provide minimal support to refugees, offering only limited financial and medical assistance. This aid is primarily directed towards particularly vulnerable groups, such as unaccompanied children, single mothers, and victims of refugee trafficking. Additionally, local charitable organisations lack the resources and capacity to meet the refugees' needs. Employment opportunities in these countries are limited, as is access to education and political participation. As a result, refugees must rely on remittances from abroad or are forced to embark on dangerous journeys in search of a safer and better life.

The asylum process is deeply traumatising for people seeking declaratory refugee status. Not only does it fail to provide basic protections, but it also exacerbates the vulnerability of refugees (Yohannes, 2023). Ironically, the asylum system remains closely linked to the security apparatus of the host country, further entrenching the refugees' precarious relationship with state violence. Trapped in this system of structural and institutional violence, refugees remain stranded in poverty, disability, and homelessness, with only poignant stories to share after years of living in refugee camps or informal settlements. Many are subjected to various forms of vulnerability, including the daily reality of police brutality. Unfortunately, we also came across stories of refugees who tragically died by self-immolation in front of the UNHCR office while seeking asylum (Daily News Egypt, 2016). The UNHCR, the organisation mandated to protect refugees, watches these tragedies powerlessly. Despite refugees' pleas for protection, the UNHCR can only offer an asylum (yellow) card or refugee (blue) card and replace them when they expire or go missing. This raises the question: what is the purpose of the UNHCR if it only administers the establishment of refugee status based on 'fear of persecution' and disregards refugees' testimonies stored in its vast archives? How does having refugee status or a blue card actually help people without adequate protection? These are questions refugees often ask.

Generally, the self-settlement of refugees in neighbouring countries such as Sudan, Ethiopia, and Egypt provides little respite in terms of protection. The appeals for protection made by refugees merely reinforce their essentialised vulnerability and perpetuate their insecurity. The ineffectiveness of declaratory protection and humanitarian assistance highlights the violent origins of 'carceral humanitarianism' (Oliver, 2017), which is deployed alongside the exclusionary and racialised bordering policies of the womb-abyss.

Refugee trafficking across the desert

Whether refugees choose to remain in the camps, venture into urban areas, or continue their journey within the region and beyond, they are exposed to the dangers of being targeted by traffickers and their accomplices, who engage in illicit activities such as torture, ransom extraction, and organ harvesting. Refugees are frequently targeted by traffickers who operate across both their home countries and the countries where they seek refuge.

Recruitment into the trafficking chain is facilitated by a complex network of organised criminals, private individuals, government entities, and non-governmental actors at various stages along the journey. This includes abductions and kidnappings from the refugees' home countries, during border crossings, in refugee camps, while travelling, in urban areas, and even from detention centres, with the help of prison security personnel who collaborate with traffickers.

Once victims fall into the hands of traffickers, they are turned into valuable commodities and traded for ransom, organ extraction, and sexual exploitation within the highly profitable enterprise of refugee trafficking. Those of us who have endured the traumatic journey of refugee trafficking are burdened with the pain of our own open wounds and the perpetual loss of our fellow refugees, some of whom have left no remains at all. We have witnessed our friends' bodies disfigured and bleeding, seen lifeless bodies scattered in the open, and endured the putrid stench of decomposing flesh. Radically exposed to violence, some of us requested to bury the dead, only to be told that their lives and deaths held no inherent meaning or value.

> We saw dead bodies in the desert and requested to bury them.
> One of the traffickers responded, 'No, they are Kafir bodies'.
> In broken Arabic, we asked, 'What is Kafir?'
> The trafficker replied, 'Just like a dead cow'.
> 'A dead cow?' one of us echoed.
> The trafficker loudly pronounced,
> 'They are already dead'.
> We all fell into silence.

The desert is an unmarked grave for those buried alive, those who vanished without a trace, and those who succumbed to the abyss of the journey.

Amidst this collective indignation, the brutality and inhumanity faced by women and young girls in refugee trafficking defy adequate description. On the perilous journey into unknown lands, times, and realities, we bore witness to young girls and women being raped for the sadistic pleasure of traffickers. The relentless cries of refugee women and girls haunt our sleep, transforming nights into an endless procession of nightmares. Some of us recall the traffickers' chilling declaration: 'Every virgin woman will be treated well during the journey'. A woman found to be a virgin becomes the 'property' of one trafficker until her virginity is lost, at which point she is passed on to the next in the chain. The violation of a virgin is considered an added prize, sometimes sparking disputes among traffickers. We also heard mothers humiliated before their children, and brides humiliated before their husbands. We learned of sisters and cousins tortured to death for refusing to sexually abuse one another. We have already recounted the horrors of those 'buried alive', as if their existence had been of no consequence. In the belly of refugee abyss, refugee women and girls endure death, despair, and isolation.

In the past two decades, nowhere has the trafficking of refugees been more notorious than in the Sinai Peninsula and the ongoing tragedy in Libya. From 2006 to 2014, tens of thousands of Eritreans, escaping pervasive violence in their homeland, found themselves on the Sinai Peninsula (see Simpson, 2014). These victims were subjected to severe torture, including electrocution, rape, burning with melted plastic and cigarette butts, hanging upside down from barbed metal, mutilation with knives, alleged organ harvesting, and starvation (see Reisen et al., 2012; Fisseha, 2015; Yohannes, 2023). The Sinai hostages were treated as 'human incubators' for organ trafficking (Fisseha, 2015, p. 7), sold to whoever paid the highest price among traffickers (Bahlbi, 2016), and extorted for ransoms amounting to tens of thousands of US dollars (Reisen and Mawere, 2017; Yohannes, 2023). Disturbingly, many survivors recounted instances where traffickers derived pleasure from inflicting pain and humiliation upon them. Sergel recalled the unimaginable acts of violence their forsaken bodies were compelled to perpetrate against one another:

> They would tie our hands behind our backs
> and force us to engage in dirty stuff,
> such as raping and abusing each other,
> while they watched and laughed at us.
> If anyone dared to refuse,
> they would subject us to severe torture.
> They would electrocute us, or even mutilate us
> by cutting off our fingers with their knives.
> That was how my friends lost their lives.

When asked about the deaths of his friends, Sergel struggled to hold back his tears and spoke in a hushed voice. He described how two traffickers approached one of his friends and demanded that he engage in sexual acts with his 16-year-old cousin in front of the hostages. For the hostages, it is both immoral and unacceptable to engage in sexual relations with a close relative under any circumstances. Naturally, Sergel's friend refused to participate in the sexual acts the traffickers requested of him. Enraged by his refusal, Sergel described how the traffickers used a long knife to sever two of his friend's fingers while the friend was restrained. Despite this horrific act, the traffickers demanded that he rapes his cousin. Once again, the victim adamantly declined while screaming in pain. 'At this point', Sergel described, 'one of the traffickers turned to the girl and instructed her to remove her clothing and engage in sexual act with her cousin'. She too firmly refused. Infuriated, Sergel recounted how the second trafficker left the room momentarily and returned with a heated knife. The trafficker proceeded to hang the girl upside down, fastened to the wall by metal chains, and mercilessly cut through the middle of her breast with the knife: 'The sight of this was unbearable and caused all of us [the hostages] to scream in agony'. Sergel further explained: 'We felt an overwhelming desire to end our own lives, but we were unable to do so as we were bound by handcuffs'. Realising their desperation, the traffickers chained the hostages' limbs together to prevent any further suicide attempts. The two cousins succumbed to excessive bleeding, and the traffickers disposed of their bodies in the sea. Their deaths were not reported to their families and relatives until they had been deceived into paying a total ransom of US$20,000.

Sergel was held hostage in the Sinai Peninsula for approximately nine months, during which he witnessed the tragic deaths of more than a dozen victims. Eventually, after his family and relatives paid a ransom of US$25,000, he was finally released from captivity. Although he expressed gratitude for surviving, Sergel admitted that he still struggles with recurring flashbacks of the torture he endured and the events he witnessed. In tears, Sergel suddenly removed his shirt, revealing his recent and old wounds.

> Look at my wounds,
> still bleeding.
> These are my scars,
> my old wounds.

We saw that Sergel's upper body was covered in dotted scars from molten plastic that had been poured onto his skin, as well as broken ribs that had been crushed by the butt of a Kalashnikov. However, there was an aspect of his experience that we could not fully grasp, as Sergel explained: 'You see, my inner being remains numb. Nightmares still haunt me'. He went on to share that this numbness in his psyche, along with the physical pain in his body, is something nearly all of his friends who survived the Sinai trafficking have also endured. The trauma of witnessing their companions subjected to torturous deaths, as well as the horrific acts of rape committed by a group of sadistic traffickers against young girls and boys in their presence, has infected their bodies like 'venom' from 'a snake'. 'This experience', Sergel confessed, 'will forever remain deeply ingrained within us'.

The painful deaths, open wounds, and scars explored in this book are not isolated tragedies; rather, they are the harsh realities endured by thousands of refugees who have perished within the chains of trafficking, such as those orchestrated in the Sinai Peninsula and beyond. In the case of the Sinai trafficking alone, estimates cited by CNN and Reisen et al. (2012, p. 19) reveal that over 4,000 refugee bodies were counted between 2007 and 2012, with many more vanishing without a trace. Furthermore, survivors who managed to escape or were released by their captors often faced a cruel fate, as they were frequently murdered by border security guards. As Reisen et al. (2012, p. 19) note, 'Many refugees die after their release (after their ransom is paid), shot by border control on the Egyptian or Israeli side'. This grim reality exposes how, whether at the hands of traffickers or state agents, these victims were treated as disposable human commodities, relentlessly subjected to necropolitical exploitation.

It seems there is no hope of healing the survivors' shattered hearts or restoring their broken minds and bodies. As we write these words, new refugees continue to be ensnared within the expanding network of trafficking that has spread throughout the region since the days of the Sinai trafficking. Nearly a decade after the horrors of the Sinai trafficking, the cycle of refugee exploitation continues unabated in Sudan, Ethiopia, Libya, and other countries in the region and beyond. In Libya, for example, refugees must navigate perilous routes controlled by rogue powers, militias, human traffickers, and border guards, before they can even glimpse the sea. Tragically, countless lives are lost at the hands of these unaccountable forces, as Ariam's account demonstrates. Ariam also bore witness to the tragic death of a pregnant woman, an event she described as an 'enduring haunting memory'. The woman, expecting a child and already a mother to a five-year-old, succumb to injuries sustained in a car accident on her way to the Mediterranean coast in Libya. Overcome with profound sorrow, Ariam lamented:

> The woman died,
> her son and I
> survived.

The torture camp, controlled by traffickers, exists as a place where life is commodified, violated for pleasure, murdered for gratification, and ultimately erased from existence. There is perhaps no more desolate and 'abject' of camps than the torture camp, where unimaginable acts of cruelty and inhumanity are inflicted upon those seeking refuge. The function of 'abject spaces', as Isin and Rygiel (2007, p. 184) argue, 'is to treat people neither as subjects (of discipline) nor objects (of elimination) but as those without presence, without existence, as inexistent beings, not because they don't exist, but because their existence is rendered invisible and inaudible through abject spaces'. The torture camp is a necropolitical site, where refugees are reduced to raw corporealities. Once stripped of their humanity, the living bodies of refugees are subjected to suffocating brutality. The refugees kidnapped and held hostage in the torture camps are forced to disown their own bodies, as they are possessed by their traffickers. The traffickers, in fact, are at liberty to do as they please with these masses of bodies, as evidenced in the harrowing accounts of survivors.

Refugee trafficking is a unique and grotesque form of exploitation, in which the vulnerable are commodified, held hostage, and subjected to ransoming, organ harvesting, refugee trading, and sexual violence, all under conditions of extreme brutality. At a fundamental level, the ontological states of being and non-being for trafficked refugees blur into a realm of indiscernibility and violability, where the living dead become inseparable from the vicarious existence of the physically dead. As revealed, some victims may ultimately succumb to a slow, agonising death, but until then, they continue to exist in a limbo, waiting for their ransom to be paid or their organs harvested.

The ransom, which signifies the market value of their violable bodies, marks the liminal threshold where the physically dead and the surviving victims intersect. Here, at this point of intersection, the living dead and the dead living enter a zone of indistinction where the bodies of refugees confront the politics of death, or necropolitics. It is here that the radical violability and disposability of refugees are realised.

Tortured to death, the bodies of the hostages are stripped of their dignity, with valuable body parts including organs harvested for profit and organ transplanting. The excavated bodies are often subjected to mutilation, extortion, burning, and the disposal of their flesh in the open air. Once discarded in the desert or in a torture camp, their bodies are left scattered across the desert, exposed to the organisms, elements and the things of nature. There is no proper burial, no ritual of mourning or grief to honour their death. Their flesh becomes sustenance for beasts and insects, while their bones lie visible, strewn upon the ground, exposed to the open air. News of their deaths, if communicated at all, reaches their families only when there is no longer any value to be extracted from withholding such information (e.g., after a ransom is paid or organs harvested), or when the traffickers have reached the point of maximum exploitation. The confirmation of their deaths signifies the total collapse of their physical and vicarious existence. These victims, stripped of the most basic rights, were not recognised as lives worthy of dignity nor afforded proper burials. They exist in a liminal space between life and death, confined to the belly of the refugee abyss. Their personal and collective stories are remembered with profound anguish until their eventual death, even if that death is one of living in a constant state of suffering.

For the survivors, the past is a relentless memory of pain, and our future remains scarred, a painful testament to wounds that refuse to heal.

Detention and deportation

The detention and forced removal of people seeking refuge, including victims of refugee trafficking, have become increasingly widespread across the globe. The carceral infrastructures of detention span from the stark prison structures in refugee-sending countries like Eritrea to the underground cells and military prisons in larger refugee-hosting nations such as Sudan, Ethiopia, and Egypt. Furthermore, hotspots, detention centres, floating barges, and remote offshore facilities are scattered across continents, from Europe to the Americas, Australia, Asia, and Africa. These physical structures are upheld by legislative frameworks, exclusionary necropolitics, and an unsettlingly mundane operation of carceral humanitarianism. Together, these physical and juridico-political systems intensify the violence inherent in a carceral world.

Throughout this study, we had the privilege of engaging with numerous Eritrean, Sudanese, and Ethiopian refugees trapped in prisons across Aswan, Cairo, Alexandria, and other remote towns in Egypt. We witnessed the deportation of over a dozen Eritrean refugees, expelled without due regard for legal or asylum procedures. Before their deportation, we visited these refugees, and our encounters revealed stories of suffering that lays bare the limits legality, political understanding, and morality. Some shared their experiences in the following words: 'I was trafficked by people connected to both the Eritrean and Egyptian authorities, which is why they decided to deport me so quickly, tomorrow'; 'look at my back, covered in wounds that still bleed'; 'this is our life, soon returning to the open prison we escaped from'; 'our hopes vanished the moment we were arrested'; 'we may think we exist, but how can one exist in such a torturous life?'; 'I no longer have tears because I exhausted them through crying in solitude'. These raw accounts reflect the reality for countless Eritrean refugees who have been deported back to Eritrea from neighbouring and regional countries, such as Sudan, Ethiopia, and Egypt. This cycle of detention and deportation creates a continuous carceral orbit, endlessly shifting between the country of origin (Eritrea), where a dignified life is impossible, and the neighbouring countries.

Following detention, the process of deportation is a spectacle of bureaucracy, corruption, and arbitrary decision-making. Refugees, upon their capture, are compelled to contact the embassy of their country of origin, Eritrea, to verify their identities, pay administrative fees for their deportation, and are then transported to the airport in prison vehicles. They are taken to the Eritrean embassy by prison security, where they undergo a procedure involving evidence collection, identity verification, and documentation, all under the watchful eyes of guards. This occurs only after the detainees' families or relatives have gathered or agreed to raise sufficient funds for airfare (ranging from $300 to $500 at the time of writing) and for the issuance of their temporary travel documents (ranging from $30 to $50, depending on the staff member handling the process, though often recorded as $30 on official receipts). Once the embassy is satisfied with the paperwork, the refugees are returned to prison until their flight is confirmed and their deportation is finalised by either embassy staff or prison officials. On the day of deportation, they are once again transported in prison vehicles, accompanied by prison security, before being escorted onto the plane, only to return to the country they fled. They are deported to Eritrea with wounds still fresh, scars visible, and clothes torn and ragged.

Another issue that remains rarely discussed, at least to our knowledge, is the plight of what we have referred to in the introduction as stateless refugees. These individuals, whose ties to home, family, and community have been severed beyond recognition, experience a profound crisis of identity and a loss of belonging. Many of them were born in neighbouring countries such as Sudan, Ethiopia, and Egypt before Eritrea gained independence. They have lost all contact with their families, including their parents. We spoke with over half a dozen stateless refugees, who shared their harrowing stories of trafficking, detention, and deportation. As illustrated in the introduction through Hatem's story, a significant number of these refugees have no parents and are entitled to no citizenship in any nation. They attribute their parents' deaths to either the casualties of the war of independence or to covert assassinations carried out by the various factions of the liberation movement or Ethiopian colonial agents, targeting individuals based on their affiliations.

With no family and no country to claim them, the stateless refugees are cast outside the realm of the womb-abyss, effectively excluded from ethical and political life. Their existence is unknown, their bodies reduced to mere vessels of suffering. They are trapped in an endless cycle of trafficking, detention, and deportation, a cycle that reinforces their dehumanisation and denies them the right to be. When abducted by traffickers, they have no one to confide in or appeal to for rescue. In detention, they vanish without a trace, and when deported, no state is willing to receive them. Even when they make asylum claims, their testimonies are often dismissed as lacking credibility, failing to meet the established criteria for well-founded fear of persecution. Alex described this tragic reality with chilling clarity when he said, 'I did not exist; I de-existed'.

Though Alex was once connected to a state for which he fought and suffered, his family and country had recorded him as deceased; to them, Alex no longer existed. His story, therefore, mirrors that of the stateless refugees, condemned to a necropolitical existence and denied a place in the world. As Hatem described, for them, the world is a 'living hell'. Yet they cling to a fragile hope, yearning for a life beyond this suffering, a world that might take their existential questions seriously.

It bears repeating that the trafficking, detention, and deportation of refugees are intrinsically linked to the failure of states to address the atrocities committed by traffickers and their powerful partners in border security across East and North Africa and beyond. These rogue actors, including traffickers and associates from government institutions and humanitarian organisations, operate across (b)orders, exploiting vulnerable refugees in search of safety. As evidenced in the case of Sinai trafficking, the involvement of border security officers, police, military commanders, humanitarian staff (including UNHCR personnel), and local communities is well-documented. Yet, there have been no investigations to hold accountable those responsible for the mass killings of thousands of refugees, carried out with impunity. The dehumanising exploitation and mass murder of refugees, with no consequences, has unfortunately become a grim reality in many parts of the world, from the countries of origin to the countries they seek refuge in.

Conclusion

We have shown that the condition of becoming a refugee arises when people find themselves entangled in a state of perpetual indignity and servitude, subjected to the state's self-preserving violence. The core elements of the rule of no law nor rights—namely, indefinite national service, arbitrary detention, and forced disappearance—are used to create compliant, exploitable, violable, and disposable individuals under the guise of state preservation. In the womb-abyss, citizens and the state blur into a realm of indistinguishability, with the former enduring incessant violence and exploitation at the hands of the latter. This unrelenting violence, governed by the womb-abyss, makes it exceedingly difficult to live a life of dignity within the postcolony. Fleeing the postcolony has become a necessity for the continuation of both physical and political existence.

For Eritreans, the decision to flee our country and enter a foreign land is a desperate attempt to escape the omnipresent and all-powerful carceral state. Our decisions to flee not only acknowledges our status as suffering people but also represents a plea for a life of dignity. However, even after leaving our country, this quest for a dignified existence and political recognition continues to be undermined. When fleeing across the (b)order, prospective refugees are burdened with the enduring effects of marginalisation, illegality, incarceration, and potential deportation. The (b)order becomes the convergence point for various forms of marginalisation, incarceration, and uncertainty, ultimately resulting in a violent state of stagnation. Subjected to this ongoing violence of racialised (b)ordering, we treated as what Da Silva (2014) describes as 'No-bodies'—bodies whose ethical and political existence is disregarded.

As we have observed, once we cross the (b)order, we are confronted with the belly of the refugee abyss. Despite their differences, the refugee camp, the police city, the desert, and the torture camp all share the same underlying reality: the refugee abyss. What is ultimately at stake within the belly of the refugee abyss is the very essence of our lives. State and non-state actors, who often profit from and derive pleasure from human suffering, inflict open wounds upon significant portions of humanity. Faced with lacerations and injury, we are condemned to a necropolitical existence that can only be imagined in a realm of indistinguishability between being treated as less than human [(de)humanisation] and not being acknowledged at all [(de)existence], without the possibility of juridico-political existence within the framework of the womb-abyss. This abyssal reality of being caught between (de)humanisation and (de)existence occurs when the state has complete control over life and death (Mbembe, 2003). The womb-abyss, through its instruments of sovereignty and governmentality, decides who falls outside the protection of the womb-abyss and is condemned to the belly of the refugee abyss. The violence exercised in the refugee abyss clearly neither preserves life nor exhausts it to a state of pure death but instead keeps it suspended between life and death, where both life and death are constant threats and occurrences. It suspends our lives in a state of perpetual (de)existence.

Consigned to this state of perpetual (de)existence, we contemplate our status within the abyssal world and its inherently colonial logic of intelligibility and consciousness. During a group discussion in Cairo, some of us expressed their profound weariness as follows:

> Does the world know we exist?
> To the world, we are not recognisable, and
> our suffering is unintelligible to its consciousness.

These words were uttered by survivors of refugee trafficking, in a fading tone, as an expression of their (de)existence in a world that remains existentially indifferent to them. As shown, neither sovereign states nor the futile efforts of humanitarian organisations could rescue these lives trapped within the refugee abyss. While transit states relentlessly camouflage their indifference and (b)ordering violence directed towards refugees, the 'humanitarian organizations—which today are more and more supported by international commissions—can only grasp human life in the figure of bare or sacred life' (Agamben, 1998, p. 133). The lives of refugees do not seem to count as lives, and our bodies are exploited and discarded once they no longer serve any purpose (Mbembe, 2019).

The refugees, whose displaced voices this book draws upon, used the Tigrigna term ሕሰም (h'sem), which literally translates to 'plight', to describe the realities of being trapped in the refugee abyss. In Tigrigna, h'sem refers to a precarious state of being, in which pain and suffering surpass language, beyond words. It signifies the collapse of all positive experiences and relationships into a condition of absolute brutality and precarity, leading to the negation of human existence within the abyssal world. In conditions of h'sem, occurrences of (de)humanisation and (de)existence are endless; murder is not unusual, nor is it a crime. The lives of those condemned to h'sem are neither liveable nor grievable, as Butler would argue. No utterance of pain, misery, or lawlessness lies beyond the realm of h'sem.

Condemned to h'sem, as Arendt (2017) argues, we are stripped of the capacity to belong to our home, community, or nation-state. Arendt rightly points out that this results in a triple loss: first, refugees become displaced, deprived of their right to live in their homeland and denied the opportunity to establish a new home elsewhere; second, they lose control over their bodies, becoming disposable corporealities existing outside communal life; and third, they lose their political status, rendered outside the realm of political imagination, yet remaining at the heart of necropolitics. Trapped within this violent spectacle of triple calamities, our political and ethical lives are indefinitely negated.

So far, we have traced the journey of Eritrean refugees to the edge between the lifeless desert and treacherous waters. We continue to be radically exposed to the h'sem of the desert and the brutality of trafficking and (b)ordering, while yearning for a dignified existence. Let us conclude the chapter with a poem that reflects our profound longing for life in the desert. The poem expresses our existential lamentations of the refugee abyss. We originally wrote it in the Blin language, while working with refugees in Egypt.

For an oasis
Scorching heat from beneath the surface,
piercing rays from above, the sun,
this world, a lifeless world, burns.
Torture, misery, carnage,
screams echoing mirage,

tears, streaming down the face.
The young girl yearns,
for an oasis,
for life in the desert.

In the end, what remains of the capacity for existence is tested by yet another belly of the refugee abyss: the sea-camp. Refugees risk their lives in densely packed, fragile boats to reach the imagined safety on the horizon. However, as will be explored in the following chapter, the prospect of a dignified existence, even upon arrival in the metropole, seems increasingly remote, both spatially and temporally.

References

Aas, K.F. (2006) 'The Body Does Not lie': Identity, Risk and Trust in Technoculture. *Crime, Media, Culture*, 2, 143–158.
Agamben, G. (1998) *Sovereign Power and Bare Life, Homo Sacer*. Stanford, California: Stanford University Press.
Amoore, L. (2006) Biometric Borders: Governing Mobilities in the War on Terror. *Political Geography*, 25, 336–351. https://doi.org/10.1016/j.polgeo.2006.02.001
Andom, N.G. (2018) Post-independence Eritrean Migrants Transiting Through/Living in Sudan: Driven by Politics or Economics. *Journal of Cultural and Religious Studies* 6(10). Available from: https://www.davidpublisher.com/Public/uploads/Contribute/5c4a76cf85741.pdf (accessed 11.3.19).
Arendt, H. (2017) *The Origins of Totalitarianism*. London: Penguin Classics.
Bahlbi, Y.M. (2016). Human Trafficking and Human Smuggling to and from Eastern Sudan: Intended and Unintended Consequences of States' Policies. *Academic Journal of Interdisciplinary Studies*, 5, 215.
Bernal, V. (2001) From Warriors to Wives: Contradictions of Liberation and Development in Eritrea. *Northeast African Studies*, 8, 129–154.
Bernal, V. (2004) Eritrea Goes Global: Reflections on Nationalism in a Transnational Era. *Cultural Anthropology*, 19, 3–25. https://doi.org/10.1525/can.2004.19.1.3
Bernal, V. (2024) 'Diaspora and the Afterlife of Violence: Eritrean National Narratives and What Goes Without Saying', in Mlambo, O.B., and Chitando, E. (Eds) *The Palgrave Handbook of Violence in Africa*, pp. 141–166. Cham: Springer Nature Switzerland. https://doi.org/10.1007/978-3-031-40754-3_6
Bozzini, D. (2015) The Fines and the Spies: Fears of State Surveillance in Eritrea and in the Diaspora. *Social Analysis*, 59, 32–49.
Daily News Egypt (2016) 2 Ethiopians Reportedly Set Themselves on Fire in Front of Cairo's UNHCR Office [WWW Document]. Daily News Egypt. Available from: https://dailynewsegypt.com/2016/07/28/2-ethiopians-reportedly-set-fire-front-cairos-unhcr-office/ (accessed 28.8.20).
Da Silva, D.F. (2014) *No-Bodies: Law, Raciality and Violence*. Belo Horizonte: Meritum, Revista de Direito da Universidade FUMEC.
Fanon, F. (1963) *The Wretched of the Earth*. New York, New York: Grove Press.
Fisseha, M. (2015) Organ Trafficking of Eritreans in the Sinai: Perpetration or Provision of Service? *SSRN Journal*. https://doi.org/10.2139/ssrn.2609329
Foucault, M. (1998) The Will to Knowledge, Amended reprint. ed, *The History of Sexuality*. London: Penguin Books.

Foucault, M. (2020) *Discipline and Punish: The Birth of the Prison*. London: Penguin Books.
Hirt, N. (2010) "Dreams Don't Come True in Eritrea": Anomie and Family Disintegration Due to the Structural Militarization of Society. *SSRN Journal*. https://doi.org/10.2139/ssrn.1541908
Human Rights Watch (2016) Sudan: Hundreds Deported to Likely Abuse [WWW Document]. *Human Rights Watch*. Available from: https://www.hrw.org/news/2016/05/30/sudan-hundreds-deported-likely-abuse (accessed 23.8.20).
Isin, E.F. and Rygiel, K. (2007) 'Abject Spaces: Frontiers, Zones, Camps', in E. Dauphinee and C. Masters (Eds) *The Logics of Biopower and the War on Terror*, pp. 181–203. New York, New York: Palgrave Macmillan US. https://doi.org/10.1007/978-1-137-04379-5_9.
Kibreab, G. (1996) Eritrean and Ethiopian Urban Refugees in Khartoum: What the Eye Refuses to See. *African Studies Review*, 39, 131. https://doi.org/10.2307/524946
Kibreab, G. (2017) Sexual Violence in the Eritrean National Service. *African Studies Review*, 60, 123–143. https://doi.org/10.1017/asr.2017.5
Kok, W. (1989) Self-Settled Refugees and the Socio-Economic Impact of Their Presence on Kassala, Eastern Sudan. *Journal of Refugee Studies*, 2, 419–440. https://doi.org/10.1093/jrs/2.4.419
Maldonado-Torres, N. (2016) *Outline of Ten Theses on Coloniality and Decoloniality*. Paris: Frantz Fanon Foundation.
Mbembe, A. (2003) Necropolitics. *Public Culture*, 15, 11–40.
Mbembe, A. (2019) Bodies as Borders. *From the European South*, 4, 5–18.
Mekonnen, D.R. and Estefanos, M. (2011) *From Sawa to the Sinai Desert: The Eritrean Tragedy of Human Trafficking*. Available from: https://papers.ssrn.com/sol3/papers.cfm?abstract_id=2055303 (accessed 9.8.24).
Miller, S. (2022) Nowhere to Run: Eritrean Refugees in Tigray. Washington DC: Refugees International. Available from: https://www.refugeesinternational.org/reports-briefs/nowhere-to-run-eritrean-refugees-in-tigray/ (accessed 27.8.24).
OHCHR (2023) UN Experts Urge Ethiopia to Halt Mass Deportation of Eritreans [WWW Document]. OHCHR. Available from: https://www.ohchr.org/en/press-releases/2023/07/un-experts-urge-ethiopia-halt-mass-deportation-eritreans (accessed 2.8.24).
Oliver, K. (2017) *Carceral Humanitarianism: Logics of Refugee Detention, Forerunners*. Minneapolis, Minnesota: University of Minnesota Press.
Plaut, M. (2024) Eritrea's Foreign Festivals: Clashes Within the exile Community. *Review of African Political Economy*, 20240009.
Reisen, M., van Estefanos, M., and Rijken, C. (2012) *Human Trafficking in the Sinai: Refugees between Life and Death*. Oisterwijk: Wolf Legal Publishers.
Reisen, M. van Estefanos, M. and Rijken, C. (2013) The Human Trafficking Cycle: Sinai and Beyond [Draft]. Oisterwijk: Wolf Legal Publishers. Available from: https://humantraffickingsearch.org/wp-content/uploads/2017/07/Small_HumanTrafficking-Sinai2-web-4.pdf.
Reisen, M., and Mawere, M. (Eds) (2017) *Human Trafficking and Trauma in the Digital Era: the Ongoing Tragedy of the Trade in Refugees from Eritrea*. Bamenda: Langaa Research & Publishing CIG.
Research and Evidence Facility (2023). *Forced displacement and social cohesion in Ethiopia*. London: EU Trust Fund for Africa (Horn of Africa Window) Research and Evidence Facility.
Salter, M.B. (2004). Passports, Mobility, and Security: How Smart can the Border Be? *International Studies Perspectives*, 5, 71–91.
Siegfried, K. (2016). Sudan and Eritrea Crackdown on Migrants Amid Reports of EU Incentives [WWW Document]. *The New Humanitarian*. Available from: https://www.thenewhumanitarian.org/news/2016/05/25/sudan-and-eritrea-crackdown-migrants-amid-reports-eu-incentives (accessed 23.8.20).

Simpson, G. (2014) *"I Wanted to Lie Down and Die": Trafficking and Torture of Eritreans in Sudan and Egypt*. New York, New York: Human Rights Watch.

Smith, A. (2017) The Million-Dollar Boat Ride Across the Mediterranean. Available from: https://www.memopublishers.com/publications/digital/item/the-million-dollar-boat-ride-across-the-mediterranean (accessed 19.8.20).

Sorenson, J. (1991) Discourses on Eritrean Nationalism and Identity. *The Journal of Modern African Studies*, 29, 301–317.

UNHCR (2020a) Ethiopia Country Refugee Response Plan (ECRRP) 2020-2021 [WWW Document]. UNHCR Operational Data Portal (ODP). Available from: https://data2.unhcr.org/en/documents/details/73572 (accessed 19.8.20).

UNHCR (2020b). Sudan 2020 Country Refugee Response Plan | Global Focus [WWW Document]. Available from: https://reporting.unhcr.org/sudan-2020-country-refugee-response-plan (accessed 19.8.20).

UNHCR (2022) Deteriorating Conditions Putting Eritrean Refugees at Grave Risk in Tigray [WWW Document]. UNHCR. Available from: https://www.unhcr.org/news/briefing-notes/deteriorating-conditions-putting-eritrean-refugees-grave-risk-tigray (accessed 2.8.24).

UNHCR (2025) Sudan Situation [WWW Document]. Global Focus. Available from: https://reporting.unhcr.org/operational/situations/sudan-situation (accessed 3.1.25).

Yohannes, H.T. (2021) Refugee Trafficking in A Carceral Age: A Case Study of the Sinai Trafficking. *Journal of Human Trafficking* 1–15. https://doi.org/10.1080/23322705.2021.1885005

Yohannes, H.T. (2023) Refugee Trafficking in A Carceral Age: A Case Study of the Sinai Trafficking. *Journal of Human Trafficking*, 9, 33–47. https://doi.org/10.1080/23322705.2021.1885005

Yohannes, H.T. (2024) 'Autobiographic Reflections on Loss, Longing, and Recovery', in Bosworth, M., Franko, K., Lee, M., and Mehta, R. (Eds) *Handbook on Border Criminology*, pp. 311–327. Northampton: Edward Elgar Publishing.

5 From Sea-camp to Metropole

Introduction

Let us begin this chapter by recounting a personal experience of returning to Egypt as part of the fieldwork for this study. Upon our arrival in Egypt, we travelled to the Mediterranean coast in Alexandria, where we had previously been involved in recovering bodies found floating in the sea. This time, burdened by our own wounded bodies and haunting memories, we sat on the shore of the vast sea. Around us, locals and tourists swam with their families and loved ones, mingling with strangers. We could not summon the courage to swim in those waters. Instead, we found ourselves reflecting on memories as our thoughts became entwined with the ordeals of lost lives, unheard cries, and unhealed wounds.

Sitting on the shore
Sitting on the shore,
we gaze out at this vast sea,
full of mysteries
and stories untold.
As we take in the view,
our minds drifts to the lives
of friends and strangers
who have perished in the abyss.
We find ourselves wondering,
where are our friends?
With a deep breath,
our thoughts dissolve
into the unknown.

The sea is a graveyard, a fluid-tomb for those cast aside by the world. For centuries, the oceans and seas have claimed the lives of enslaved people whose remains were never found, and today they continue to swallow refugees travelling in fragile inflatable boats in search of safety. Within the osmosis of the sea lie the blood, tears, and bones of our relatives, friends, and

DOI: 10.4324/9781003437192-6

strangers. The cries of refugees calling for help still echo in our minds. We often ask ourselves: what can one say or write about the torment of this 'sea-camp'? We put this question to our younger brother during a visit to Cairo in September 2024. His response was immediate: 'You like poetry, don't you? Let's write one together'. Our brother, himself a refugee in Cairo, is deeply attuned to the stories of countless lives lost to the sea. In a silent communion with those swimming in the waters where friends, relatives, and strangers have vanished, we composed a poem as a shared act of mourning for those whose remains, we believe, either drift or rest silently beneath the waves, leaving no other trace. We wrote the poem in Blin, our mother tongue, and later translated it into English. We then borrowed a pen and a piece of paper from the tourists and wrote the poem by hand. Placing it gently on a pole by the shore, where the sea meets the sand and tourists and locals gather, we waited. One by one, people stopped to read. Their gazes shifted, their voices softened, and they began asking us questions. Some joined us in an open circle, their faces reflecting moments of reckoning, confronting the unspoken truths carried by the sea. The poem stands as both our shared expression of haunting rage and an invitation to reflect deeply on the torment of the sea and its shores.

Imagine for a moment...
The sea where you swim,
its waters thick with blood,
flesh and bones.
The air you breathe carries weight,
infused with anger born of pain,
thick with grief for losses forgotten.
The water you drink is heavy,
with fugitive and painful memories,
the aches of haunting souls.
The ground beneath is fertile,
nourished by decomposing bodies,
scattered in the open or buried beneath.
Now awaken to this stark revelation;
these are all real, and
they demand your trust...

Across the 'sea-camp' lies the metropole, a city of dreams and possibilities in the imagination of the colonised mind. Its colonial history presents the metropole as a place where concrete towers rise as the homes of the colonialists who 'discovered' Africa and its impenetrable lands and uncivilised savages. In its most arrogant portrayals, the metropole emerges as a bustling hub where past and present worlds blend, and where beginnings and endings find their centre. In reality, however, this is not what the metropole is; these projections are, in fact, the deceptive mirage of a violent reality. Yet, from the world of death and the shores of the sea-camp, every distant call reaches out to the diaspora in the metropolis, urging relatives and friends to raise funds for the journey across the sea. What is it like to embark on a perilous journey to the metropole—the very source of violence—in a desperate attempt to save oneself? How can one explain the structural violence of asylum that renders resistance against violence itself impossible? What lies beneath the masks of 'integration' in the metropole?

Building on the previous chapters, this chapter examines the encounters between people seeking asylum and the sea-camp, as well as the metropole with its border architecture and asylum policies, which either force them back into the belly of the sea or confine them within the refugee abyss. We begin by conceptualising the Mediterranean Sea as a 'sea-camp', where overcrowded boats, carrying those in search of refuge, navigate towards the metropole amid overwhelming peril. The conditions experienced by refugees in the sea-camp resemble the experiences of slaves forcibly transported across the transatlantic. Next, we discuss the journey of those who survive the dangers of the sea-camp. We then explore the bureaucratic process of seeking asylum in the metropole, arguing that asylum primarily serves to dehumanise those seeking refuge, reducing them to disposable subjects of necropolitics. In this section, we highlight the 'no-asylum' system in the UK as an example of a refugee abyss within the metropole. Finally, we examine the practice and concept of 'integration' as a rhetorical tool, a juridico-political disguise, and ultimately as a means of suppressing refugees' capacity for social, intercultural, and political existence through a strategy of white-masking. In essence, this chapter encourages readers to imagine and contemplate beyond the confines of the sea-camp and the colonial projections of the metropole.

The Sea-camp

> We are caught between two worlds.
> One world has displaced and tormented us,
> forcing us into this impossible situation.
> The other world is where we hope to find refuge,
> and it, too, may not have our best interests at heart.
> A vast dark hole stands between these two worlds,
> creating a treacherous divide.
> We find ourselves on the brink of the dark hole.

We discussed the plight of those who refused to be trapped in the belly of the refugee abyss and longed to cross the Mediterranean when circumstances and resources permitted. Together, we composed the above statement, which we have then restructured into a poetic form, word for word. Sadly, we have since learned that of the nine people who participated in the discussion, only four are still alive. The others have either perished at 'sea-camp', succumbed to the harsh conditions of the desert on their way to Libya, or vanished without a trace.

This apparent 'divide' between the death world and the metropole is what we refer to as the sea-camp. However, it is not merely a divide. The sea-camp is an abyss with no bounds, a treacherous cosmos encompassing the seabed's depths and sharp edges, the vast sky with its countless stars and piercing sunlight, relentless tides and winds, and merciless creatures devouring one another. Within this abyss, one finds floating and drifting objects and creatures. It both separates and unites, harbouring life and death within its vastness, depths, and breadth, as well as through perpetual motion. The sea-camp is also a stage of splendour and a realm of opulence, adventure, and exploration. It dazzles with touristic luxury and immense wealth, creating scenes of paradox and irony. The world reacts with alarm when a luxury yacht, carrying fewer than two dozen crew and passengers, sinks (see Al Jazeera, 2024). Satellites scour the seas, and navies race to rescue survivors and recover bodies.

Yet, in these same waters, refugees drown every year. Reminiscent of the Transatlantic slave trade, thousands of weary and wounded refugees are packed into inflatable boats that can barely accommodate them, let alone navigate the treacherous sea. Every year, these boats both float and sink in the sea, appearing and disappearing, giving rise to life and death. Within these boats, children are born only to perish in an instant, as exemplified by Yohanna's ordeal of sinking off the Island of Lampedusa, still attached to her newborn baby by the umbilical cord. These tragedies create suffering and displaced voices that are often abandoned and unheard. These are some of the enduring paradoxes written in blood, salt, and history.

If we manage to survive the violent traps and tangled spaces within the belly of the refugee abyss in the death world, we then face perilous journeys across the sea-camp to reach mainland Europe. Despite the constant risk of drowning, we have no choice but to risk our lives in an attempt to sail across the sea. Drawing from our own experiences and as a collective, we describe the impossible choices refugees must make before embarking on these maritime journeys as follows: 'People are fully aware of the dangers of attempting to cross the sea in overcrowded and fragile boats, but they feel they have no alternative', 'I knew there was a chance I could disappear in the deep waters, but what other option did I have when I was trapped in a hopeless place [refugee camp]?', 'I would rather be swept away by the tides than suffer in a detention centre in Libya, be burned alive by traffickers in a torture camp, or wait for nothing in the refugee camp', and so on. We are all acutely aware of the violent role the metropole has played in shaping the Libya we see today. We know that waiting turns into stagnation when there is nothing to wait for. This temporal and spatial state of stagnation involves enduring brutal conditions imposed by both state and non-state actors, such as border regimes and organised criminals. The stuckness and ordeals within the belly of the refugee abyss force desperate refugees like us to undertake perilous sea-camp journeys.

However, it is important to note that not all refugees have the means or resources to choose between being stuck or continuing their journey. Refugees are more likely to undertake such journeys if they have the necessary resources and social connections. For example, Amal, who had been living on the streets of Cairo for nearly 20 years with no end in sight to her situation, expressed her frustration:

> I was born into poverty
> and then paralysed,
> unable to walk properly.
> I do not have any relatives
> to help me resettle in a safe place.
> I wish I was not disabled and had
> the money to travel to Europe by boat.
> Life has been unforgiving.
> I feel hopeless.

Amal shared that she relied on the kindness of friends who had managed to migrate to relatively safe countries, such as Canada and Australia, through sponsorship programmes, to provide her with food. Tearfully, Amal summed up her situation: 'For refugees like me, there is no opportunity for a better future. There is nothing to look forward to except endless waiting'.

This state of 'endless waiting', or being stuck, has been a recurring theme in our conversations. Whether speaking with residents of refugee camps, those living in police cities, or people in transit, the sentiment of feeling endlessly stuck remains the same. Many of us spoke of friends who had been trapped in carceral spaces for years due to a lack of financial support for their journey. Others have faced deportation to countries where their safety is at risk. Some are still confined to detention facilities, enduring this state of being stuck indefinitely. For all of them, the future is on hold, and life itself is constantly at risk. They are perpetually exposed to unconditional vulnerability and the threat of death. These conditions leave them with no choice but to continue their journey at any cost. It is important to note that the vast majority of refugees on this perilous journey find themselves in situations of ransom, where their families—both in the diaspora and in their home countries—are forced to contribute everything they have and can find to relieve their loved ones from their ordeals. Often, these rescue efforts take place at a community level. We must also note that many of us come from modest backgrounds, spending years in transit, saving money, and then continuing our journey. Many of us have fallen into debt, with families back home selling everything they own, while relatives in the Global North, working in harsh conditions, take on debts to fund the rescue of those of us who have been abducted.

In this search for safety, we find ourselves confronted with the treacherous depths, unpredictable currents, and chaos of the Mediterranean Sea, which has become an abyssal sea-camp. With no other option, we rely on intermediaries and traffickers, who place us in overcrowded, fragile inflatable boats, leaving us to face an uncertain fate. Wulud, alongside fellow refugees, described their experiences in the following words:

> The intermediaries took us to the coast in Libya,
> where we spent the day at a beautiful villa,
> listening to Arabic music on an MP4.
> The villa belonged to a military commander.
> A week later, the traffickers placed us on a boat,
> four hundred of us crammed onto a small boat.
> They sailed us for nearly ten hours,
> then abandoned us in the middle of the sea.
> Luckily, search and rescue found us
> and brought us to Italy, to the shore.

Once we find ourselves adrift on the open sea in fragile inflatable boats, our only guides are the stars and the tides. Beneath unfamiliar skies, we must either master the art of navigation or place our trust in someone who can guide our journey. Often, in bright sunlight and catastrophe, we must surrender to the natural forces of the sea and let tides decide our path. It has been said that the Mediterranean sea-crossing 'remains a largely unmonitored sea crossing where boats may disappear without trace' (Laczko et al., 2019, p. 11). Our experiences tell a more nuanced story: the sea-camp is both highly monitored and unmonitored, making some lives survivable and others perishable. Drifting and floating in this sea-crossing abyss, the overcrowded boats, filled with people stripped of their rights and human dignity, become necropolitical spaces where the lines between life and death are blurred. In moments of calamity, the fragile boats often capsize, leading to chaos, unimaginable screams, and unprecedented loss of life. In these moments of profound vulnerability, refugees can only prepare themselves for the possibility of death at any moment. Wulud shed tears as he described the moment when the traffickers abandoned them in the middle of the sea as the 'darkest moment' of his life: 'I felt like it was the end of the world, being stranded on an overcrowded inflatable boat in the vast sea'. Wulud recalled, 'You pray that the high tides do not come your way, and if they do, you are defenceless: the tides overturn the boat'. The image of being stranded in the sea-camp stayed with him, but he also felt a 'deep sense of relief' upon safely reaching the Italian coast. However, he could not forget the deaths of more than a dozen childhood friends, relatives, and former colleagues who had perished, some of whom had simply disappeared without a trace.

Over the past decade, the number of refugee deaths during perilous journeys has reached unprecedented levels, yet their deaths remain largely overlooked. According to data from the IOM Missing Migrants Project (2024), as of 31 December 2024, over 70,938 migrants have either died or gone missing since 2014, with more than 41,000 drowning. The remains of 29,127 people who perished during these hazardous journeys have not been recovered. A significant proportion of these tragic incidents occur in the Mediterranean Sea, where 31,180 of the recorded deaths and disappearances are reported. While obtaining accurate data on the nationality and demographics of those who have died or gone missing can be challenging, it is evident that a large number of fatalities in the Mediterranean involve refugees from Eritrea. The tragic event of 3 October 2013, near the island of Lampedusa, is a sombre reminder of the immense loss of Eritrean lives in this region (see Catania, 2013). Internationally, these deaths of refugees at sea are often regarded as inconsequential and are not mourned as human losses. They are placed beyond the realm of human imagination and the collective consciousness of the current necropolitical world, yet they remain real, at least for their grieving families.

As the tragic sinking of migrant boats continues each year, families in Eritrea and the diaspora endure the anguish that accompanies the seasons of obituaries. In Eritrea, families who once held hope for news of their loved ones safely reaching their destinations are instead met with the silence of their disappearance, leaving no trace behind. Their unburied remains may be consumed by the salt, the earth, or the beasts that roam. The fortunate few are handed the lifeless bodies of those they loved, wrapped in white sheets. Zainab, an Eritrean mother who lost her son to human traffickers, poignantly expressed that her son and many others 'leave their country with no rights and return to it with no lives'. In these moments of profound loss and grief, neighbours move from house to house, offering support to families in mourning. With every toll of the death knell in the community, mothers are overwhelmed with grief, fearing it could signal their own child's obituary. Fathers and adults of draft age are primarily serving in national service, making them the last to receive the devastating news. In the diaspora, families, relatives, and friends who have sacrificed their possessions to aid their loved ones' survival are plagued by constant sorrow. The pain and grief are intensified by the knowledge that many perish without a trace, as Farés' brother sorrowfully lamented and as we repeat:

> We have heard nothing of him [Farés] since...
> We know he is no longer alive,
> yet we refuse to accept it.
> He perished without a trace, forever lost.
> We will carry the burden of tracing,
> for the lost until our last breath.

Similarly, Ariam, who had witnessed her friend being buried alive, expressed her belief that the lives of refugees are not valued, 'even by the angels and saints who no longer seem to listen to our prayers'. She spoke of the impossibility of recovering the remains of those buried undignified in the desert and those drowned at sea, including her friend and the pregnant woman whose five-year-old son she had been entrusted with, as well as the many friends who perished in the Mediterranean sea-camp. For the unfortunate, the journey across the sea-camp becomes either the final end of their lives, when death is confirmed, or an endless abyss as they vanish without a trace. The only remaining traces of those who perished and were never found are their names and memories (see also Chapter 6).

> Héluf, Hassen, Haben,
> the named and unnamed,
> the numbered and unnumbered,
> the buried and unburied,
> all born rightless, died rightless.

In this struggle for survival, refugees face not only the abyss of the sea-camp itself but also the maritime and territorial borders of Europe, which aim to prevent refugees from entering the continent's territorial limits (see Ambrosini, 2018; Mainwaring, 2019). Europe seeks to expand and enhance its border infrastructure by incorporating modern surveillance technologies to effectively detect, intercept, and repel incoming refugees. One of the latest technologies employed for border control is the use of 'aero-naval assets with the dual aim of protecting borders and national interests and rescuing lives in danger' (Ambrosini, 2018, p. 105). With the deployment of advanced technology, the border has become increasingly 'smart' (Salter, 2004), yet also more 'violent' (Jones, 2019). It can now detect, monitor, and intercept movements across these areas, either by repelling them or refraining from intervention. For instance, boats carrying migrants are often stopped from crossing the Mediterranean Sea. Those found near Europe's southern coastline are increasingly deported back to Libya, where the refugees are detained incommunicado. According to a press release from Médecins Sans Frontières (MSF, 2020), nearly 8,000 refugees were intercepted at sea and subsequently returned to Libya between January and September 2020 alone. Italy and Greece, along with other southern European countries, have been implicated in these forced deportations, which violate international legal frameworks and human rights norms. A 2009 report from Human Rights Watch, for example, highlights Italy's breach of the 'legal principle of nonrefoulement when it interdicts boats on the high seas and pushes them back to Libya with no screening whatsoever' (pp. 7–10).

In addition to preventing boats carrying refugees from safely landing on the shores of Europe, there has been widespread reluctance in recent years to rescue abandoned forced migrants in dangerous waters. As Spijkerboer (2017, p. 26) correctly points out:

> States act as if they have no responsibility to prevent risks to life of irregularised travellers because they die outside their territory and rely on non-state actors such as smugglers... Because these travellers do not

> comply, states feel they do not have to protect the right to life of the people concerned beyond search and rescue—an obligation which is only triggered when the risk to life already has materialised.

It is important to note that states not only deprive refugees of sovereign protection but also make it illegal for non-state actors to attempt rescues or provide humanitarian assistance. For example, Italy and Greece have enacted restrictive and punitive laws that prohibit private rescue operations. The UNHCR highlighted this in its briefing notes of 6 August 2019:

> Under changes approved by [the Italian] Parliament, fines for private vessels that undertake rescue of persons and do not respect the ban on entry into territorial waters have risen to a maximum of €1 million. In addition, vessels will now be automatically impounded.
>
> (UNHCR, 2019)

There is a simultaneous prohibition on charitable organisations and private rescue initiatives from rescuing sinking boats carrying refugees, alongside the suspension of emergency services aimed at assisting survivors. International and non-governmental organisations involved in rescue missions have faced allegations of colluding with traffickers and illicit mafia groups (see Ambrosini, 2018). For example, according to Cusumano (2018), the Italian government has accused the non-governmental humanitarian organisations Cap Anamur and MSF of complicity in facilitating the illicit crossing of irregular migrants. These charges have been strongly denied by the organisations themselves. In a press release issued in September 2020, MSF condemned the EU's approach to refugees and expressed severe criticism.

> Across the Mediterranean, from preventing rescues at sea to purposely holding people in Moria refugee camp, the EU's current approach to migration is to systematically trap, push back and abandon people; whether that is leaving them to die at sea or trapping thousands of men, women and children in appalling conditions in camps on the Greek islands.
>
> (MSF, 2020)

As a result, private rescue ships, NGOs, and humanitarian organisations are increasingly confronted with restrictive and punitive laws, and are threatened by the juridico-political powers of sovereign nations. In his analysis, Edler (2020, p. 23) applies Agamben's concept of the camp to argue that the Mediterranean Sea has become a highly regulated camp, determining 'who lives and who dies', and who is included or excluded from the population of the European Union. Europe, according to Edler (2020), holds the authority to decide matters of life and death both within and beyond the sea-camp. Through its racialised and necropolitical borders, the continent traps refugees in a state of perpetual indifference and vulnerability. They exist in a limbo between the world of death and the metropole. The abyss of the sea-camp both divides and unites these worlds. However, our existence and quest for a dignified life cannot be entirely contained by either the world of death or the metropole. Our humanity is neither fully negated by nor fully assimilated into the necropolitical system. Instead, we cling to a glimmer of hope for the possibility of emerging from these circumstances.

From sea-camp to metropole

Despite the challenges encountered in the death world and sea-camp, a significant number of Eritrean refugees persist in their efforts to reach mainland Europe. Eritrean refugees typically choose between two primary 'routes to Europe': 'the central Mediterranean route, through Sudan, Libya and by boat to Lampedusa, Sicily or Malta' and 'the land route through Ethiopia, Sudan, Egypt, Israel or Jordan to Turkey and Greece' (Brekke and Brochmann, 2015, p. 4). Among these main routes, the latter (the land route) proves exceedingly arduous for many refugees due to heavily fortified borders and state interventions marked by violence. For example, Israel's construction of a border fence in 2012 and increased Egyptian government intervention in the Sinai Peninsula have severely restricted refugees' mobility, effectively confining them to the central Mediterranean route. As of October 2023, the century-old Palestinian struggle for self-determination faces a genocidal war waged by Israel, armed and shielded by its Western allies. Palestinians, particularly those in the Gaza Strip and the West Bank, are enduring existential threats to their lives, land, and aspirations for self-determination. They experience multiple catastrophes while living under siege.

Returning to the focus on Eritrean refugees, a few who manage to navigate stringent immigration regulations enter Europe through legal avenues, such as family reunion visas and resettlement programmes like the UK Gateway Protection Programme (see Darling, 2009; Platts-Fowler and Robinson, 2011). Yet, regardless of how they arrive, these refugees face racialised and necropolitical forms of bordering. They are compelled to live in a 'hostile environment' as a condition of existence (Yohannes et al., 2024). We return to this point below.

Majority of the refugees travel across the sea-camp to the shores of mainland Europe, where they encounter a sophisticated bordering regime that aims to politically and physically exclude refugees from what is perceived as the 'inside'. Politically, the arrival and presence of a large number of undesirable refugees is viewed as a threat to the safety of European citizens and is used to falsify and justify national security concerns. European governments often exploit this fear by promoting exclusionary and racialised discourses aimed at forced removal, offshore containment, abandonment, and even the systematic destitution of refugees (Ambrosini, 2018; Mainwaring, 2019). Physically and legally, the refugees are subjected to the Dublin Regulation, which was established to determine the first country of asylum (Grant and Domokos, 2011). The Dublin Regulation effectively traps refugees in the initial country they arrive in, regardless of their personal circumstances or preferences. According to Brekke and Brochmann (2015), this presents two main issues: firstly, it places a 'disproportionate burden' on countries of arrival, particularly those situated on Europe's southern border; and secondly, it triggers 'competition' due to 'differences in reception conditions, processing ability, and access to social rights' (p. 3).

The majority of refugees travel across the sea-camp to reach the shores of mainland Europe, where they encounter a complex border regime designed to politically and physically exclude them from what is perceived as the 'inside'. Politically, the arrival and presence of a large number of refugees, often deemed undesirable, is framed as a threat to the safety of European citizens and used to fabricate and justify national security concerns. European governments frequently exploit these fears by promoting exclusionary and racialised narratives that support forced removal, offshore containment, abandonment, and even the systematic destitution of refugees (Ambrosini, 2018; Mainwaring, 2019). Physically and legally, refugees are subject to the Dublin Regulation, which was introduced to determine the first country of asylum and effectively restrict the right to asylum to the first country they arrive in, regardless of their personal circumstances or preferences (Grant and Domokos, 2011). This creates two main issues: firstly, it places a 'disproportionate burden' on countries of arrival, particularly those on Europe's southern border, and secondly, it leads to 'competition' arising from 'differences in reception conditions, processing ability, and access to social rights' (Brekke and Brochmann, 2015, p. 3).

The Dublin Regulation confines refugees to the country where their biometric data is collected, effectively creating a permanent exception for the rest of the European zone. As a result, refugees whose biometrics are recorded in one country are deemed inadmissible in others, making their claims for protection and support unintelligible. In this exception, the Dublin Regulation both fixes the border within the body and confines the body-border to the refugee abyss, specifically the 'asylum colonies' within the metropole (Yohannes et al., 2024). The asylum colonies, often under the watchful eye of the state, range from reception spaces with limited resources and excessive bureaucracy (such as reception centres, entry points, arrival ports, and hotspots) to violent spaces for containing refugees (such as makeshift camps, detention centres, barges, and removal centres). These asylum colonies, as we have argued elsewhere, represent a precarious state of 'double negation', where refugees' existence is reduced to 'unliveability and ungrievability' (Yohannes et al., 2024, p. 11).

Upon arrival, refugees are sent to these asylum colonies. For instance, Wulud shared his experience of being arrested in Italy and taken to a reception centre in Milan. He described these centres as functioning like 'police stations', where strict control is enforced and access to basic needs is limited.

Despite suffering from injuries sustained during his journey, Wulud was denied even basic pain relief at the centre. In excruciating pain and without information about the asylum process or its duration, he felt both uninformed and abandoned. This negligence and abdication of responsibility make refugee voices and stories incomprehensible both epistemically and politically. Even if refugees choose to remain in the first country of asylum where their fingerprints are recorded, they are often trapped in bureaucratic processes, deprived of basic necessities and any hope for the future.

The poor reception and asylum conditions in first asylum countries are not the primary challenges identified in this study. In fact, many refugees pointed to the EURODAC system of registering and storing fingerprints as the main obstacle, which they refer to colloquially as 'fish'. Refugees view 'fish' as the key barrier to continuing their journeys to their preferred destinations. Under the Dublin Regulation, those who travel beyond their initial country of entry are often seen as deceptive, illegal, or criminal. For example, Yonas explained that in the summer of 2002, he crossed the sea and arrived in Italy before travelling to the UK to join his sister. However, his asylum claim in the UK was rejected because his fingerprints had already been registered in Italy. He was subsequently arrested and deported back to Italy after spending a year in hiding with his sister. Yonas struggled to find work in Italy for almost a year, so he decided to move to Switzerland. To avoid deportation by Swiss authorities, he changed his name and date of birth. Fortunately, his fingerprints went undetected by Swiss immigration officials, and he was eventually granted refugee status.

Avoiding 'fish' is crucial for travelling to other European countries. Various strategies are employed to bypass the challenges posed by 'fish'. As Yemane (see Yemane, 2023, Chapter 5) extensively demonstrates, many refugees also resort to burning their fingertips to avoid identification. For example, Zenawi, like Yonas, had his fingerprints taken in Italy but managed to obtain residence papers in Sweden by burning his fingertips and rubbing them against a rough surface. Zenawi explained that burning fingertips was a common strategy used by many refugees to evade identification and prevent deportation. Some even recounted rubbing garlic cloves on their bodies to confuse sniffer dogs during their journey to their preferred destination.

From the abyss of the sea-camp,
where survival seems unlikely,
to the 'fish' that stores fingerprints,
a trace of unsettling evidence
blocks the path to imagined safety.
To evade this 'fish', the burdened claim,
'You need a garlic clove and toxic acid'.

The fact that refugees are forced to harm their own bodies, such as their fingertips, in order to erase the borders imposed on them is dehumanising.

In a 2016 report, Human Rights Watch criticised the Dublin Regulation as 'inefficient and inhumane' for forcibly deporting people seeking asylum to their countries of first arrival, without properly assessing their asylum claims or ensuring a fair distribution of responsibility across the continent (Human Rights Watch, 2016). Unfortunately, the bodies and dignity of refugees appear to be subordinated to border security. In fact, their bodies and humanity have become sites for sophisticated bordering technologies.

It is worth noting that many people seeking refuge remain stranded in refugee camps and at transit borders throughout Europe. They face significant challenges as they attempt to navigate the 'inflexible and insufficient' protection measures offered by the EU (Davies et al., 2017, p. 1264). The Moria refugee camp in Greece, which was destroyed by a fire in September 2020, and the Calais camp near the French border with the UK are just two examples of places where refugees are left without support. The camps in Europe confine and immobilise forced migrants, while also subjecting them to destitution and illegality. Those forced to endure such conditions are both physically and conceptually treated as exceptions within political discourses. They are often defined by what they are not, rather than by the realities they face and the capacities they possess. This leads to refugees being rejected by local community groups, often supported by extremist politicians, media outlets, and other factions. The following poetic composition, developed from a conversation involving Andit, Saba, Desale, Wolde, and Hayat, reveals a prevailing indifference towards those seeking refuge.

> We believed the sea would be our final trial,
> but instead, we faced hostile local groups
> protesting with banners that bore messages:
> 'Refugees Go Home',
> 'Refugees Not Welcome',
> 'Stop Illegal Migration'.
> This encounter was utterly terrifying,
> reminding us of our racialised attributes –
> our black skin and our Otherness.
> These markers are indelible, impossible to evade.

Thus, both during transit and upon arrival in their preferred destinations, such as the UK, the asylum regimes reveal a bureaucratic necropolitical experiment that further marginalises and dehumanises those seeking refuge, turning hope into a haunting struggle and dreams into shadows on foreign land. In this relentless spectacle, the prospect of refuge becomes either a swift rejection or a bureaucratic nightmare, where the displaced are condemned to exist on the margins, stripped of dignity and reduced to mere statistics in an indifferent system.

Asylum in the metropole

While those trapped within the confines of EURODAC are caught in a state of orbital confinement, suspended between the initial country where their fingerprints are registered and stored (i.e., the first country of asylum) and the rest of Europe (i.e., a zone of exception), those who have managed to elude or evade the biometric identification system find themselves entangled in a complex necropolitical asylum regime in the metropole. Once the epicentre of colonial power, the metropole continues to function as the heartland of coloniality. The matrices and veins of coloniality still pulsate beneath the foundations of its institutions of sovereignty and governmentality that decide who enters and exits, lives and perishes, or must be removed. The metropole combines brute force with sophisticated technology and legislation to maximise its grip on the undesirable Others who have sneaked into the polity.

The UK is a prime example of a hostile environment. Since Brexit, UK immigration legislation has undergone significant structural and legal changes. These include the introduction of the points-based immigration system in 2021, the Nationality and Borders Act in 2022, the Illegal Immigration Act in 2023, and the recently scrapped Rwanda Deal. The current UK government has established a Border Security Command, overseen by a former police, military, or intelligence chief who directly reports to the Home Secretary. The Border Security Command is intended to coordinate the efforts of multiple agencies to secure the borders, bringing together the National Crime Agency (NCA), intelligence services, police, Immigration Enforcement, and Border Force (see Brown, 2024). The phrase 'smashing smuggling gangs facilitating small boat crossings' has become a government mantra. The Command is entrusted with new counter-terrorism powers and enhanced measures to confront these organised networks, blurring the lines between terror and asylum in a regime of ever-tightening control.

The primary objectives of these pieces of legislation and the Border Security Command are threefold: first, to enable the government to selectively recruit skilled workers for public institutions using a filtering system; second, to prevent the entry of undesirable individuals seeking asylum and to make asylum inadmissible for those who have entered the country by irregular means; and third, to reduce net migration. These objectives form the basis of the 'hostile environment' framework, which includes immigration detention, unlawful asylum refusals, forced removals, forced evictions, extreme destitution, and visa restrictions, all while recruiting skilled labour from abroad for sectors in greatest need, such as the National Health Service (NHS). For those seeking refuge, as Webber (2019) argues, the purpose of the hostile environment is 'to weaponise total destitution and rightlessness, so as to force migrants without the right to be in the country to deport themselves, at low or no cost to the UK' (p. 77). Politically, this is achieved by labelling people seeking refuge as socially and culturally unassimilable, racially incongruent, economically burdensome, and politically unintelligible. The use of polarising, racialised, and toxic rhetoric by government officials exemplifies these sentiments. These views are clearly echoed by various politicians, right-wing media outlets, and white extremists and nationalists. The consequences of this rhetoric became evident during the summer of 2024, when racist and violent riots spread across the UK (see Boukari and Devakumar, 2024).

For those who survive the militarised border and reach the metropole, they are then confronted with navigating a bureaucratic vetting system without the necessary resources or skills. The asylum system is designed to make asylum difficult or even impossible. Upon arrival, those seeking refuge must claim asylum at ports of entry or at an asylum intake unit in Croydon. They then undergo a screening interview with an immigration officer. The officers gather information from asylum claimants, including documents and other sources, to determine the outcome of their claims. People seeking refuge often describe a pervasive institutional culture of disbelief and disregard for their identities and testimonies during interactions with immigration officers. Andit's personal testimony, for example, reveals how deeply ingrained this culture of disbelief is. Upon arrival, Andit was uncertain about what to expect but knew he had to claim asylum. In the asylum reception unit, Andit recounted, 'I encountered an immigration officer who treated me unkindly, questioning my age and doubting my claim'. When asked about his age, Andit stated that he was seventeen. However, the officer remained sceptical and dismissive, insisting that Andit provide identification documents to verify his age, nationality, and identity. Andit attempted to explain that obtaining such documents was not possible, but the officer insisted that Andit undergo an age assessment conducted by social services to determine his age. This process lasted eight months. Unfortunately, by the time the assessment was completed, Andit had turned eighteen, and he lost his rights as a child. 'The system dictates', Andit explained, 'that I can only be treated as an adult, erasing my childhood and incarcerating my adulthood'.

The experience of Andit appeared to be quite common among young people seeking asylum. These children often go through extremely difficult and traumatic experiences that shape their maturity and behaviour. During their journeys, they face complex situations such as trafficking, border violence, and life-or-death decisions. This exposure to adult situations can lead to what is known as 'childhood adultification', where children are 'prematurely, and often inappropriately, exposed to adult knowledge and assume extensive adult roles and responsibilities' (Burton, 2007, p. 329). As a result, the behaviours of adultified children may not align with what is considered appropriate for their age. On one hand, children seeking asylum may demonstrate greater maturity than their age suggests, but on the other, their circumstances can make them highly vulnerable. Both situations can negatively affect their asylum claims when age disputes arise. The focus on the maturity and demeanour of children during age assessments not only increases the chance of error, but also overlooks their challenging experiences, socio-cultural backgrounds, and lived realities. These age assessments reflect the Home Office's discriminatory policies targeting young people seeking asylum, whom they regard as undesirable and a burden on the taxpayer (see McLaughlin, 2018).

Immigration lawyers who have worked with young people seeking asylum in the UK, including unaccompanied children and refugees, have described the practice of age assessments as an 'endemic problem'. They expressed deep frustration with the Home Office's questioning and dismissal of children's ages. It troubled them that state institutions, such as social services and local authorities, which are unfamiliar with these children's backgrounds, were entrusted with determining their ages while dismissing the credibility of their testimonies. Using physical features and behaviour to estimate the ages of vulnerable children is practically impossible, and the margin of error for age assessors is immeasurable. After years of frustration with the age assessment process, the determination of young people's ages by public institutions was challenged in the Court of Appeal. In May 2019, a case involving a young Eritrean child led to the Court of Appeal ruling that the age assessment policy in place at the time was 'positively unlawful'. The court also suggested that 'any policy must seek as far as possible to avoid the Secretary of State acting unlawfully' (EWCA Civ 872, 2019, Paragraph 57). Lord Justice Underhill, the Vice-President of the Court of Appeal (Civil Division), further stated:

> In my view this defect in the policy/guidance gave rise to a real risk of children being (unlawfully) detained. That conclusion would in my view be justified even without evidence of specific cases where that had occurred: in the absence of guidance as to the width of the margin of error there is inevitably a real risk that immigration officers will place too much trust in their own assessment that a particular young person is "significantly" over 18.
>
> (EWCA Civ 872, 2019, Para 68)

After the Court of Appeal's decision, the Home Office claimed that the government had revised its age assessment guidance. However, it appears that these revisions, if they were made, have had little impact on the experiences of children seeking asylum. In fact, the treatment of these children has become even more dehumanising due to the legislative and procedural changes resulting from Brexit since 2020. One example of this worsening situation is the cessation of transfers of children seeking asylum from other European countries to the UK under the Dublin Regulation, to reunite with relatives (Neidhardt, 2022). The full consequences of these changes, both in terms of the legal and practical aspects of asylum under new legal frameworks such as the Nationality and Borders Act and the Illegal Immigration Act, are yet to be fully understood.

As these practical and legal difficulties suggest, children seeking asylum are placed beyond the reach of the law, denied their childhood, and treated as people devoid of basic knowledge, including an understanding of their own ages. Under the violent, panoptic gaze of the state and its asylum institutions, they are viewed merely as Others who must endure state-sanctioned scrutiny, marked by biometric borders, assigned arbitrary ages, and offered conditional asylum. They cease to exist as children and are permitted only to exist in a state of (de)existence and (de)humanity. For them, as Andit's experience illustrates, time is juridical, experienced while awaiting the ever-present possibility of being subjected to racialised Othering, criminalisation, detention, and deportation. In juridical time, the future becomes a period of pre-criminality, pre-illegality, and pre-deportation, while the present is marked by hostility and necropolitics. Life is lived in the nakedness of existence, bearing witness to the unbearable, confirming the powerlessness of one's existence and the vulnerability or absence of joy.

Adult claimants also face significant challenges within the asylum system. During the screening interviews, they are expected to provide details of their backgrounds, identities, family relationships, and journeys. They are regularly required to affirm their compliance and disclose their immigration and criminal histories in order to be deemed admissible and safe, even to be eligible to make an asylum claim. The anatomy of the hostile environment, Canning (2020) writes, 'relies heavily on compliance, including opening up interpersonal experiences to scrutiny in the main (or substantive) interview, and weekly or monthly signings at the Home Office' (p. 266). Furthermore, people seeking asylum may face immigration detention and forced removal if they have passed through another country deemed safe by the UK government, are suspected of committing crimes, or come from a country that the UK considers safe. Overall, the screening interviews are structured to enable the government to gather extensive information about claimants while offering minimal prospects of protection. This reduces the number of people eligible to seek asylum and ultimately obtain the right to remain in the UK.

After the screening interview, adults seeking asylum undergo a substantive interview, during which they must demonstrate a well-founded fear of persecution, as defined by the 1951 Refugee Convention. This requires them to disclose their experiences of victimisation and substantiate their fear of persecution. Claims of persecution are assessed through detailed questioning and cross-examinations, with some cases involving mediation by legal representatives and interpreters. Participants have reported that their testimonies are often viewed as not credible, and their vulnerability is seen as less compelling in establishing a claim of persecution or fear, even when supported by legal representatives and interpreters. For instance, Hayat shared her experience of surviving trafficking as a single mother, only to remain trapped in the asylum process for 13 years. She expressed her frustration with the asylum system as follows:

> I have been in the asylum system for thirteen years
> and am still claiming asylum without success.
> For countless days and nights, I succumb to fears
> of imminent detention and deportation.

What else can one do if denied asylum?
Live on freezing streets forever?
Contemplate death?
What else…?
What else?

Following the substantive interview, Home Office caseworkers make decisions regarding asylum claims based on their assessments of the testimonies gathered during subsequent interviews with people seeking refuge, as well as relevant information about their countries of origin. The claimants' testimonies are evaluated in the context of international refugee law, humanitarian provisions, and applicable regional or national legislation before granting status. In the decision-making process, caseworkers focus on any inconsistencies or implausible elements within the testimonies. This process results in first-instance decisions, which may include the refusal of the claim, the granting of leave to remain, or the provision of humanitarian protection.

Failure to establish persecution, or a well-founded fear of it, leads to the rejection of asylum claims, denying people seeking refuge the limited rights conferred under domestic laws and the 1951 Refugee Convention. Typically, those whose claims are rejected by the Home Office can appeal the decision in the First-tier Tribunal, with appeal hearings organised within the Asylum and Immigration Tribunal. The rejected claimants may be supported by legal representatives during these hearings, which generally involve the claimants, their representatives, Home Office presenting officers, clerks, an interpreter, and immigration judges. Hearings are generally open to the public, except in exceptional circumstances. The judges preside over the legal proceedings in the asylum court. The burden of proof rests with the person seeking refuge, who must substantiate or clarify the grounds on which the Home Office based its negative decision.

However, while people seeking refuge whose asylum claims have been refused have the right to appeal negative decisions, the exhaustion of their appeal rights effectively places them outside legal protection. In this situation, their presence becomes illegal, stripping them of their rights to seek refuge. Once their appeal rights are exhausted, they become trapped in an ongoing cycle of legal liminality. If they are not deemed suitable for forced removal, these rejected claimants may submit fresh asylum claims. They then face the traumatic and dehumanising process of reapplying for asylum, burdened with the need to present new evidence, as the evidence they provided during their interviews with the Home Office has either been disbelieved or deemed insufficient for protection.

According to the government's asylum support guidelines (see GOV.UK, 2024), people seeking asylum rely on an allowance of £49.18 per week per person to meet basic needs such as food and clothing. If food is provided (as in asylum hotels where people have no access to a kitchen), this allowance is reduced to £8.86 per week. If a mother is pregnant, she receives an additional

£5.25, and another £5.25 is provided for a child between the ages of one and three years. For children under one year, the additional amount is £9.50. For those whose asylum applications have been refused, the allowance is even lower, at £47.39 per week per person, and they are provided with temporary accommodation. These people often experience ongoing instability as they are moved between various accommodations and asylum regimes, resulting in severe deprivation and insufficient support. This is the case for Harnet, who arrived in the UK as a child with her mother. Her mother later died while they were navigating the asylum process (see Chapter 1). Since her mother's death, Harnet has remained in the UK without recognised status for over two decades. 'I made several fresh claims and provided new evidence, but I was rejected every time', Harnet recounted. Reflecting on her grandmother's saying, 'The soul belongs to God, and the body belongs to the land', Harnet expressed her ordeal:

> In a grave, your body decays
> until it turns to dust and debris.
> If you're a destitute asylum seeker,
> both body and soul wither away,
> until you become a lacklustre.
> The asylum system fears
> neither God nor land;
> in this unjust system,
> no one seems to care.

Harnet counted more than half a dozen friends who found themselves in situations similar to hers, constantly moving between asylum housing and emergency accommodations for years without adequate support. These friends are often prohibited from working for at least a year after submitting their asylum application, facing significant challenges in accessing basic necessities or securing employment. They encounter difficulties such as opening bank accounts and obtaining national insurance numbers. Positioned at the margins of the law and the state-private alliance, they are stranded in destitute asylum colonies. While their bodies endure destitution in these colonies, their souls are 'anxious and depressed', suffering 'every day while waiting' (Topak, 2020, p. 1863). Trapped in carceral spaces and juridical time, they experience depression, anxiety, and a profound sense of hopelessness. Neither their asylum claims, appeals for protection, nor their cries for help seem to resonate within the necropolitical reality of seeking asylum in the metropole.

The asylum in the metropole unfolds as an abyss, stretching from no-asylum to state-sanctioned asylum, regulated by an alliance between state and private interests in a hostile environment. This no-asylum becomes a chasm of precarious exile, leading to life in asylum colonies where existence itself is perpetually under threat. As we have seen, those seeking refuge are only able to feel the weight of their racialised and impoverished existence, along with the precarity of their legal status. As Arendt (2017) famously argues, the torments of exile within the metropole are compounded by the loss of home, estrangement from one's community, and the absence of sovereign protection. This experience of exile fosters an enduring sense of loss, longing, and solitude. For those of us contributing to this study, what we have shared so far is our reality; for those of us still trapped in perilous journeys, we know all too well what to expect, yet we have no choice. For all of us, what is at stake is our dignity, our futures, and our lives. Through our lived experiences, we are painfully aware that our lives are rendered violable and expendable.

Integration as white-masking

Those who navigate the asylum system and secure legal status embark on a journey of what is often referred to as 'integration'. For us, 'integration' is an elusive concept, both in theory and in practice. We do not even have an equivalent term for 'integration' in our languages, such as Tigrigna, Tigre, and Blin. In exploring this term and its meanings, over a dozen of us, all multilingual, were unable to translate the word 'integration' into our mother tongues. Zenawi, a former journalist from Eritrea who reported extensively in Tigrigna and Tigre, noted that terms like 'integration' simply do not exist in Eritrean languages. He acknowledged that many Italian and English words have entered Tigrigna and other local Eritrean languages, largely due to the colonial period. Though people often use these borrowed terms, creating a confusing blend of words, it remains challenging to find translations for concepts that are foreign to our languages, our culture, and our way of life. For this reason, Zenawi argued, terms like 'integration' can only find sanctuary in the 'languages of the colonisers'. This was a challenge he faced in his previous work as a journalist. Similarly, Aman, a native Tigrigna speaker and author of several works in Tigrigna, described 'integration' as a 'practical but untranslatable term'. Others, fluent in Blin, Tigrigna, and Tigre, also found it impossible to identify a word that describes, or even closely approximates, the meaning of 'integration' in these languages.

That said, our intention here is not to delve into a linguistic or semantic analysis of the word 'integration', but rather to understand the meanings that people seeking refuge, including ourselves, attach to it. In practical terms, integration is often seen as a continuum of encounters, engagements, and adaptations within the destination society. In group discussions, as illustrated in the diagram below, we created a list of adaptation and engagement activities, which some referred to as 'elements of integration' (Figure 5.1).

These layers (Figure 5.1) reflect the various stages and levels that are linked to the legal status in the UK—from seeking asylum to the granting of a residence permit, settled status, and for a few of us, 'naturalised citizens'. This connection between the 'elements of integration' and the shifting contours of legal status reveals that integration is inextricably linked to the legal position

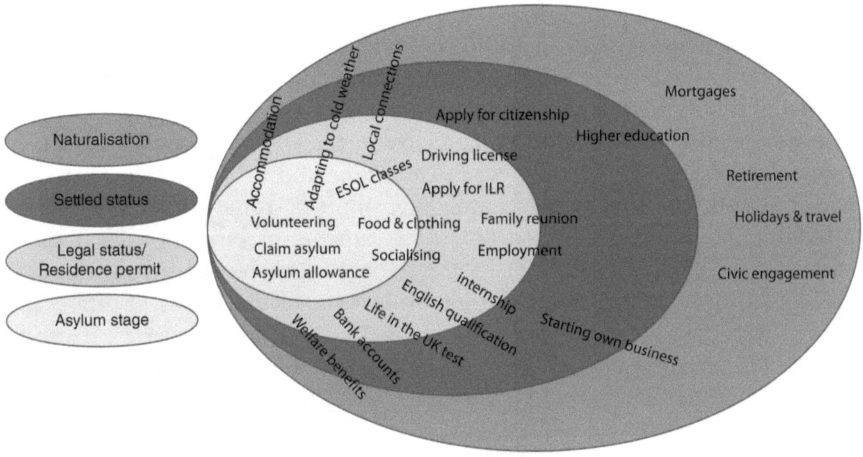

Figure 5.1 'Elements of integration'.

of the immigrant population. This relationship stems from the reality that 'most rights conferred upon refugees and immigrants remain predicated on their immigration status and subsequently on citizenship, should they become naturalized' (Lomba, 2010, p. 419). As illustrated, those seeking asylum are often deprived of fundamental rights, such as access to employment, education, and welfare. Their enforced unemployment and lack of essential support not only subject them to severe destitution but also hinder their capacity to 'integrate', whatever that term may mean. As Lomba (2010, p. 424) further clarifies:

> [...] the balance of rights and restrictions that characterizes the status of asylum seeker engages two principles relating to the concept of integration. First, it engages the multidimensional nature of integration. Indeed, asylum seekers are excluded from key domains of integration, such as employment, and their access to others, such as education, is limited. Secondly, it conflicts with the principle that integration starts upon arrival.

From this practical perspective, integration becomes a selective process, deeply shaped by the legal status of the immigrant population. This renders the rhetoric of 'integration starts upon arrival'—a mantra of the New Scots Integration Strategy in Scotland (Scottish Government, 2024)—all but impossible to implement; the rest of the UK remains, at best, far behind. For us, integration is not only untranslatable into any language we understand, but it is also seldom reflected in practice of human relations. It exists solely through its practical absence and rhetorical dominance. As McNeill (2019) observes from the viewpoint of prisoner reintegration: 'social integration has become well-nigh impossible in these conditions, but sustains a rehabilitative fiction or imaginary in and through their professional or occupational discourses and practices' (p. 144). Integration is this fictitious imaginary, applied with all its assimilationist connotations. Even those of us who have acquired legal status permitting us to live in the UK are not immune to the challenges posed by this assimilationist regime and its deliberate conflation with legal status. Within the hostile environment framework, immigration discourse, law, and practice become instruments of biopolitical exclusion and control. They are wielded to create conditions of Otherness, docility, and destitution, even when the right to remain in the UK is granted. The aim of fostering a hostile environment is clear: to use power to degrade, disqualify, disempower, discourage, and expel those deemed undesirable. In examining the 'harm' inflicted by the UK asylum system, Canning (2020, p. 272) affirms:

> While at the surface it embodies the ideals of welfare by providing financial support and housing, at the micro-level, it erodes human autonomy, infantilizes adults, and enforces dependency. Complicity is the foundation of a relationship built on unequal power, and non-adherence to (often unclear) instructions or expectations bears punitive results from an increasingly authoritarian set of actors, state as well as corporate.

Our shared experience reveals that the hostile nature of immigration laws and policies is felt at every stage of adapting to life in the UK. Laws concerning family reunion, and their application by entry clearance officers, were particularly harsh and discriminatory. For instance, Andom shared how it took him and his wife three years to convince the Home Office officers of their marriage. Their application for family reunion was rejected twice, simply because the officers were not convinced of the genuineness of their union. The second rejection was partly due to Andom's wife forgetting to include her bank statements in the application. 'It was a nightmare', Andom lamented. He further reflected on how fortunate they were to meet the high-income threshold set for family reunion by immigration regulations. Under the rules introduced in 2012, the minimum income requirement increased from £18,600 per annum to over £29,000 per annum by 2024. Given their enforced unemployability during the asylum process and the unlikelihood of finding a job that meets this high threshold, these regulations effectively deprive many refugees of their right to family life. Two participants in this study recalled friends who had divorced their spouses because they could not meet the financial requirements for reunion. This income-based discriminatory practice highlights a 'hierarchical ordering of acceptable and less acceptable family formations which explicitly links rights to family life with levels of income, creating those who are seen as more or less "deserving" of such rights' (Sirriyeh, 2015, p. 19).

Moreover, family visa applicants are required to establish their identities and relationships with their sponsors, a daunting task for many. Refugees, often lacking the necessary documentation, such as identity cards, passports, marriage certificates, struggle to validate their identities and relations. This challenge is especially pronounced for Eritrean refugees, who face significant barriers due to the absence of passport provisions and other vital documents in their homeland, compounded by the perilous nature of their journeys. During fieldwork, we attended several family reunion appeal hearings at immigration tribunals in Yorkshire and Glasgow. These experiences offered a poignant glimpse into how disputes over identity and familial ties can unfold into a complex spectacle of legal obscurities. The following excerpts illuminate the intricate struggles faced by those seeking to prove their connections amidst an unyielding bureaucracy.

> I sit in a courtroom at the [X], waiting for an appeal hearing concerning a family reunion case to begin. Earlier, I spoke with the appellant's husband in the reception area. He shared that the Home Office had denied his wife's application for entry clearance to the UK. With a heavy heart, he showed me the refusal letter, which cited insufficient evidence to prove her identity and their relationship. The hearing commenced at 10:11 a.m. The judge first asked the interpreter to clarify the language spoken by the appellant's sponsor, but the interpreter struggled to communicate effectively. For about fifteen minutes, the judge, the respondent, and the appellant's representative exchanged words, ultimately agreeing to adjourn the hearing – despite the appellant having submitted new evidence, including two witness statements and numerous wedding photos. The judge informed the appellant that the case would be adjourned pending further evidence, and the court session concluded at 10:36 a.m. The entire hearing struck me as bizarre. The sponsor remained excluded from the decision to adjourn the appeal, bewildered as to how it had been reached. He sat in a state of constitutive absence throughout the proceedings, leaving the courtroom lost and confused after the session ended.
>
> (Fieldwork notes, November 2019)

As these fieldwork notes suggest, appellants without passports or identity cards are expected to submit various alternative documents, such as witness statements, private messages, wedding photos, remittance records, and more. In their pursuit of the right to family life, they must disclose every aspect of their existence, exposing both their private and public lives in a vulnerable bid for recognition and reunion. From this perspective, the notion of refugee integration appears both conceptually misleading and practically invasive. It remains little more than a rhetorical device, used to categorise and delineate marginalised groups of people. In brief, integration defines the distance, as Lomba (2010) illustrates, 'how remote' one's relationship with the nation-state is, depending 'on the status ascribed to the immigrant or refugee' (p. 420).

What does it mean to 'integrate' into the illusion of homogeneity and colonial coherence of the womb-abyss, with mantras such as, at best, 'integration starts upon arrival'? How can one find a place in a hostile environment marked by systemic racism and the punitive realities of unjust immigration laws? In the grammars of coloniality, 'integration starts upon arrival' suggests that refugees are oblivious to the histories and languages of the metropole. But how could this ever resonate with those who arrive, bearing the wounds and scars of past and present colonial ravages, marked by the pain of their devastated communities and lands? What do these tropes of integration signify for those who have adopted colonial tongues, who have learned the histories woven through generations of struggle? And what of the Other, not merely an outsider, but the slave, the colonised, the displaced, all woven into the very fabric of the metropole's history? In the depths of irony, one must learn the tongue, read histories written in favour of masters, where colonial kings and queens are memorialised, their bellies filled with the blood, tears, and labour of the enslaved, sacrificed on the altar of empire. All for the chance of becoming a naturalised British citizen, to become a racialised figure within the heart of the metropole. If this is the price of integration, is it not a masquerade, a white-masking exercise in the theatre of coloniality? To our humble minds, unquestionably so.

The price of integration is clearly evident to those of us with second-generation children, or those born to refugee parents in the diaspora, as well as to those who arrived in the metropole at a young age. In the name of integration, we observe our children growing up in a culture of white masking, navigating the complexities of living with Black skin concealed beneath white masks, as Fanon alluded to. We witness the disappearance of our languages, the erosion of our cultures before our eyes, and the severing of our generational ties. Our languages, cultures, histories, and places of origin become the unknown, the unknowable—an imagined realm of trauma and deprivation. We represent the border, the limit, the last to tell our story, speak our language, savour our culture and food, and uphold our community's guiding wisdoms. While we may still inhabit the border, we bear witness to our children growing up in the metropoles of empire, gradually drowning in the abyss of colonial masks. As is the case for many Eritreans in diaspora, when we die, our bodies may return to our place of origin for burial in our family graveyard; yet the fate of our children remains uncertain. This is why we urge for multilingual education. By teaching children in the languages of their parents, as well as the languages of the communities in which we live, as Zenawi put it, 'We believe we are writing our languages, cultures, and histories into the future'. Through such an education, our children could become the multilingual poets of tomorrow, carrying the traces of both their ancestors' and their new communities' languages, cultures, and histories within them.

Finally, a profound question arises: what comes next? Do we submit to the White-masking machine known as integration, perpetually bearing its visceral wounds and scars, or rise in onto-epistemic decolonial restoration, contemplating the shedding of masks? What lies beneath the surface of the skin, beyond the borders of time, space, and flesh, in the face of such profound reality? These questions must be repeated, even if they do not have satisfactory answers in the current state of affairs. Hold on to them for further exploration and insight in the following chapter.

Conclusion

We began the journey of this chapter from the shores of the sea-camp, where many of us remain stranded at a crossroads, embarking on a journey with no map or guide for any place or time, with our dreams still trapped in their raw state. There is no definitive conclusion to be drawn here, but the conundrum we face upon reaching the sea-camp is this: either perish in the deserts and dungeons of time and space, or move forward, knowing that the shadow of death follows us until we find the possibility of relative safety. With no other choice, when possible, we begin our audacious journeys through the perils of the sea-camp under the cover of darkness. As we have shown, some perish and some survive, yet all endure the suffocating ordeals it imposes. Whether here or there, on either side of the sea-camp, in the depths or the heights of the abyss, in camps or cities, we struggle to find safety. We strive to grasp hope and realise our dreams.

For those of us who survived the sea-camp, we remain trapped in the refugee abyss, where despair threads its way through the bordering regimes and asylum systems of the metropole. The metropole embodies the origins of violence: slavery, colonialism, and imperialism. Within the metropole, we learned that the womb-abyss is confined within its halls of colonial power, which unapologetically refuse to confront the weight of the brutal past. This fortress of arrogance—the refusal to apologise for centuries of brutality or to acknowledge the ordeals it inflicted—is the hallmark of coloniality, deeply embedded in the fabric of the metropole. While the sun has set on the British Empire, its tainted legacy remains ever-present. What differs now is that the remains of those enslaved, along with their ordeals and histories, are surfacing beneath their feet, while the cries of the forgotten weave through the air. Descendants can only yearn for voices that dare to speak softly, to heal, to acknowledge, to relate, and to weave love into loss (Hartel, 2024).

As refugees, we are all too familiar with the metropole's portrayal of a glorious past and its denial of both past and present crimes. Upon our arrival, we found what we had already knew deep in our bones laid bare on the streets, walls, and in the buildings: monuments erected to honour former enslavers, colonisers, and military figures who committed untold atrocities, alongside emperors, queens, kings, religious leaders, and pseudoscientists. Amid these monuments, mummified in cement and stone, and the colonial wounds they inflict upon us, we encounter police officers trailing us with sniffing dogs, chains, and lock batons at transport hubs, on the streets, in public spaces, and within asylum colonies. Occasionally, we see officers on horseback patrolling the city. The most alarming of all are the immigration raids, marked by aggressive behaviour, racial profiling, and brute physical force that resemble settler tactics. We do our best to avoid the racist and extremist rioters who engage in organised violence and terror against our very existence. But the metropole is accustomed to this.

The law is often wielded like a lethal weapon, sharpened to inflict wounds upon us and to dissuade people like us from embarking on the journey to the metropole. In the last three years alone, as we have shown, the UK has passed several immigration laws. These laws aim to make seeking asylum an impossibility, to detain those of us seeking refuge indefinitely, to forcibly deport some of us to offshore detention, and, most recently, to empower newly established command posts to patrol the borders and prevent entry. A multitude of walls, techniques, technologies, resources, intelligence, and power have been mobilised to dismantle our existence, movement, and establish a state of impermanence. Invasive border control measures, such as biometrics, have now penetrated our bodies—our fingerprints, the iris of our eyes, the features of our faces. As Aas (2006) demonstrates, the body has become both a site and a means of enforcing border control, alongside passport checks, biometrics, and electronic surveillance. These borders of time, space, law, and flesh are often laced with linguistic vulgarity, including from those in government, which we have chosen not to repeat here.

Despite these spectacles of bordering, we seek refuge because that is why we are here. However, seeking refuge is one thing, while being granted it is quite another. The asylum system demands that we expose our deepest wounds to meet the criteria of the well-founded persecution formula, with its many variations, misinterpretations, subjective credibility assessments, and pervasive cultures of disbelief. Even after our open wounds are examined, we are more likely to be denied asylum or remain trapped in legal limbo within asylum colonies. If we are fortunate enough to be granted asylum, we are expected to hide ourselves behind white masks. That, in essence, is the story of the asylum process. Amid all this, we too long to find our friends and relatives who perished in the refugee abyss and to support those in need to help them survive.

The question then becomes, as Butler (2006) invites us to consider: 'If we stay with the sense of loss, are we left feeling only passive and powerless, as some might fear? Or are we, rather, returned to a sense of human vulnerability, to our collective responsibility for the physical lives of one another?' (p. 30). We are still contemplating, and this is why we invite you, dear reader, to join us on a journey towards what we call acentric relationality in the pages that follow. In the next chapter, we begin to imagine the poetics of refuge, shifting away from the refugee abyss and moving from open wounds to poetic traces. We offer poetic remarks as invitations for world-writing and world-building.

References

Aas, K.F. (2006) 'The Body Does Not Lie': Identity, Risk and Trust in Technoculture. *Crime, Media, Culture*, 2, 143–158.

Al Jazeera (2024) Last Body from Superyacht Sinking Off Sicily Found: Italian Coastguard [WWW Document]. Al Jazeera. Available from: https://www.aljazeera.com/news/2024/8/23/last-body-from-superyacht-sinking-off-sicily-found-italian-coastguard (accessed 31.12.24).

Ambrosini, M. (2018) 'Becoming a Borderland: The "Refugee Crisis" in Italy and Beyond', in *Irregular Immigration in Southern Europe*. Cham: Springer International Publishing, pp. 89–129. https://doi.org/10.1007/978-3-319-70518-7_4

Arendt, H. (2017) *The Origins of Totalitarianism*. London: Penguin Classics.

Boukari, Y. and Devakumar, D. (2024) Far-Right Riots in the UK: The Culmination of Years of Rhetoric and Policies. *The Lancet*, 404, 931.

Brekke, J.-P. and Brochmann, G. (2015) Stuck in Transit: Secondary Migration of Asylum Seekers in Europe, National Differences, and the Dublin Regulation. *Journal of Refugee Studies*, 28. https://doi.org/10.1093/jrs/feu028

Brown, T. (2024) UK Update. The Institute of International and European Affairs [Preprint], (172). Available from: https://www.iiea.com/images/uploads/resources/UK_Update_172.pdf (accessed 1.1.25).

Burton, L. (2007) Childhood Adultification in Economically Disadvantaged Families: A Conceptual Model. *Family Relations*, 56, 329–345. https://doi.org/10.1111/j.1741-3729.2007.00463.x

Butler, J. (2006) *Precarious Life: the Powers of Mourning and Violence*. London: Verso.

Canning, V. (2020) Corrosive Control: State-Corporate and Gendered Harm in Bordered Britain. *Critical Criminology*, 28, 259–275. https://doi.org/10.1007/s10612-020-09509-1

Catania, T. (2013) Lampedusa: "An Island Full of Pain; It Carries the Weight of the World's Indifference." *The PostColonialist.*

Cusumano, E. (2018) The Sea as Humanitarian Space: Non-Governmental Search and Rescue Dilemmas on the Central Mediterranean Migratory Route. *Mediterranean Politics*, 23, 387–394. https://doi.org/10.1080/13629395.2017.1302223

Darling, J. (2009) Becoming bare Life: Asylum, Hospitality, and the Politics of Encampment. *Environment and Planning D: Society and Space*, 27, 649–665.

Davies, T., Isakjee, A., and Dhesi, S. (2017) Violent Inaction: The Necropolitical Experience of Refugees in Europe: Violent Inaction. *Antipode*, 49, 1263–1284. https://doi.org/10.1111/anti.12325

Edler, I.A. (2020) The Mediterranean Sea as a Camp. Khamasin Issues, pp. 18–25. Available from: https://aucegypt0.sharepoint.com/sites/documents/HUSS/Forms/AllItems.aspx?id=%2Fsites%2Fdocuments%2FHUSS%2FKhamasin%20ISSUE%20%2D%20Spring%202020%20%2D%20Final%2Epdf&parent=%2Fsites%2Fdocuments%2FHUSS&p=true&ga=1

EWCA Civ 872 (2019) BF (Eritrea) v Secretary of State for the Home Department [2019] EWCA Civ 872 (23 May 2019) [WWW Document]. Available from: http://www.bailii.org/ew/cases/EWCA/Civ/2019/872.html (accessed 5.1.21).

GOV.UK (2024) Asylum Support [WWW Document]. GOV.UK. Available from: https://www.gov.uk/asylum-support/what-youll-get (accessed 1.1.25).

Grant, H. and Domokos, J. (2011) Dublin Regulation Leaves Asylum Seekers with Their Fingers Burnt. *The Guardian* 7.

Hartel, L.E. (2024) Legacies of the Slave Trade: An Analysis of Demands, Apologies and Reparations in Britain over the Last 25 Years (Master's Thesis). NTNU.

Human Rights Watch (2009) *Pushed Back, Pushed Around Italy's Forced Return of Boat Migrants and Asylum Seekers, Libya's Mistreatment of Migrants and Asylum Seekers*. New York, New York: Human Rights Watch.

Human Rights Watch (2016) EU Policies Put Refugees At Risk [WWW Document]. Human Rights Watch. Available from: https://www.hrw.org/news/2016/11/23/eu-policies-put-refugees-risk (accessed 2.1.21).

Jones, R. (2019) From Violent Borders: Refugees and the Right to Move. *NACLA Report on the Americas*, 51, 36–40. https://doi.org/10.1080/10714839.2019.1593688

Laczko, F., Black, J., and Singleton, A. (eds) (2019) *Missing Migrant Children*. Geneva: International Organization of Migration.

Lomba, S. d. (2010) Legal Status and Refugee Integration: a UK Perspective. *Journal of Refugee Studies*, 23, 415–436. https://doi.org/10.1093/jrs/feq039

Mainwaring, Ċ. (2019) *At Europe's Edge: Migration and Crisis in the Mediterranean*, 1st ed. Oxford: Oxford University Press.

McLaughlin, C. (2018) 'They don't look Like Children': Child Asylum-Seekers, the Dubs Amendment and the Politics of Childhood. *Journal of Ethnic and Migration Studies*, 44, 1757–1773. https://doi.org/10.1080/1369183X.2017.1417027

McNeill, F. (2019) *Pervasive Punishment: Making Sense of Mass Supervision*, 1st ed. Bradford: Emerald Publishing Limited.

Missing Migrants Project (2024) International Organization for Migration [WWW Document]. Deaths During Migration Recorded Since 2014, by Region of Incident. Available from: https://missingmigrants.iom.int/ (accessed 31.12.24).

MSF (2020) Detaining of Fifth Search and Rescue Ship in Five Months Condemns People to Die at Sea | MSF [WWW Document]. Médecins Sans Frontières (MSF) International. Available from: https://www.msf.org/detaining-fifth-search-and-rescue-ship-five-months-condemns-people-die-sea (accessed 27.11.20).

Neidhardt, A.-H. (2022) 'Post-Brexit EU–UK Cooperation on Migration and Asylum: How to Live Apart, Together', in *Brussels: European Policy Centre*, pp. 1–15. Available from: https://repository.uantwerpen.be/docstore/d:irua:17476 (accessed 13.9.24).

Platts-Fowler, D. and Robinson, D. (2011) An Evaluation of the Gateway Protection Programme. Sheffield: Sheffield Hallam University.

Salter, M.B. (2004) Passports, Mobility, and Security: How Smart can the Border Be? *International Studies Perspectives*, 5, 71–91.

Scottish Government (2024) New Scots Refugee Integration Strategy: 2024 [WWW Document]. Available from: https://www.gov.scot/publications/new-scots-refugee-integration-strategy-2024/ (accessed 1.1.25).

Sirriyeh, A. (2015) 'All You Need Is Love and£18,600': Class and the New UK Family Migration Rules. *Critical Social Policy*, 35, 228–247.

Spijkerboer, T.(2017) Wasted Lives. Borders and the Right to Life of People Crossing Them. *Nordic Journal of International Law*, 86, 1–29. https://doi.org/10.1163/15718107-08601004

Topak, Ö.E. (2020) Biopolitical Violence and Waiting: Hotspot as a Biopolitical Borderzone. *Antipode*, 52, 1857–1878. https://doi.org/10.1111/anti.12676

UNHCR (2019) UNHCR Concerned at New Measures Impacting Rescue at Sea in the Central Mediterranean [WWW Document]. UNHCR. Available from: https://www.unhcr.org/news/briefing/2019/8/5d49370e4/unhcr-concerned-new-measures-impacting-rescue-sea-central-mediterranean.html (accessed 27.11.20).

Webber, F. (2019) On the Creation of the UK's 'Hostile Environment'. *Race & Class*, 60, 76–87.

Yemane, T.H. (2023) We Are Here Because You Are Still There. *Coloniality of British Soft Power and Eritrean Forced Migrants in the UK* (PhD thesis), University of Leeds.

Yohannes, H.T., Yemane, T.H., and Wangari-Jones, P. (2024) 'Chapter 1: The Hostile Environment, Covid-19, and the Creation of Asylum Colonies in the UK', in Bhambra, G.K., Mayblin, L., Medien, K., and Viveros, M. (Eds) *The Sage Handbook of Global Sociology*, pp. 1–16. London: SAGE.

6 Poetics of Refuge

Introduction

Throughout the pages of this book, we have charted the subjection of forcibly displaced people to the refugee abyss, veiled under the pretext of safeguarding the body politic and its ostensibly protected constituents. We have traced the displaced voices of the naked, the hungry, and the suffering, their pain rendered into a poetics of the abyss and open wounds. The preceding chapters also uncover the resistance that stirs within these wounds as poetics of defiance born in the struggle against the containment of life within realms of death. Through acts of moving, dying, fighting, and protesting, survival becomes a form of radical resistance under the shadow of pervasive violence and death.

Yet beyond the poetics of open wounds, we have contended that the systems which call our humanity into question are woefully inadequate. Humanity, fragmented and narrowly conceived, must be reimagined. The physical and metaphysical impositions of (de)humanity and (de)existence cannot continue to erode the essence of our being. At the core of our argument is a rejection of racialised and colonial constructs that divide and diminish. In their place, we envision the refugee as a decolonial agent, striving not merely to survive but to cultivate a poetics of human relations that attends to the inviolable dignity of all, one that insists on perpetual mutuality, multiplicity, relationality, and the essential right to opacity.

This compels us to ask: what alternatives might the displaced voices of the persistently marginalised offer to a world predicated upon their death? This chapter explores this pressing question through an exploration of what we term poetic traces and acentric relationality. In envisioning the poetics of refuge, we begin with tentative reflections on four poetic traces: the body, movement, face, and memory. These traces are explored in the second section, following an initial reflection on the poetics of refuge. It is essential to stress that our observations are not definitive; they are left open to interpretation, reflection, and even rejection.

In the third section, we propose the concept of acentric relationality as both a means of world-writing and world-building, anchoring it in the poetic

DOI: 10.4324/9781003437192-7

imagination of our contemporary moment. The chapter concludes with further reflections on the poetics of refuge and acentric relationality, presented as emergent political imaginaries. These final thoughts, like the poetics they describe, are deliberately vulnerable and profoundly open invitations to understanding, transformation, and action.

Poetics of refuge

The poetics of refuge can be envisioned as a luminous thread within Glissant's poetics of Relation, where human communities, including those displaced, weave spaces of mutuality, intercultural exchange, multilingualism, and opacity. These poetics name the emergence of human relations between peoples and nations, citizens and non-citizens, across dialogues of knowledge, culture, and language, and through the diverse temporalities, geographies, and causes that unite or differentiate them. It is a poetics grounded in the necessity as well as fragility of human relations while celebrating their resilience, revealing how shared existence can persist even amid rupture and estrangement (Akomolafe, 2020). In these fugitive yet enduring relations, a profound sense of belonging may arise, shaped not by uniformity but by the intricate interplay of differences and opacities.

Yet, from the outset, it must be acknowledged that such poetics may seem nearly impossible for refugees trapped in the belly of the refugee abyss. For those detained in the unyielding confines of carceral spaces, their existence becomes a relation with violence, imprisoned indefinitely. At the borders, they navigate a maze of brutality under conditions of exception. In the camps, they endure unending deprivation and a paralysing stasis of time and space. Within the police city, they are relentlessly hunted by state and non-state forces alike. In torture camps, they are commodified, reduced to mere objects of trade, locked in harrowing relations reminiscent of the horrors of past abysses. On the open sea, in the perilous expanse of the sea-camp, they vanish into the apocalyptic void. Even in the metropole, those who survive find their dignity eroded within the cold machinery of a (de)humanising asylum system. This stark reality leads to an urgent question: how might the poetics of refuge emerge amidst prisons, at borders, in the desolation of camps, in lifeless deserts, within police cities, across sea-camps, in the heart of metropoles, or beneath the shadow of an unyielding asylum regime?

Though death lurks within the refugee abyss as an ever-present shadow and an inevitable fate for so many, refugees also navigate its belly, defying what seems insurmountable. Despite the overwhelming ordeals, at least in our poetic visions, the abyss is not entirely bereft of the poetics of refuge, for such poetics challenge the very notion of impossibility. Throughout the writing of this book, we are reminded that breathing bodies endure, even in the darkest of underground cells, as Alex's story so vividly reveals. Though we may be rendered invisible and violable, we refuse to relinquish our grasp on life, holding fast to the hope that one day we shall breathe freely. We chase our poetic visions, gazing towards a world beyond the abyss of the present and the reverberations of the past. From beneath these subterranean spaces, our displaced voices rise, calling for a different kind of human relations in a world where the inviolability of dignity prevails. The translation that follows reflects the defiance of survivors of detention, as shared during our collective discussions on the strategies of survival.

> We would not let our minds dwell in that darkness.
> We chose to learn new languages with the prison guards,
> celebrating our own through letters from afar.
> We prayed to reach beyond the human worlds,
> singing to walls and listening to their echoes.
> We recalled memories of the life we once knew.
> Through it all, we remained calm and alive.

The phrase *'we remained calm and alive'* emerged as a recurring theme in our conversations and encounters with those seeking refuge. It speaks to the indomitable human capacity to endure, adapt, and uphold a sense of dignity, even within the dehumanising depths of despair. It is a reminder of our fugitive and abyssal (de)existence in a world overwhelmed by violence and systemic marginalisation. Yet, *'we remained calm and alive'* also invokes the poetics of life that rise beyond mere survival. Calmness becomes not a passive state but a profound expression of active resilience, while remaining alive signifies the determined effort to breathe, to preserve dignity, and to hold onto the opacity of our own humanity even amidst the most profound challenges. '*We remained calm and alive*' thus embodies not only a commitment to sustaining life with dignity in the face of adversity but also an enduring endeavour to transform the world around us by fostering poetics of relation. This spirit is reflected in the traces of relations found within the lives of refugees, as seen in their acts of resilience and community-building. Many run businesses, such as restaurants and shops, where refugees and locals alike gather for coffee ceremonies, share intercultural meals, engage in multilingual conversations, and enjoy friendly games. Whether in camps, cities under heavy surveillance, or bustling metropoles, refugees celebrate religious rituals and festivals, play football, and partake in everyday activities that link them to the wider human experience. These are the spaces where, as we celebrated together over an Eritrean coffee ceremony in Cairo, the sentiment of *'refugees welcome refugees'* comes alive. In extending this welcome to one another, all participants agreed:

> The greatest gift we have encountered on our journey
> is the company of friends and strangers, whose
> kindness, generosity, and courage have woven
> the threads of lives made possible, bearable.

> No moment existed without sacrifice –
> through torture, ransom, or death,
> each step of the journey bore its cost.
> Yet, it is humans who make the unbearable endurable,
> who render the impossible attainable.
> In our shared acts, our lives found possibility,
> even as we mourn the countless friends
> who have perished [in the abyss].

We find resonance in these poetics of remaining calm and alive, of welcoming one another, becoming with each other, and mourning together those who have perished. In his autobiographical reflections, Yohannes (2024) describes the spaces where such poetics of refuge emerge as 'ruderal spaces', conceived as the places where the 'phenomenologies of crying, prayer, music, poetry, and encounters with those living in near-life conditions' come into being (2024, p. 324). Yohannes explains in detail:

> For me, these spaces include the impoverished community centres where I can cry on someone's shoulder; the under-resourced health care systems where I began to heal my wounded body; the faith-based organisations where I can pray for healing with family and friends; the friend zones where I share my story; the coffee ceremonies where I find solace during difficult times and a sense of belonging; the workplace where I meet like-minded colleagues committed to decoloniality; the library where I can reflect on my reality; the virtual spaces where I connect with long-separated family acquaintances; the cafes where I enjoy tea and watch football matches with friends; the desk from at which I am writing this chapter; the spaces where I listen to people's stories; the music that heals the soul; the writing through which I create my own storylines and imagine safer places; and so many other spaces, too.

These ruderal spaces are 'where refugees constantly invite us to cry, pray, dance, read poetry, and meet face-to-face with them' (Yohannes, 2024, p. 324). In our poetics, we cry out for refuge, including for those who have died. We seek justice for the lost, not in punitive terms, but as an invitation to come to terms with the unbearable through expressions of 'love and rage' (Maldonado-Torres, 2016, p. 30). Amidst the darkness of the womb-abyss and its grammars of coloniality, we find our stories, our songs, our displaced voices, our poetry, and our poetics interwoven with struggles for survival and visions of a more profound future. The whispers and memories of lost friends traverse the borders of time and space. We, the survivors and those still enduring, alongside their loved ones, recount their ordeals and deferred dreams. Those who bear witness to the lives of the perished remind us that their companions were caught in the storms and turbulence of the refugee abyss, much like the enslaved who perished at sea or on plantations.

With every fragment adrift, every name named, and every displaced voice remembered, traces of their stories rise to the surface, sustaining the currents of their abyssal realities, keeping them 'calm and alive', resting in peace. These realities illuminate the potential for the body, movement, face, and memory to emerge as poetic traces not solely of the survivors but also of those who perished, as we reflect upon below.

Poetic traces

Poetic trace embodies an idea of incompleteness that seeks not to complement itself but to become-with in a totality of perpetually evolving relations. Poetic traces flourish in the soil of resilience, resourcefulness, and relationality, where even the catastrophe of the abyss can nurture seeds of possibility for the restoration of human and nonhuman relations. Our poetic traces stand against the refugee abyss, linking incomplete survivals, fragmented stories, severed threads of life, pained bodies, ungrieved losses, haunting memories, and the unknown dimensions of the abyss. These are not merely physical imprints or empirical realities but conceptual allegories, inviting us to explore encounters, histories, interculturalities, and shared experiences without the constraints of assimilation, articulation, measurability, predictability, or erasure.

Poetic traces speak through untamed voice imagined outside dominant modalities, creating space for the refugee voice to transform into a displaced voice. This displaced voice acknowledges that nothing is ever fully grasped and, in doing so, asserts the right to opacity, unintelligibility, immeasurability, and incalculability. Within it, the physical structures and metaphysical logics that seek to impose order and stability based on a singular mode of being, knowing and relating are destabilised. In this rupture, the displaced voice not only resists assimilation but also becomes a poetic vision for new ways of imagining existence, where multiplicity, relation, and difference remain irreducible. Through this, survival and solidarity emerge, affirming life beyond the refugee abyss.

Thus, poetic traces are intertwined with the inappropriable desire for freedom from the ordeals of the womb-abyss. This desire is not merely an escape or a mere relation of vulnerability but an ethical call to proximity, shared existence, and relationality. In the poetic traces, where encounters with the Other—in this case, the refugee—become possible, vulnerability weaves threads of presence and absence of relations, evoking an ethical call to relate beneath the surface of the skin and beyond the borders of time and space. With the presence and absence of relations, every glance or encounter becomes an invitation to meet and dwell at the edges of the 'borderlands' (Anzaldúa, 2012), bearing witness to the birth of relations that transcend borders, walls, and political and juridical constructs. Within the ruderal spaces, human communities intertwine, with each life appearing as a fragile, fugitive, fleeting presence inhabiting the margins of time and space (Yohannes, 2024). It is in these acentric relational spaces that beings, non-beings, entities, and things meet in relationships of mutuality, conviviality, interculturality, and multilinguality. In the context of the refugee abyss, these poetic traces find their most prominent expression through the body, the face, movement, and memory, emerging beyond the confines of the womb-abyss.

Bodily existence

Each time we attempt to understand our bodily existence through intellectual analysis, we are confronted by the realities of forced displacement, open wounds, and the scars inflicted upon us. These experiences underscore our ongoing exposure to vulnerability, violability, and mortality. Thus, even if we are repeating what has already been said, it is essential to explore the relationship between our displaced bodies, the experience of displacement, and the violence inflicted upon us. Our displaced bodies are ceaselessly rendered violable and disposable by the womb-abyss and its institutions of governance, with the violence of sovereign power acting upon our bodily existence to impose the coordinates of coloniality upon us, alongside the necropolitical spectacles of (b)ordering. This forced entanglement of our bodies with the structures of coloniality and raciality results, in Fanonian terms, in a profound 'experience of dispossession and dislocation—psychic and social—which speaks to the condition of the marginalized, the alienated, those who have to live under the surveillance of a sign of identity and fantasy that denies their difference' (Fanon, 1986, p. xxxv). These intertwined experiences of dispossession and dislocation have inflicted upon us a fragmented sense of bodily existence, leaving us struggling to reconcile our lived realities with the pursuit of dignity.

As shown in the preceding chapters, our bodies have suffered dispossession and dislocation as a result of the abyss imposed upon us. We experience dispossession as a deep estrangement from our bodies, histories, homes, and communities, perpetuated by state violence, displacement, and bordering (see Hirt, 2010). At the same time, we feel dislocated due to the fragmentation of our composite identities or a detachment from our sense of place, time, and reality. Our bodies are rendered bare, forcibly displaced from homes and homelands, finding no shelter, no refuge, no rights, and no rest, even in their perishability. This is exemplified in the exhumation of refugee bodies from graves intended for others, their remains discarded in mass graves or treated as unworthy of a resting place, even in death. The bodies that have sunk to the seafloor, floated with tides in the sea, or have become sustenance for marine life are also part of us. So too are the bodies that have perished without a trace, lost in the depths of the refugee abyss or languishing indefinitely in underground cells. These bodies remain entangled in what Fanon (2007) describes as a condition of 'incomplete death' (p. 128).

Our pained and displaced bodies also suffer from a lack of purpose or vocation within the confines of the womb-abyss. Our bodies exist in a perpetual state of exile, pushed to the edges and borders of space and time, inhabiting 'at the limits of life, trapped in uninhabitable worlds and inhospitable places' (Mbembe, 2019a, p. 10). These edges and borders are violent confines, deployed to regulate our bodily existence, to institute necropolitics and raciality upon us, or an incomplete death. Our bodily existence remains a form of, as Glissant (2009) poetically describes, 'persecuted errantry' (p. 20). Furthermore, as Glissant (2009) writes, our bodies endure the 'impossibility of communicating in [our] language' (p. 15), with our visceral voices excluded from the domains of politics and intelligibility. This violence of the womb-abyss, enacted for self-preservation, persists through the deliberate suspension of laws and rights, the denial of asylum, and the deployment of state-corporate-private alliances, as demonstrated in the preceding chapters.

Ironically, those who claim to express humanitarian solidarity with forcibly displaced people often limit their efforts to condemning the violence inflicted upon us without addressing the structural necessity of that violence. This is the catastrophic formula through which humanitarianism operates, celebrated for its grammar of charity, solidarity, and neutrality, yet complicit in perpetuating the violent system it claims to challenge. Under this humanitarian gaze, our bodies are reduced to mere pained corporealities—choked of breath and life, trapped in perpetual destitution, languishing in open or carceral spaces, floating in the sea, or buried in indignity. In the eyes of humanitarian organisations and their workers, our bodies exist merely as subjects in need of help, feeding, a need that justifies the creation of humanitarian organisations with vast employers, policy frameworks, funds, and power structures. These organisations, however, do not relieve our bodies of pain, hunger, or the lack of shelter; nor do they liberate us from the shackles of the womb-abyss. Instead, they sustain and perpetuate a carceral charitable imaginary in which bodies are fed, treated, and contained, only to ultimately perish beyond the bounds of the polity (see Oliver, 2017).

At this point, let us pose a different question: What poetic traces can emerge from such pained, displaced, and burdened bodily existence? More importantly, how does one reclaim a body that has been dispossessed, dislocated, or made absent from its home, birthplace, or even grave through exhumation or disappearance, leaving no physical trace? Tracing a body and a voice in such bodies may seem unbearable, exhausting, or even futile. Yet, we cannot simply abandon our bodies or yield our bodily existence to its perishability. Instead, with each breath, we persistently strive to ensure the possibility of our bodily existence. Even when we are alone and abandoned, radically exposed to brutality, unintelligibility, and perishability, we continue to grasp the poetic traces of our displaced bodies and voices, as narrated in this book. Each step becomes a burden, each breath a prayer for survival. As we wane, we weep, bleed, and perish in brutal carceral spaces where arbitrary detention is the norm; at borders where multiple forms of violence intersect; in barren deserts where the shadows of life creep; in torture camps where human bodies are commodified; and in the sea-camp where apocalyptic scenes of despair and disposability unfold. We persist and continue to exist, even if it is in a state of incomplete death, or as a trace of fading memories.

With all our being, we protest these conditions of (de)existence and (de) humanity amidst the chaos and despair of our circumstances. We move so that our bodies are not confined to carceral spaces, protest so that our bodies are not vessels for the pleasure of others, ransoms for the highest bidders, organ incubators, empty corpses to rot in the desert, the humus of barren lands, sustenance for fish, objects of humanitarian rescue. We reclaim our bodies and bodily existence so that they do not become no-bodies, or simply eradicated. Crucially, our bodies resist being appropriated by the whims of the womb-abyss. This is why each time we step into the camp, the police city, cross fortified borders, or enter the metropole, we assert our human and bodily existence against the refugee abyss. In doing so, we transform our bodies and ourselves into decolonial agents for a radical turn. These are our poetic rages, from which emerge our theoretical orientations towards the politics and ethics of life, imagination, and relationality. We are fighters who do not wage war, armed not with the arsenal of raciality and coloniality, but with the boundless possibilities of decolonial existence (see Phipps and Sitholé, 2018).

We reclaim our bodies and our very existence because, as Anzaldúa (2012) writes, 'For only through the body, through the pulling of flesh, can the human soul be transformed. And for images, words, stories to have this transformative power, they must arise from the human body—flesh and bone—and from the Earth's body—stone, sky, liquid, soil' (2012, p. 75). Our bodies stand as a testament to our capacity for survival through creativity, resourcefulness, and resilience, shaped by the weight of our pain, burdens, and the stories we carry. With weary limbs, a hungry stomach, and a heart laid bare, our bodies not only navigate the abyss of the refugee experience but also open the possibility of imagining the world anew. This is what Sergel sought to share when he laid his body bare to reveal his wounds and scars: 'Look at my wounds, still bleeding. These are my scars, my old wounds'. These words are not mere declarations of pain, nor revelations of wounds and scars, but poetic invitations to bear witness to our open wounds and scars, and to rebel against the inscription of our bodies and bodily existence by the womb-abyss, as sites of its violent (b)ordering. Staring at the sight of the open wounds turns us away from the womb-abyss, urging us to resist the thought and deployment of violence.

There is often an aesthetic dimension to our bodily existence. For us, aesthetic praxes are essential not only for our bodily being but also to find joy in life and to mourn our death amidst the abyss. We celebrate life and death through the musicality, dance, and rituals of mourning and prayer. We honour traditional coffee ceremonies, sitting in circles, face to face, sharing our struggles and hopes, praying for one another, and offering support, no matter how difficult our circumstances may appear. Through these interconnected aesthetic practices, we breathe life into our (de)existence, generate meaning to our lives, and restore our dignity by creating human spaces and times—ruderal spaces and times, to be precise. In these aesthetic practices, our bodies speak more than we can ever articulate or wish to articulate. In our poetic lamentation, the lacerations and scars on our bodies are, above all else, our archives of loss and life. Our bodies, in Fanon's (1986) terms, represent 'the open door of every consciousness' (p. 181). Our bodies embody and carry cultures, languages, crafts, and arts that sustain our lives and generate knowledge beyond the refugee abyss and the matrices of coloniality.

Figure 6.1 Roasted coffee beans, resting upon a Meshrefet at a workshop celebrating the tradition of Eritrean coffee, held within the Scottish Crannog Centre. Photograph by Karen Gordon.

Figure 6.2 A meal of Eritrean dishes at Mosob Bar and Restaurant in Glasgow. Photograph by Karen Gordon.

We often receive coffee beans and food ingredients from relatives in our home country or neighbouring lands, where these beans hold a significant place in local traditions. Today, they are sold in markets and diasporic shops in the cities. These coffee beans and food ingredients are our seeds of hope, life, care, sharing, relation, and the possibility of making life bearable once more. The traditional coffee ritual in Eritrea, Ethiopia, and other regions is a thread that unites people, culture, and nature. During coffee ceremonies, families, neighbours, friends, and strangers come together to discuss socio-political events, share food, stories, dance, perform, and celebrate the gifts of nature—rivers, arable land, forests, deserts, and mountains. The coffee ceremony creates a space where the unsaid can be expressed and the unknowable can be revealed. We gather in this space to discuss shared struggles, hidden archives, and the intertwined memories that connect our intercultural, inter-epistemic, multilingual, and natural worlds. In our encounters with others, we open the archives of our coffee beans, incense, cloth, songs, pots, dishes, and lived experiences, inviting both friends and strangers to touch, taste, and see what our bodies are made of. Most importantly, the joy of celebrating our ways of life and modes of knowing and relating has a healing effect. It is a sensory experience that engages the whole person—body, mind, and soul—through taste, smell, texture, sound, and sight.

We are irresistibly drawn to other cultures, curious as the breeze that carries the aroma of our roasted coffee beans, whispering through doors both open and closed. We are not merely open but deeply attuned to the cross-pollination of ideas, where customs, practices, and languages intertwine like a garden of shared traditions, each enriching the other as they are woven together through time. The pumpkin seeds and weaving supplies (Figure 6.3), so graciously offered during our workshops, symbolise a profound hope and relation that transcends the racialised violence of the womb-abyss. Avril Bellinger, a cherished friend and Honorary Associate Professor of Social Work at the School of Health Professions, Faculty of Health, University of Plymouth, entrusted us with these seeds of hope and life. Some of these seeds found their way to families in Eritrea, where a sister nurtured them on our forsaken farmlands, returning seeds to us accompanied by this poetic message:

> You sent us seeds,
> and we have nurtured them,
> sending you the seeds
> imbued with the taste of our lands
> and the care of our hands,
> in abundance.
> May the lands
> and the lords
> bless you all.

Through such poetic messages, we restore joy to our displaced bodily existence, freedom to immobility, and refuse to be held hostage by the refugee abyss as the sole condition of our lives. We sing with these words, however rough our lyrics and fading rhythms may be, because they enable us, as Mbembe (2015) writes, 'to write with the musicality of one's own flesh'. These poetics open new political and ethical possibilities between here and there, now and then. They carry liberatory potential, allowing us to break free from the suffocating conditions of the refugee abyss.

Finally, our bodies are our homes, unbound by fixed spatialities or temporalities (Yohannes, 2024). As argued, wherever we journey or choose to stay, our bodies carry, share, and perform our languages, cultures, and

Figure 6.3 Pumpkin seeds on a Meshrefet. These seeds, gifted by Avril Bellinger, journeyed from Scotland to Eritrea, where they were nurtured by family hands, only to return, flourishing, with an abundance of seeds. Photograph by the author.

crafts, while honouring rituals of both mourning and joy. From the traditions of food to the sacred ceremonies of life and death, to the creation of crafts and artworks, these expressions are carried, shared, preserved, and embodied within us. These embodied poetic traces manifest through our bodily expressions, performances, and actions, fostering our interconnectedness with both human and earthly worlds. Our bodies, accustomed to inhabiting ruderal spaces, adapt to new destinations, share and create knowledge, form humans and nonhumans alike, offer healing, and provide warmth. From the embodied praxes and poetics, new political and social

Figure 6.4 Weaving supplies laid before the attendees at the University of Glasgow Memorial Chapel, offered during a vigil for the victims of genocidal wars. Photograph by Karen Gordon.

realities emerge through a continuous reclamation of the body and bodily existence. Through resourcefulness, opacity, creativity, and writing, these embodied poetics challenge the 'object-subject' binary, where the refugee is often positioned as an 'object' to be known by a knower, such as a researcher. The evidence and essence of our poetic traces dissolve this binary, giving rise to displaced voices and acentric relationality. As Mbembe (2015) writes, 'The language of these genres communicates how ordinary people laugh and weep, work, play, pray, bless, love and curse, make a space to stand forth and walk, fall and die'.

Movement

'Everything and everyone moves – so why shouldn't we?' This question frequently arose in our conversations with friends trapped in the refugee abyss. These friends often associated immobility with losing their 'way home'. For them, movement becomes an existential inquiry, prompting reflection on what it means to move in an age of violent borders, frontiers, and the prisons of time and space. When does one begin, if a beginning even exists, to move—to arrive home? And most importantly, how do we liberate the body from the shackles of borders, (b)ordering, and homelessness? These questions are central to the poetics of refuge, which seeks to address the question: 'Why shouldn't we move?' This questioning pertains to reclaiming the necessity and urge to move, rather than merely seeking to understand the fictitious rationale for (b)ordering, with which we are all too familiar through our lived experiences.

'Why shouldn't we move?' is a poetic lament for the fundamental necessity to move—a necessity frustrated by the legitimacy and stability of (b)orders, whether territorial, biometric, physical, or metaphysical. The violence of (b)ordering confines the body's natural impulse to navigate through space and time. The immobilising effect of (b)orders and (b)ordering is particularly terrifying for our displaced selves. In response, we rush and rage with our bodily existence trapped in multiple states of (im)mobility while yearning for freedom of movement. Despite the obstacles and dangers we face, movement enables us not only to carry and sustain our pained bodies and masked faces but also to glimpse the possibility of healing our wounds and shedding masks within ruderal spaces, however fleeting these moments may be. As we co-write elsewhere: 'For migrants, mobility has existential value; to move is to live, to survive, to connect, to resist, to exist, and to enjoy' (Yohannes and Phipps, 2024, p. 138). Movement fosters meetings and encounters, each of which opens new possibilities for overcoming closures, borders, and dungeons, making life and joy in life conceivable (Mbembe, 2015).

Movement embodies the poetic traces of life-making and life-living. It is a desire for freedom to live, to become-with, to conjure, to relate to, and to encounter the Other in relation. This desire to move, to move in order to be free, is inappropriable and ineffaceable. It is this desire, along with creative and innovative resourcefulness, that enables refugees to survive the refugee abyss. In an interview with Goldberg, Mbembe explores people's creative capacity for survival within the (im)mobilities of the postcolony:

> For once, to get out of the hole and to break through the wall, the captured subject must actively engage in a relation of multiple doubles and multiple selves. He or she must develop an extraordinary capacity to become imperceptible and unassignable, to continually shift from one self to its alternate, to inhabit the tiniest of cracks and fissures.
>
> (Goldberg, 2018, p. 212)

Like other refugees, who, by the very nature of their flight, traverse the borders of time, space, and language, we master the art of knowing when to hide, where to move, and how to navigate (b)orders. After all, it is through movement that we endlessly drift across the borders of time, space, and flesh, slipping through the very spectacle of (b)ordering. Constantly shifting between multiple identities, we strive to remain unnoticed, undefined, and beyond absolute control. In the darkness of night and the blindness of day, we slip through cracks between (b)orders of death, prisons of time, dungeons of walls, and checkpoints of police, unseen by the panoptic gaze of the womb-abyss. We travel across borders without passports, identification, or travel documents; walk the streets of metropoles that deny our existence, our visibility, and our capacity to make a home; move between informal jobs and temporary shelters in shantytowns and police cities; speak from the underground and the underbelly through a displaced voice woven from our poetic vision of the world.

We often find refuge in the smallest gaps, openings, movements, things, and traces of life. We find refuge in the offering of bread from a nomad's hand, in the wild maize along the Nile, mangoes and bananas from gardens, and in each piece of food shared in the quiet, haunting moments. We find refuge on the back of a camel, a donkey, or in dusty cars; resting in each other's arms, a silent promise to never let each other down during crowded perilous journeys, a shared breath, prayers whispered in our mother tongues, and small jokes that nourish and carry us forward. With movement, life pushes through the dust, muddied waters, walls, camps, and vast seas. Our movement is not tied to place but to our mobile bodies, to traces of footsteps taken one at a time, to becoming-with, to making a life reborn in the ruderal spaces where the seeds of life grow, however slowly.

As we move, we find inspiration in the smallest of things and beings. For instance, after a lengthy discussion over Eritrean coffee in Cairo in September 2024, we decided to walk along the banks of the Nile as a quiet act of defiance against the (im)mobilities imposed upon us. As we mingled and strolled beside the river, Rozina suddenly burst into tears, her voice breaking as she called for our attention: 'Look, look here! Even the ants move to make a home', she exclaimed, gesturing towards a line of ants, their tiny procession weaving life into the sands along the river's edge. Another participant, Wolde, responded softly: 'Back home, my family had a bee farm. We all know a bee cannot make honey unless it moves'. We all wondered how they never lost their way home. Perhaps it is because they move. For refugees who have lost their way home, movement becomes a modality of creating a home beyond any notions of geography or temporality. Like the ants and bees, whose movement allows them to make both home and sustenance, movement offers refugees the possibility of making home and belonging, even when that belonging means existing in a space of non-belonging created by the womb-abyss that is predicated upon their constitutive exclusion and death.

Movement as home-making is, in fact, a relationship of belonging that refuses to conform to a system designed to immobilise bodily existence and confine the body within realms of death. Movement as home-making resists the domestication of the body and its subjugation to structures of control and violence. It rejects territorially rooted identities and the confinement of belonging to the womb-abyss. Beyond spatial, temporal, and carceral constraints, movement enables bodily existence and opens possibilities for emergence and perpetual becoming-with. It creates lives that are liveable, places that are habitable, and relationships that are profound and meaningful. When the coordinates of here and there, now and then, and later are radically disrupted through movement, borders lose their grip and become porous. When the boundaries between us and them, self and Other, are softened with a measure of opacity, othering and (b)ordering transform from exclusionary forces to contemplative operatives.

Movement is essential to all these possibilities, enabling both survival and flourishing. In its various forms (physical, metaphysical, and sociopolitical), movement signifies the freedom to act against the refugee abyss, enabling us to express our desires and discover new ways of relating and becoming-with others. It allows us not only to navigate the world but also to confront its limits, constantly redefining what it means to be human. It is our mode of survival, home-making, and human relation. We cannot reduce its errantry and poetics to the limits of our own writing or understanding, nor can we fully grasp the refugees' resourcefulness, creativity, or their remarkable ability to move, build a home, and find joy, however precarious life may be. In Glissantian terms, the poetics of movement is an itinerancy of errantry, not exile. It allows us to meet the other and each other life to life, both in human place and human time, free from the masks imposed by the womb-abyss.

The face

The face represents a physical, metaphorical, and ethical dimension that mediates the relationship between the self and the Other. According to Levinas (2011), the face signifies a direct call to responsibility and embodies an irreducible ethical obligation. More than just a physical appearance, the face serves as a gateway between the self and the being before us, presenting itself as an ethical and ontological presence that establishes a fundamental intersubjective relation. Levinas consistently emphasises that the vulnerability and humanity conveyed by the face of the Other demand recognition and compel us to confront our ethical responsibilities to one another. This recognition challenges the self, disrupting its arrogance, individuality, and its objectifying gaze towards the Other. Levinas explains that the face interrupts the self's solitude, or the state of 'being at home with oneself' (2011, p. 39), and initiates an encounter with the Other, whose presence is inescapable, irreducible, and irreversible. In this ethical relation, which Levinas refers to as the '*face-to-face*' encounter (2011, p. 39, emphasis in original), the face appears as an 'order' that transcends all other orders and borders, including those of the responder. Within this non-linguistic framework of signification and responsibility, Levinas (1985, p. 89) writes:

> The first word of the face is the "Thou shalt not kill." It is an order. There is a commandment in the appearance of the face, as if a master spoke to me. However, at the same time, the face of the Other is destitute; it is the poor for whom I can do all and to whom I owe all. And me, whoever I may be, but as a "first person," I am he who finds the resources to respond to the call.

The face, with its dual gaze of simultaneously appearing as an order and signifying defenceless frailty, reveals a dimension of ethical relation that precedes both ontology and epistemology. In fact, the ethical and moral significance of the face-to-face encounter constitutes the 'first philosophy' (Levinas, 2011, p. 304). The face, as an ethical relation, invokes two inseparable dimensions: first, the relation between the self and its ethical obligation towards the Other; and second, the relation between the self and the Other, mediated by the significance of the face. These relations suggest that the face of the Other must haunt us not only with its defencelessness and vulnerability but also through its demand for responsibility and the burden of obligation it places upon us. The self must fulfil its ethical responsibility not only to the defencelessness and vulnerability of the face but, most importantly, to the call of responsibility placed upon it by the face of the Other.

Levinas' ethical propositions are, of course, deeply hopeful. They suggest that the ethical command of the face—not to kill—will always be upheld, or at least must be upheld. Yet, in reality, the face has often failed to uphold anything in countless contexts. Clearly, the face has lost both itself and its ethical power in the abyss of slavery, colonialism, and forced displacement. As Fanon (1986) reminds us, in the colonial imagination, the face of the Other must wear a mask, always appearing as a black skin beneath a white mask. In effect, the faces of the enslaved, colonised, and displaced are reduced to mere (sur)faces. 'What began on the surface', Mbembe (2017) writes, 'became stratified, transformed into a framework and over time a *calcified shell*—a second ontology—and a canker, a living wound that eats at, devours, and destroys its victim' (p. 39, emphasis in original). According to Mbembe, a face reduced to a surface, or one hidden behind a mask, signifies an existence bound to an imaginary ontology, which dissociates itself from reality and reason the moment it appears. This image ontology, Mbembe (2001) writes, 'is sustained by an imaginary—that is, an interrelated set of signs that present themselves, in every instance, as an indisputable and undisputed meaning' (p. 175). Viewed through this imaginary, the face is relegated to a mere surface, stripped of the ethical obligation Levinas claims. If anything, it invites violence through its defenceless facelessness, unreality, and unreason.

Moreover, in today's world, beyond its symbolic and figurative appearance, the (sur)face has increasingly become a site of ethical, socio-cultural, and juridico-political scrutiny by the womb-abyss and its institutions of governmentality and sovereignty. As argued, the womb-abyss holds a monopoly on legitimate violence and engages with the face (especially that of the Other) in a perpetual relation of violence. This is why the faces of racialised Others (i.e., Black people and other people of colour, including displaced people) can only appear as (sur)faces within the colonial and necropolitical world order in which we live. If such faces have been historically disfigured, they are now refigured into a relation of ongoing violence, necessary for preserving the nation-state's monopoly over legitimate power (Da Silva, 2014). As such, the faces of racialised Others, including displaced people, have always been positioned as the darkest foundation of the violence of sovereignty, or, as Mbembe (2017, p. 72) puts it, the 'nocturnal face' of the womb-abyss. In any case, as demonstrated by the example of Eritrea, the womb-abyss is not bound by the ethical demands of the face of the Other or the citizen; rather, it is primarily founded on securing its own continued survival through its monopoly on power and legitimate violence. Even the citizen it claims to protect is so powerless that it cannot escape this relationship of violence and may only die in service to it, as seen in wars.

That said, however, there is a paradoxical resistance hidden in the encounter with the surface or masked faces. If the self only perceives a surface on the Other, the face of the Other remains beyond the grasp of the self. The face of the Other unveils itself as what we might call the untamed face beneath the surface. The untamed face is one whose guiding principles are opacity and emergence, in the Glissantian sense of the terms. It is a face whose truth lies beyond the fleeting transparency and distorted imagery of the womb-abyss and its racialised gaze. The untamed face defies any simplistic notion of transparency or articulation; it cannot be fully understood without confronting the unease of its opacity. It may bear scars and remain silent, yet such a face speaks of radical opacity, stripping away the violent gaze of the self or responder. The untamed face, in its quiet inaudibility and unknowability, invites us to listen with a different kind of understanding, recognising the intelligibility in what lies hidden and the knowledge in what remains unsaid.

Through endless struggles for decoloniality, often concealed in opacity and hidden within underground spaces, the masked face seeks to clear a path for decolonial possibility, not through simple exposure or defencelessness, but through its opacity and unknowability. At least in poetic vision, the untamed face emerges in opacity from the undergrounds and underbellies, mocking the facelessness and racial distortions cast by the womb-abyss. It challenges the individuality of the self, which carries the weight of the disfigurement and vulnerability reflected in the face of the Other. The mask may veil the face, blurring the lines between reality and appearance. Yet, as Mbembe (2017) writes, 'if being and appearance combine in the mask, it is true as well that, because of the impossibility of seeing the face hidden by the mask, of peering through the miniscule gap, the mask always denounces itself as a mask' (p. 51). In this denunciation of the mask, the person beneath it gazes outward from beneath the surface, neither fully seen nor entirely unseen, quietly asserting the right to opacity. Thus, Mbembe (2017) declares: 'The face of the mask doubles as the face of the flesh and transforms itself into a living, figurative surface' (p. 133). Through this doubling of the (sur)face, the body of the Other is 'always on the verge of exceeding the real' (Mbembe, 2017, p. 134).

As such, the untamed face, through its opacity and unknowability, challenges the colonial logics of knowledge and contests the power of the womb-abyss to inscribe the face within its own measures of intelligibility, transparency, and docility. On the one hand, the disfigurement of the refugee creates an abyss; yet on the other, it rebukes this very abyss by speaking in a displaced voice and asserting the right to opacity in the face of adversity. Despite its defencelessness, its nakedness, and its raw exposure, the untamed face, to borrow from Levinas (1985, p. 87), 'renders possible and begins all discourse'. This discourse is underpinned by a displaced voice, emanating from the act of living and moving through the abyss, and from the ruderal spaces that allow it to gaze towards the distant possibility of an irreducible relation that binds us to one another. Having journeyed through darkness and the nocturnal days, the untamed face learns to see in the dark, to navigate it, and to guide us towards a new light. When Fanon repeatedly writes 'look' in *Black Skin, White Masks*, for instance, it is a direct plea for a gaze that turns towards the face of the pained yet living body as a source of relation—or, in Fanon's (1986) case, a 'new humanism' (p. 1). In this way, the untamed face shifts the foundations of relations, from one of violence to one that destitutes violence and proclaims the emergence of human relation beyond it.

In essence, the untamed face is the transcendental face of the human. It emerges beyond the reach of the racialised gaze and the violence of unreality and unreason mediated by the womb-abyss. In the face of the refugee abyss, it remains our ineffable and inviolable face, always shrouded in opacity. After dribbling past the fences and dangers in our path, when we finally reach a place of relative safety from the borders of space, time, and flesh, we erupt into noisy clapping, drumming, singing, and dancing as signs of life and joy. We also mourn our friends, offering prayers whispered softly, and performing rituals of grief, where every gesture is a song of endless mourning. There, in the ruderal spaces, our untamed faces may appear with a measure of opacity, compelling the womb-abyss and its citizen subjects to confront their own limitations in encountering the Other, flesh to flesh, face to face. This may force them to acknowledge the fallibility of their knowledge of the Other and the falsity of their assumptions about the Other's experience. The self, whose knowledge and existence are premised on transparency, is confronted by the power of unknowability and the opacity of the face of the Other. In doing so, the untamed face invokes what Glissant (2009) calls the 'mockery of the image' (p. 205). Both the distorted image and the violence of the imaging are playfully reduced to poetic expressions, with all their contemplative and destituent potential. Seen from this perspective, the untamed face opens the possibility for a new relation by weaving a new ethical and political imaginary. When condemned to each other's exposure, untamed faces offer the possibility for a poetics of refuge to take root in a rhizomatic weave.

If one conducts the same analysis of the untamed face on the body, one arrives at a similar conclusion: the self that sees nobody in the Other's body is both incapable of grasping the humanity of that body and unable to constitute a human body itself. It has confined itself to a relationship with objects and surfaces; it has become a mere human-object. In denying the bodily existence and face of the Other, it forfeits its own humanity, trapped in an unyielding cycle of objectification, racialisation, unreality, and unreason. Only by recognising the untamed life of the Other can the self discover its own capacity and opacity for authentic existence and relation. We return to this point in the conclusion of the book.

Memory

Memory, as understood here, is a poetic trace woven from the names, symbols, and experiences of refugees, preserved in the world's archives and deeply embedded within the refugee experience itself. It cradles the pain endured and the joys cherished, the traces left behind and those carried forward. These fragments are assembled from scattered evidence: exhumed bodies, unmarked graves, unattended cries, untold stories, fleeting encounters, and fragile relationships—from moments of disconnection, separation, and the rare gift of reunion. Memory lingers in the remnants of its own abyss, stretching across places and non-places, through times both remembered and judicially marked. At its core, memory is the archive of life and death, entwined with the rituals and poetics that breathe through both.

Within the abyss of memory, some archives are partial and provisional, others incomplete. Some are empirical, others theoretical or contemplative. Some endure, while others have been erased beyond recall, as this book illustrates. It is for this reason that we have sought, through these pages, to name what has been rendered nameless and to recount what has been displaced. We have endeavoured to gather fragments of memory from the scattered evidence. A sacred wish, shared by many friends and strangers—and our solemn promise to them—was this: those who perished had names given to them at birth, and we must never allow them to be reduced to mere numbers. As an act of naming the unnamed, each of us, each participant, offered the name of a friend, a stranger encountered on their journeys, or individuals who, at the time of writing, remained trapped in the bellies of the refugee abyss. We tell their stories so that they are remembered, their sufferings acknowledged, and their poetics clear a path towards dignified existence.

Some had already succumbed to the cruelty of the refugee abyss, including those who perished in sea-camp. Although their cries may have gone unheard, their pain unattended, and their silence unbroken, the names and memories of the missing remain cherished by their fellow refugees, loved ones, and communities. In many Eritrean homes, including those in the diaspora, images and objects belonging to missing loved ones are prominently displayed. Moreover, as seen in the stories of Ariam, Alex, Fares, and many others, there is a deep determination to retell and remember the lives of those lost to the abyss. The images hanging on walls, tucked into wallets, or preserved in photo albums, along with treasured objects, are tangible reminders of their (de)existence. For the families and communities of the missing, preserving these traces is an act of defiance against forgetfulness, lack of accountability, and disregard for the disappeared.

We named these missing friends and strangers and shared their open wounds, scars, and fragility as poetic traces, whose imaginings gesture towards a world beyond the borders, camps, and metropoles of our time. In reading our poetics, you have encountered names such as Haben, symbolising pride and hope; Héluf, representing those who departed; Hassen, signifying a better future; Hiwet, meaning life; Wolde, meaning birth; and others. These names were deliberately chosen not only to liberate the participants from the reductive numbers and letters often employed in migration scholarship under the guise of confidentiality and methodological rigour but also to activate and honour their 'fugitive memories' (Glissant, 2009, p. 7) and unrestrained acts of resistance. In the same vein, our effort to transform our witnessings and stories into poetic form—without altering their meanings—seeks to articulate the untold and challenge the dominant narratives that reduce such voices to mere headlines of vulnerability, threat, or disposability. In doing so, we free our poetic traces to emerge as archives capable of imagining, writing, and creating.

The memories of refugees, along with those preserved about them, are poetic traces through which their displaced voices reach a world beyond the womb-abyss. As we have argued, the humanity of refugees and their displaced voices represent poetic traces that remain unintelligible within the existing juridico-political framework of the womb-abyss. Agamben (2000) reminds us that a 'stable statute for the human in itself is inconceivable in the law of the nation-state' (p. 19). He explains that the treatment of refugees, whose status is consistently regarded as a 'temporary condition' requiring either 'naturalization' or 'repatriation', provides the clearest evidence for the absence of an 'autonomous space' within the juridico-political structure of the nation-state for the idea of 'the pure human in itself' (Agamben, 2000, p. 19). Agamben warns that assimilation into the violence of the nation-state may result in a condition even worse than the refugee abyss, as it reinforces the structures of governmentality and sovereignty responsible for both the violent origin of the womb-abyss and the refugee abyss.

Since violence is a necessary condition for the foundation of the womb-abyss, destitution, or what Agamben refers to as the 'inoperativity' of this violent structure, is a precondition for the emergence of a new politics and ethics of life, being, and knowing. 'Inoperativity', Agamben (2014, p. 69) writes, 'must not be understood as the cessation of all activity, but as an activity that consists in making human works and productions inoperative, opening them to a new possible use'. The purpose of this inoperative activity is to expose and dismantle the violence of the womb-abyss and its matrices of coloniality through what Agamben calls 'destituent power', which is 'a force that, in its very constitution, deactivates the governmental machine' (Agamben, 2014, p. 65). Agamben asserts that 'Only a power that is made inoperative and deposed is completely neutralized' (2014, p. 71). Our individual and collective experiences converge to resist the workings of the womb-abyss and its violent foundations. We have affirmed that our practices of remembering, storytelling, commemoration, language, music, and art have never succumbed to the structures of the womb-abyss. Our struggles for survival, our efforts to heal open wounds, transform scars, shed masks, care for one another, move forward, and create the conditions for survival and flourishing have endured. The tears we shed, the wounds we bear, the silence we observe with dignity, and the joys we celebrate all testify to our resourcefulness, resilience, and capacity to thrive—qualities that have often been denied to us.

These activities refuse to submit to the womb-abyss, resisting transparency, measurability, and predictability. Through their opacity, they exist beyond the grasp and articulation of the womb-abyss and its systems of knowledge and power. They are our archives, remaining inoperable, unintelligible, and inaccessible to systems that prioritise structure, knowledge, and transparency over unpredictability and obscurity. In the face of the abyss, which seeks to articulate our worst nightmares and dehumanise us, our fugitive memories preserve and transmit our displaced voices, keeping our stories and humanity alive. Through these memories, we assert our presence, dignity, and the traces of having once lived in this world, even when the womb-abyss refuses to recognise us as fully human. This preservation, whether through oral traditions, photographs, objects, or written stories, becomes an act of defiance against the sovereign power whose function is to control, define, erase, and contain our poetics.

Moreover, memories enable cultural, familial, and communal bonds and rituals to persist, even after our loved ones have passed away. This is what Sada's indomitable memory teaches us: although his brother, Farés, is no longer alive, the family remains determined to search for any traces of him. What does it mean to wait for a loved one lost in the abyss, seemingly gone forever? For Farés' family, the line between the known and the unknown has dissolved into an indistinguishable opacity marked by memory and the silence of absence. For them, memory evokes a profound void, marked by the lack of knowledge, the absence of bodily existence—if any—and the inability to communicate. The family struggles to begin rituals of mourning or preserve hope, as these remain fleeting memories with no clear starting or ending point. Mourning becomes a perpetual wound, while hope diminishes in the face of an uncertain and unknowable future. The only way for both mourning and hope to reach resolution is through the return of Farés' remains, if he has indeed died. This act would confirm his death and allow for burial alongside his umbilical cord, completing the rituals of death and anchoring their memory. Until then, the family remains stuck in the abyss of memory.

For the families of the missing, all that remains are their loved ones' names and fragments of memories that have always been both present and absent. When people flee, they often leave behind traces of their physical selves, such as umbilical cords buried in their homeland, alongside traces of their identities such as names, stories, and other memories. They also leave behind loved ones, material possessions, memories, letters, writings, and more. More often than not, they leave behind personal and family images and objects, symbols of their shared existence. All these traces contribute to reassembling an archive through which displaced people find themselves remembered and can remember. The essence of their (de)existence persists within their families and communities through the traces that remain. Both their presence and absence are felt, mourned, and expressed. As Agamben (1999) reminds us, memory reopens 'the past, making what happened incomplete and completing what never was' (p. 267). It is not simply what occurred or what did not, but 'their potentialization, their becoming possible once again' (Agamben, 1999, p. 267).

For us, memory enables us and our families to express our shared experiences and reassemble traces of care, family life, and an irreducible desire for freedom. Like Farés' family, many of us, in our conversations, reflected on countless losses, with memories still burdened by unfound remains, unmarked graves, and unspoken sorrow. In the silence of absence, and in the quiet moments when flashbacks arise, the loss of friends and strangers, along with the enduring pain of that loss, lingers beyond the boundaries of time and endurance. With every breath, we remember lives consumed by relentless pain, grief, and loss; their cries for help haunt our fading fugitive memories. At the site of their ruins, we have witnessed the exhumation and disposal of the remains of both friends and strangers, cast into the unknown while their families endure unending grief, hoping to find their loved ones and lay them to rest in their own graveyards. We regularly receive inquiries from families seeking to trace the whereabouts of their loved ones, as one mother recently lamented:

> I have one dream in life
> before I pass away:
> to find the remains of my son
> and bury him next to his father,
> who died in a war, and his sister,
> who was killed trying to cross the border.

Our families wait in silence, their hope dissolved into despair, their hearts filled with impossible longing, their lives wounded and laid bare. In dreams, they roam through shadows of darkness and distance, but dawn reveals the harsh reality: their loved ones have perished in the abyss. Far from our families and communities, we stand still in the silence of absence, bearing witness to the truth that our friends and loved ones are lost forever. The world moves on around us, yet we feel these existential wounds tearing at our being. This tearing, as Fanon (1986) so eloquently describes, is 'an amputation, an excision, a haemorrhage that spattered [the] whole body' (p. 85). And yet, we continue to breathe, to move, and to hold on to their memories, carrying them forward in a world incapable of feeling the weight we bear. The reworking of these memories' potential, while respecting their opacities, creates opportunities to forge new relations, relate to new beings, and imagine new possibilities for becoming-with and (un)knowing.

The stillness of fugitive memories suggests that absence is not merely a void but something that carries its own weight and significance. The silence created by such profound loss is often louder and more impactful than the presence of something tangible or audible, such as a marked grave or the performance of mourning rituals. Our memories refuse to surrender to forgetting, letting go, or moving on; they linger beyond the bounds of time and space. Beyond the confines of linearity and historicity, as Mbembe reminds us, time is experienced '*as lived*, not synchronically or diachronically, but in its multiplicity and simultaneities, its presence and absences, beyond the lazy categories of permanence and change beloved of so many historians' (2001, p. 8, emphasis in original). He argues that 'subjectivity itself' is constituted 'as temporality...by a set of material practices, signs, figures, superstitions, images, and fictions that, because they are available to individuals' imagination and intelligence and actually experienced', forming 'life worlds' against necropolitical existence (Mbembe, 2001, p. 15). In the ruderal spaces, time and place are experienced as memories, or as remembered. Our life worlds are sedimented into memory, resisting the complete erasure of the lives we have lost. For the missing, the memory of their vicarious (de)existence transcends both life and death. This memory becomes inseparable from the subjective experiences of their families. Their memories take on a poetic, displaced voice, whose opacity renders it inappropriable by temporal and spatial metrics.

Finally, the praxes of reworking these memories involves shedding masks, opening cracks, inhabiting ruderal spaces, healing lacerations, and more. The emergence of displaced voices from the traces and memories of our conditions of (de)existence and (de)humanity creates poetic spaces for reflection, thought, and potential change. These spaces become sites of inoperativity and resistance to the matrices of coloniality and the womb-abyss. As argued, our memory archives cannot be appropriated by the existing body politic; they are untamed voices whose unpredictability, opacity, and unrestrained nature disrupt the security, transparency, and integrity of colonial systems. Engaging with memory as a displaced voice invites us to pause and reflect in a state of inactivity, allowing us to explore what remains inoperable within current structures of power, being, and knowledge, without the pressure to actualise or assimilate into them. This form of reassembling memory challenges us to reconsider what it means to live fully and freely, beyond the womb-abyss that seeks to tame, control, and dominate us. We reiterate: memory is an abyss, untamable and impervious to the whims of the womb-abyss.

Towards acentric relationality

The purpose of tracing our displaced voices through the poetics of the body, movement, face, and memory is not merely to critique the structures of raciality and coloniality that underpin the womb-abyss and the experience of the Other. Critique often produces answers that confine us within the framework of coloniality, whereas questioning opens up new possibilities, even if only through writing. Our aim is to fundamentally question the scholarly practices of seeking answers within the confines of colonial logic and to move beyond them. At the heart of recounting our open wounds lies a praxis of radical questioning (Chapter 1). Through such questioning, as Anzaldúa (2012) reminds us, we create a world through thinking and writing that compensates for the colonial world, which fails to offer us a home. Mbembe (2017) reminds us that 'Thinking through what must come will of necessity be a thinking through of life, of the reserves of life, of what must escape sacrifice' (p. 179). The kind of thinking Mbembe calls for is '*a thinking in circulation, a thinking of crossings, a world-thinking*' (2017, p. 179, emphasis in original). This kind of thinking invites world-writing and world-building, born out of necessity and grounded in the depth of relationality and the appeal for Relation.

The process of world-writing and world-building begins with imagining acentric relationality. In spatial terms, acentric relationality is not about redistributing centres or transforming peripheries into new centres; it is not concerned with centring, recentring, or decentring, or any concept of centres at all. Poetically, acentric relationality calls for dissolving the womb-abyss, along with its death worlds and metropoles, into a relational world without fixed centres, but with perpetually evolving traces and relations. As Mbembe (2001) articulates:

> What a certain rationality, claiming to be universal but in reality mired in the contingent and the particular, has never understood is that all human societies participate in a *complex* order, rich in unexpected turns, meanders, and changes of course, without this implying their necessary abolition in an absence of center.
>
> (p. 8, emphasis in original)

Against the fixity of order and rationality, acentric relationality invites us to dissolve centres, whether metaphysical, physical, spatio-temporal, or otherwise, into irreducible and continuously evolving threads of relations.

In essence, acentric relationality represents a relationship of transcendence. From Fanon, we learn that this relationship is 'haunted by the problems of love and understanding', or what he describes as 'aberrations of affect' towards racialised people (1986, p. 2). For a relation of transcendence to take root, the racialised Other must be freed from the logic of raciality and coloniality that underpins these 'aberrations of affect'.

Acentric relationality embodies this transcendental relation of interwoven possibilities, where each thread carries the weight of history and the promise of renewal. Metaphysically, this implies that relation precedes ontology and that the unknown underpins relation. In other words, the foundation of knowledge begins with the unknown. For knowledge to remain a perpetual possibility, the unknown must exist. The unknown is a beginning without an end, a web of contingencies, potentialities, and possibilities. Knowing is a relational process characterised by perpetual encounter, convergence, and the emergence of the known in interaction with the unknown. Without the unknown, knowing cannot occur; without knowing, there can be no knowledge. For knowing to be possible, there must be an ongoing relationship with the unknown. In this way, the unknown precedes both knowing (epistemology) and knowledge (ontology). Relation comes before ontology, preceding both knowing and knowledge, as Glissant (2009) argues.

At the structural and systemic level, acentric relationality resists the social and political structures rooted in violence, alongside other associated frameworks of rights and the grammars of raciality and coloniality. It rejects the emptiness and violence inherent in laws, rights, and the fictitious grammars of universal humanism. These structures and grammars must be challenged for their violent foundations and racially differentiated functions, reduced to potentiality, and 'contemplated as such in order to liberate the inoperativity that has remained imprisoned in them' (Agamben, 2015, p. 278). As Agamben demonstrates, this strategy of deactivating and reducing the violence of the womb-abyss, along with its violent powers and laws, to a 'destituent potential' is a necessary precondition 'in order to allow a different use of them' (2015, p. 273). This demands a radical reimagining and envisioning of new relational forms of governance aimed at dismantling the violent power structures upon which the womb-abyss is built. The lessons from both past and present abysses reveal that human dignity requires a new anchor, one that can only be attained through a fresh foundation for human relations, grounded in the rhizomatic roots and the thought of Relation. Through this strategy, the womb-abyss can be transformed into a suspended and inoperable topia and telos for the politics to come.

Politically, acentric relationality can be understood as an exercise in what might be called a politics of abnegation. This politics begins with a conscious suspension of the violence of the womb-abyss and its institutions. As Gordon (2018) explains, it necessitates 'a teleological suspension' of the political, the ethical, and the disciplines associated with them. When politics is reduced to necropolitics and ethics to 'necroethics' (Schaffer, 2020), the only course of action is to suspend both without hesitation and delay. 'One must act', Gordon insists, 'on the basis of what one cannot know' (2018, p. 12). Such a politics requires envisioning a world free from rooted identities, monolingualism, and rigid particularities. Acentric relationality seeks to release human beings and communities, along with other beings, things, and entities, into what Glissant (2020) describes as the 'Whole-World'. The Whole-World is where life is lived without determination, without inscription into the whims of power, and without affiliations to necropolitics. Building and inhabiting this Whole-World is not about seeking identity or establishing membership. Instead, it is about engaging in the exchange of finding and sharing, giving and receiving, within relationships of mutuality, interculturality, and multilinguality. It is about forming lives, voices, and communities that remain untameable to the violence of the womb-abyss and its necropolitical institutions and powers.

At a communal level, acentric relationality is a metaphor for radically open, fertile, and non-exclusive modes of life, knowing, and relating, focused on communal growth, sharing, and mutuality. It envisions a communal praxis where life is understood as a relation, rather than being racially classified (with differential value placed on human beings), bordered (separating the included from the excluded), or annihilated (subjected to necropolitics).

Figure 6.5 Offering bread to a colleague as part of a welcome ritual at Mosob Bar and Restaurant in Glasgow. Photograph by Karen Gordon.

Figure 6.6 Offering coffee to a colleague seated in an open circle, celebrating the Eritrean coffee ceremony at Mosob Bar and Restaurant in Glasgow. Photograph by Karen Gordon.

This vision of communal life opens the possibility for a politics of abnegation through resignation, teleological suspension, and the emergent restoration of world-writing and world-building. It is worth noting that acentric relationality is not an appraisal of existing notions of integration. Rather, it insists on the radical exposure of unmasked human beings to one another in all their nakedness, without imposing any particular language or modes of being and knowing.

In practical terms, this involves, first and foremost, refusing to go to war, rejecting servitude, resisting stagnation in the womb-abyss, and, instead of creating conditions that compel the seeking of refuge, embracing togetherness and conjuring new possibilities with one another. It entails rejecting fixed identities such as nationalities, races, classes, or genders and, rather than perpetuating the conditions that differentiate us, focusing on relational forms of existence beyond the constraints of borders, genders, and classes. It calls for the rejection of hierarchies, choosing instead to engage with the world without domination or subordination. It entails the freedom to express oneself in a language of one's choice, embracing all their composite identities, multilingualism, and interculturalities. In these poetics of relation, we find not only freedom but the birth of the Whole-World, where every voice, unbound and unafraid, sings the song of our shared human and nonhuman multiplicities.

Poetics of acentric relationality also demand that we no longer judge one another by our relation, or lack thereof, to the sheer insanity of past abysses. Nor can we ignore the centuries of suffering, for their open wounds and scars remain fresh in our bodies and the realities we inhabit. As Arendt (2017) reminds us, the past is not merely 'heritage', or 'a dead load which by itself time will bury in oblivion' (p. xi). Since the past is a colonial wound that still 'bleeds' (Anzaldúa, 2012, p. 25), this wound is what we live today and what the womb-abyss seeks to project into the future. This bleeding must be stopped, the wound healed, and its continuity suspended, both practically and theologically. Interrupting, healing, and restoration involve resigning from the reproduction or maintenance of systems of wounding and, instead of sustaining them, enabling poetic freedoms that transcend colonial projections of the open wounds and scars. It includes refusing simplistic binaries of right and wrong, and, rather than perpetuating them in public discourse or written works, fostering communal relations grounded in mutuality, radical openness, and a shared acknowledgment of vulnerability. It encourages living, knowing, and acting not for specific political ideals or moral attributes, but practising relationality as a way of life founded in Relation, care, and shared existence.

Finally, the being cultivated through these poetics, dispositions, and guiding beliefs of acentric relationality is, as Agamben eloquently pronounces, 'whatever being' (2007, p. 19). Agamben further explains that 'the manner in which [this whatever being] passes from the common to the proper and from the proper to the common is called usage—or rather, ethos' (2007, p. 19). This embodied praxis of world-writing and world-building fosters becoming-with caring and sharing commons beyond war and peace, where life is lived as it unfolds. In the flow of becoming-with, whatever beings live radically exposed to one another, where every poetic trace contributes to the creation of the Whole-World that is shared, nurtured, and endlessly in the process of becoming. Here, the Whole-World is not an entity or 'raw material' to be owned (Mbembe, 2019b, p. 79), but a flow to be honoured and inhabited in its fullness. In this flow, we can find a life unburdened by the ownership and dominion of the womb-abyss, woven together in a collective ethos of care and mutual growth.

Conclusion

Let us conclude the chapter with a few reiterations that resonate throughout the book. We have consistently demonstrated the vulgarity and lewdness of the racialisation and coloniality through which the womb-abyss strives to annex our bodily existence, our faces, movements, memories, and realities, subjecting them to its spectacle of (b)ordering and the matrices of coloniality and raciality. Historically, the enclosure within the appearance of a mask has led to a condition where the enslaved, the colonised, and the displaced alike find themselves 'prostrate in a postulate of unreality' (Mbembe, 2001, p. 178). This forced entanglement with unreality is also an entanglement with inhumanity and its enduring violence, as reflected in the refugee abyss. For the womb-abyss, the refugee is a newly formed racial and juridico-political category onto which it can impose what Mbembe (2001, p. 178) describes as the 'pre-ordained madness' necessary for its existence and assertion of its sovereignty. The refugee abyss is a madness in which refugees are physically and epistemically confined within a realm of thinghood and animistic savagery, from which they strive to break free. The womb-abyss and its fictitious project of humanism are entangled in a relationship with this madness and the violence it breeds through time, space, and unreason.

Alongside exposing the violence and madness of the refugee abyss, we have summoned 'whatever beings', including the displaced, to come together in spaces of relation, ruderal existence, and unpredictability. We find ourselves in urgent times, caught in intensified interactions and encounters that lead to forced displacement, genocidal wars, and their catastrophic consequences. Faced with this reality, we have offered provisional gestures that we believe can guide us away from the violence of the womb-abyss and its institutions of law and rationality. The abyss imposed upon us, with its immense depths, painful ordeals, and poetic traces, remains elusive and difficult to comprehend as a foundation for reimagining and rebuilding the world. It is neither transparent nor readily grasped. Yet, as we have demonstrated, we cannot abandon the effort to reflect upon or move towards a poetics of relation. If there is key lesson to draw from our experience of the refugee abyss, it is, as Mbembe (2017) writes, 'the idea that in every human subject there is something indomitable and fundamentally intangible that no domination—no matter what form it takes—can eliminate, contain, or suppress, at least not completely suppress' (p. 170).

Emerging from this untamed existence, we have briefly explored how the body, movement, face, and memory allow us to express our displacement, name ourselves, share our stories, and sustain a sense of calm and vitality. Our poetic traces are interwoven into a thread of relationships that resist reduction to any systematic or transparent framework defined by the coordinates of time, space, and language. The true purpose of poetic tracing is not to create a fleeting and masked encounter, as often occurs in the project of integration, but to honour the irreducible entanglement of life's limits and fragilities without imposing any particular desires. Integration finds its meaning only when it embodies the perpetual process of becoming-with 'whatever beings', embracing their differences and irreducible rhizomatic relations. Without difference, relation itself becomes unimaginable, as Glissant (2020, p. 64) so eloquently explains:

> Because if there are no differences, there is no relation. For instance a people that has been assimilated into another people cannot participate in a world-wide relation. For it to do so, it has to put up a resistance. But if it puts up this resistance by being closed in on itself, and this is the crucial point, then it is doing the same thing, neither more nor less, than its oppressor. It does not enter into a world-wide relation.

This is why we offer our poetic traces and displaced voices as acts of resistance against the violence of the refugee abyss and the bestiality and (b)ordering it enforces. Following Glissant, we insist that true restoration and global relation can emerge only through the resistance of what he calls 'conjoined poetics' (2009, p. 17). We contend that the most pressing and vital action is to create the conditions for acentric relationality to arise as a crossroad of irreducible relations. Acentric relationality, as a concept, represents the process where the refugee abyss is destituted, enabling human communities to rebuild what Glissant describes as 'composite societies' (2009, p. 22). This is why we have cried, and continue to cry, our poetic cries born from our lacerated flesh, bone marrow, and tears of pain, love, and rage. This is both our demand and our shared principle, as we explore in the Conclusion.

References

Agamben, G. (1999) *Potentialities: Collected Essays in Philosophy*. Stanford, California: Stanford University Press.

Agamben, G. (2000) *Means Without End: Notes on Politics*. Minneapolis, Minnesota: University of Minnesota Press.

Agamben, G. (2007) *The Coming Community*. 6th printing. Minneapolis, Minnesota: University of Minnesota Press.

Agamben, G. (2014) What Is a Destituent Power? *Environment and Planning D: Society and Space*, 32 (1), 65–74.

Agamben, G. (2015) *The Use of Bodies*. Stanford, California: Stanford University Press.

Akomolafe, B. (2020) Coming Down to Earth • Writings – Bayo Akomolafe [online]. Available from: https://www.bayoakomolafe.net/post/coming-down-to-earth (accessed 1.9.25).

Anzaldúa, G. (2012) *Borderlands: la frontera: The New Mestiza*. 4th ed. San Francisco, California: Aunt Lute Books.

Arendt, H. (2017) *The Origins of Totalitarianism*. London: Penguin Classics.

Da Silva, D.F. (2014) *No-Bodies: Law, Raciality and Violence*. Belo Horizonte: Meritum, Revista de Direito da Universidade FUMEC.

Fanon, F. (1986) *Black Skin, White Masks*. London: Pluto Press.

Fanon, F. (2007) *A Dying Colonialism*. New York, New York: Grove Press.

Glissant, É. (2009) *Poetics of Relation*. Ann Arbor, Michigan: University of Michigan Press.

Glissant, É. (2020) *Introduction to a Poetics of Diversity*. Liverpool: Liverpool University Press.

Goldberg, D.T. (2018) 'The Reason of Unreason': Achille Mbembe and David Theo Goldberg in Conversation About *Critique of Black Reason. Theory, Culture & Society*, 35 (7–8), 205–227.

Gordon, L.R. (2018) Teleological Suspensions for the Sake of Political Life. *Social Alternatives*, 37 (4), 12–17.

Hirt, N. (2010) 'Dreams Don't Come True in Eritrea': Anomie and Family Disintegration Due to the Structural Militarization of Society. Working Paper No 119.

Levinas, E. (1985) *Ethics and Infinity*. 1st ed. Pittsburgh: Duquesne University Press.

Levinas, E. (2011) *Totality and Infinity: An Essay on Exteriority. 23rd Printing*. Pittsburgh: Duquesne University Press.

Maldonado-Torres, N. (2016) *Outline of Ten Theses on Coloniality and Decoloniality*. Paris: Frantz Fanon Foundation Paris.

Mbembe, A. (2001) *On the Postcolony*. Berkeley, California: University of California Press.

Mbembe, A. (2015) The Value of Africa's Aesthetics. *The Mail & Guardian*, 14 May. Available from: https://mg.co.za/article/2015-05-14-the-value-of-africas-aesthetics/ (accessed 20.7.22).

Mbembe, A. (2017) *Critique of Black Reason*. Durham, North Carolina: Duke University Press.

Mbembe, A. (2019a) Bodies as Borders. *From the European South*, 4, 5–18.

Mbembe, A. (2019b) *Necropolitics*. Durham, North Carolina: Duke University Press.

Oliver, K. (2017) *Carceral Humanitarianism: Logics of Refugee Detention*. Minneapolis, Minnesota: University of Minnesota Press.

Phipps, A. and Sitholé, T. (2018) *The Warriors Who Do Not Fight*. Glasgow: Wild Goose Publications.

Schaffer, S. (2020) 'Necroethics in the Time of COVID-19 and Black Lives Matter', in J.M. Ryan (Ed) *COVID-19: Global Pandemic, Societal Responses, Ideological Solutions*, pp. 43–53. London: Routledge.

Yohannes, H.T. (2024) 'Autobiographic Reflections on Loss, Longing, and Recovery', in M. Bosworth, K. Franko, M. Lee, and R. Mehta (Eds) *Handbook on Border Criminology*, pp. 311–327. Northampton: Edward Elgar Publishing.

Yohannes, H.T. and Phipps, A. (2024) 'What Does It Mean to Move? Joy and Resistance Through Cultural Work in South–South Migration', in H. Crawley and J.K. Teye (Eds) *The Palgrave Handbook of South–South Migration and Inequality*. Cham: Springer International Publishing, pp. 125–149.

Conclusion

Through an analysis of the refugee abyss, we have opened ourselves—our bodies, our thoughts, our struggles, our poetics, and our imaginaries—with two guiding principles: one a call for Relation, the other an invitation to resignation. Among a range of theoretical and practical perspectives, we have made small gestures towards exploring the potential for poetics of relation, of being-in-common, and of becoming-with. Let us now revisit some of these gestures in relation to these guiding principles.

First, our call for Relation

We call for Relation in the Glissantian sense, with all the depth and weight of the concept, to move beyond the open wounds and scars. For Glissant, Relation is a perpetually unfolding and evolving totality, without fixed boundaries, particular centres, or universal reason. Relation neither conforms to a fixed order nor dissolves into measurable chaos; rather, it is immeasurable and unimaginably vast, infinite in scope, and perpetually evolving through space, time, and reason. While Relation is our guiding principle, we focus on openness and opacity as mutual imperatives for the emergence of what we call untamed life. Before exploring openness and opacity, let us first briefly revisit the central theme of this book: the refugee abyss.

We have already established that the refugee abyss emerges from a precarious relationship between the Other and the womb-abyss. The Other, who in this case is the refugee, is cast by the womb-abyss into realms of violability, disposability, and chaos. Within the politics of the womb-abyss, the refugee is brought into being as, to borrow Mbembe's (2019) evocative description, 'a death that lives a human life', whose only relationship to power is 'risking one's life as a whole' (p. 69). The fundamental principle of this precarious relationship lies in constitutive exclusion and the destitution of all means of sustenance, including through the use of violent force. The states of constitutive exclusion and destitution employ violability and disposability as necessary conditions for the preservation of the womb-abyss, often at the expense of the Other. As a necropolitical condition, the refugee abyss is created and maintained through the spectacles of forced displacement generated by

DOI: 10.4324/9781003437192-8

global and local terror, underpinned by matrices of coloniality, and governed by the reification of racialised differentiation (for instance, through the labelling and categorising of migrants as refugees, citizens, and asylum seekers) and the fortification of regimes of (b)ordering (such as walls, borders, dungeons, divisive immigration laws, dehumanising asylum regimes, and hostile environments). The refugee's relationship with the womb-abyss is one of (de)existence, (de)humanisation, and necropolitical death.

Since the 'calculus of life perforce passes through the death of the Other, or that sovereignty consists of the will and the capacity to kill so as to live' (Mbembe, 2019, p. 72), the womb-abyss must ceaselessly generate violable and dispensable Others by any means necessary. It is crucial to note that the Other is not always an outsider, such as a refugee or stateless; it can also be the 'enemy'—or more precisely, the 'enemy of the state' or a 'traitor', as exemplified by the case of Eritrea. The enemy, whether insider or outsider, citizen or non-citizen, must be crushed at any cost, often to the detriment of the non-enemy, as seen in wars or other state-sanctioned violence, such as the use of police brutality. The womb-abyss deploys this relation of terror and destruction as its principal mode of sovereignty and governmentality, enforcing it by blurring the distinction between legitimate and illegitimate uses of violence with complete impunity, or, in the case of Eritrea, through the rule of no law and no rights.

In truth, no postcolonial state is immune to the rule of no law nor rights. Postcolonial states have become what Fanon (1963) not only foresaw but also sternly warned against: 'an empty shell, a crude and fragile travesty of what it might have been' (p. 147). This possibility—that the movements for independence might lead to a victory worse than defeat, or at the very least no less evil than defeat—is now a harsh reality in the postcolony. As we write this book, all of Eritrea's neighbouring countries are engulfed in their own bloody turmoil and wars. Sudan is ravaged by a brutal conflict between a powerful military faction and the national army, resulting in thousands of deaths, millions displaced, and the wanton destruction of lives and livelihoods. Only a few years into a fragile peace following a devastating war between federal and regional government forces, Ethiopia remains a battlefield for numerous internal ethnolinguistic conflicts over land, resources, and power. Somalia, too, endures as a fractured nation, with terrorist groups inflicting wounds, while the politics of separation and geopolitical tensions threaten to tear it apart. Over the Gulf of Aden, Yemen is repeatedly being destroyed and starved by a coalition of forces. Clearly, the origins, sources, and resources for these conflicts extend far beyond the region, driven by geopolitical clashes of interest, competition for resources, strategic posturing, and more.

Beyond the region, we are all too familiar with the stories of Iraq, Yemen, Syria, Myanmar, Afghanistan, and Libya, to name but a few. Reminiscent of the Cold War era, Ukraine is at the centre of geopolitical tension between the West and Russia, backed by its allies, resulting in significant costs to lives, livelihoods, and territory. One cannot overlook the ongoing genocidal war in the Middle East, primarily perpetrated by Israel and its Western allies against the Palestinians and now also against United Nations agencies. The vulgarity, bestiality, and wanton destruction caused by this war, livestreamed across televisions and media by its victims, devours life itself—even for those who bear witness (see Badwan and Phipps, 2024). The question of Palestine has exposed the terror, brutality, and destruction of life, not through the failure of the Western rights-based order, but through its enactment, deployment, and perpetuation by the very powers that created and sustain it. The project of human rights, when viewed from a perspective beyond its Western origins and context, has little to do with humanity and everything to do with violence. We shall elaborate no further, for our position is clear: this framework holds no relevance beyond its colonial grammar, lacks poetic depth, and its supposed humanism is merely a dead humanism, rooted in colonial violence—the womb-abyss. If we remain trapped within this paradigm, perpetuating its harm while bearing the open wounds and scars it has inflicted upon us, our thinking and poetics will distort reality and sustain the structures of coloniality.

The refugee abyss, with its open wounds and scars, arises from a confluence of these forces, sources, resources, and tensions. The belly of this abyss is the sites where wounds and scars are inflicted, experimented upon, and manifested on people seeking refuge as extra-territorial modes of sovereignty and governmentality. It is designed and deployed to reinforce both physical and metaphysical borders between the 'self' (the subject of rights, supposedly endowed with the power to distribute them through the apparatus of the womb-abyss and its laws and institutions) and the racialised Other, enforced through various necropolitical experiments of life and death. Creating and sustaining this relationship of 'enmity' and the perception of an external threat between the Other and the self is a fundamental function of the womb-abyss (Mbembe, 2019). The (b)ordering regimes of the womb-abyss govern the refugee by creating worlds of disposability and chaos, rendering them constitutively excluded on one hand while creating states of nominally protected citizenship on the other. The refugee abyss, as a condition of necessity, will persist until human beings are no longer required to establish a relation of exception within the matrix of the womb-abyss and until they free themselves from its dominion and its racialised, colonial gaze.

As shown in Chapter 6, the encounter between the 'self' (the citizen of the womb-abyss) and the racialised Other (consigned to realms of violability, disposability, and chaos) does not necessarily involve a meeting of human bodies or faces. Rather, it is an encounter manifest solely as unreality, with all its mirages and unreasonable reasons. Similarly, the relationship between the Other and the womb-abyss, along with its colonial mask, signifies a link to the colonial wound and the inhumanity that its unmasked vulgarity and bestiality inflict upon human relations. Mbembe explains this delirium through the figure of the 'Black man', stating: 'The Black man is the one (or the thing) that one sees when one sees nothing, when one understands nothing, and, above all, when one wishes to understand nothing' (2017, p. 2). As revealed by our displaced existence and voices, along with our open wounds and scars, the refugee abyss does not form human relations nor originate from human encounter. It is founded upon a relation of negation, whose limits and ultimate expressions are governed by the simultaneous production of thingness (mask or surface) and nothingness (a visage of unreality).

This superficial interaction between the Other and the womb-abyss neither grasps the humanity of the Other nor upholds any sense of responsibility for human relations in general. If the womb-abyss cannot recognise a human life as worthy of dignified existence in the Other, or perceives only a surface or a masked, disposable body, it is because the humanity of the Other remains either ungraspable or resistant to the violence of the womb-abyss. Through this opacity, despite the abyss, the Other renders itself untameable by the colonial logics of the womb-abyss and its institutions of law and rights-based order. While the womb-abyss may have confined the Other within a relationship of constitutive exception, it has never fully grasped the entirety of the Other's existence, nor annexed it within its coordinates of raciality and coloniality. If anything, much like the abyss of slavery and colonialism, this encounter with the Other allows the womb-abyss to wield power over, violate, and discard the Other at will, reinforcing its sovereignty and governmentality.

Likewise, if being human is intrinsically tied to human relations, then the concept of the citizen cannot claim to embody humanity or foster human relations if it can only encounter a mask or a surface in the faces and bodies of the Other, whose sole right is to exist as a 'useful thing' or to perish as a disposable threat. Such a notion of citizenship has locked itself to a relationship with thinghood—or, more accurately, with surfaces inhabited by violable and expendable bodies. It has collided with a calcified surface from which, as evidenced by the uninterrupted abyss spanning from slavery to colonialism and into the contemporary plight of refugees, it has failed to escape. A citizen socialised into a society that asserts the dominance of a particular race and seeks to derive its stability and security from maintaining this entrenched sense of racial pre-eminence, shaped and hardened by centuries of racialised violence and embedded in the structures and grammars of coloniality, inevitably becomes a body estranged from both its own humanity and its capacity for human relations with the humanity of the Other. If the varying degrees and values of mobility and nobility conferred by citizenship tell us anything, they reveal registers of racialised juridico-political pre-eminence that are perpetually mutating and spreading on a global scale. This is the crux of the matrix of the womb-abyss, giving birth to life and death, movement and immobility, nobility and inferiority within its belly.

This is why the Western concept of citizenship, rooted in the logic of state, territory, and nationality that forms the womb-abyss, cannot provide a viable foundation for supporting and sustaining human relations amidst the ruins and void perpetuated by the womb-abyss and its unchecked violence.

The West cannot position itself and its colonial matrices of power on a transcendental terrain, where it alone defines and imposes its vision of a rights-based order on the world and its humans and non-humans. The refugee abyss demonstrates that the Western universalist imposition is not only fundamentally exclusive of the West's Others but also generates such violence and vulnerability that it leaves no option to make life and reason possible other than its own eventual dissolution into acentric relationality with the rest of the world. The refugee, as a category subjected to (de)humanisation and (de) existence, starkly exposes the violence inherent in the womb-abyss and its vulnerability to the necessity of its own self-dissolution.

Untamed life, openness, and opacity

Confronted with this stark reality, we reaffirm and restore the Other and its humanity, shrouded in opacity, as a necessary principle for reimagining human relations and life itself: the untamed life. With untamed life, we propose a new conception of life as the transcendental placeholder for the poetics of relation, of being-in-common, and of becoming-with. The untamed life defies definition, eludes perception, and resists articulation, evading the grasp of raciality and coloniality, which seek to confine it within the realm of objecthood or surfaces. Beneath the visage of the Other lies the opacity of its humanity and dignity, while within the self, we demand that the seed of new thought and practice be inaugurated, emerging from the unfamiliar and the unpredictable, born of resignation and human relations. Untamed life must therefore be understood as an emergence or a break from the past and present abyss, necessitating a relation of being-in-common and becoming-with. Through the concept of acentric relationality, we have already introduced its 'fugitivity', the cracks and fissures where its emergence may take rhizomatic root, and the ruderal spaces of habitation and transformation, spaces of being-in-common and becoming-with (see Akomolafe, 2020).

Turning to the poetic demand for openness and opacity, we call for mutual recognition of each other's freedoms and existence as human beings and communities, intertwined in infinite relations of mutuality, co-existence, interculturality, and multilingualism, without imposing one's own desires. We offer openness and opacity as gestures to encounter one another—flesh to flesh, life to life, face to face—in the Fanonian sense of these terms: 'Why not the quite simple attempt to touch the other, to feel the other, to explain the other to myself?' (Fanon, 1986, p. 181). In this demand for openness and opacity, the Other constitutes the condition of possibility for sociality and relation. Raciality and coloniality aim to disrupt this foundational condition by severing the Other as the basis for sociality and relation, thereby undermining the demand for mutual recognition, openness, and opacity. Without the Other, there can be no sociality, no human relations, and no humane treatment. In our poetic forethought, we do not see an absolutely independent 'I', a self, or anything truly singular outside of language. In a relational world, the concept of an 'I' or self that signifies singularity is an illusion, for nothing is ever truly singular and independent. The 'I' or self cannot exist independently without the other—literally, biologically, and metaphysically. Both the 'I' and the self are constructs of language, names for the coordinates of traces of life and language intertwined within the totality of infinite relations.

Yet we find ourselves returning to the question that opened this book and which lingers in our thoughts: Does the world know we exist? In a world predicated on our death, how can we create life, or are we condemned to live death as our perpetual fate? Our sensibilities, instincts, and intellect reject this death-driven world, its modes of being, and its simplistic and racialised categorisation and (b)ordering of endlessly complex human communities and their activities. For this reason, we insist on abandoning the notion of a singular, territorially rooted, homogeneous identity in favour of embracing the complexity and interconnectedness of multiple, composite, and relational identities. We insist, as does Glissant—our principal interlocutor in this book—that 'identity is no longer completely within the root but also in Relation' (2009, p. 18). If no human being exists independently of Relation, and no human being constitutive of an absolute reason or meaning outside of Relation, then it is time to reject the singularity of being that has been deceptively imposed upon us. Instead, we must open ourselves and our sense of being to the multiplicity of beings that we, as humans, inherently are. For example, we are diverse physical beings within the material world of places and bodies, socially situated in a multitude of cultural and communal roles. Our past experiences, present actions, and future aspirations reflect the multiplicities of time. Mbembe's explanation is particularly insightful here, and it is worth quoting at length:

> How this is possible is, first, by being, literally, several in a single body.... In other words, the being that I am exists each time in several modes—or, let us say, several beings, which, although sometimes mutually exclusive, are nevertheless inside one another. To be several in the same body is not only to proceed to a constant enlargement of the limits of one's identity; it is, for the same unique being, to experience the possibility or actuality of several types of being, themselves taking shape and being revealed under several beings. This virtually constant passage from the single to the multiple must be performed in the very compartments of ordinary life, as circumstance and events occur.

Our ordinary lives may be filled with ordeals, but also with poetic traces and threads of relations. Our bodies may be wounded, scarred, or even killed; our faces disfigured and reduced to masks; our movements constrained; and our existence diminished. Yet our poetic traces of life remain intact through living, moving, remembering, and meeting face to face, flesh to flesh. Our ability to navigate the world, even when shadowed by death, demonstrates that we are both multiple in one and one in multiple, always intertwined in irreducible relations, including with our tormentors. Through our poetics, we have shown that we are not nameless faces, but humans with names, capable of naming ourselves, our conditions, our worlds, and our futures. We name ourselves each time we encounter a stranger or seek refuge in any society. Yet our outstretched hands, wounded bodies, and disfigured faces still wait in juridical time, in the realms of death, for the recognition of human relations and the responsibility that comes with it. We propose that this recognition and responsibility for human relations involves what Mbembe (2019) eloquently describes as a 'co-composition, of opening onto the over-there of another flesh, of reciprocity between multiple fleshes and their multiple names and places' (p. 28). Through our poetic forethoughts on acentric relationality and untamed life, we seek to inspire human relations where whatever beings encounter one another face-to-face, flesh to flesh. Confronted with our open wounds, scars, and relentless loss, we call for, as Fanon (1986) poetically demands, 'human behaviour' (p. 179).

Second, our invitation to resignation

We invite the reader to resign from the logics and structures of coloniality and raciality, and instead join whatever being in an open circle where we can collectively envision the poetics, politics, and ethics of life, knowledge, and shared existence—of emergence and becoming with. To begin with, the demand for human behaviour is also an invitation to confront loss, not with the false promise of overcoming it, but to reveal the openings and unpredictable possibilities it presents. From slavery to colonialism to forced displacement, human communities have endured countless catastrophic abysses: unprecedented human suffering, environmental devastation, and the rupture of relationships, both human and otherwise. World history, as Mbembe (2019, p. 34) aptly describes, is a chronicle of the 'squandering of human life', alongside the squandering of nature, culture, and foundational relationships.

Even today, within the belly of the refugee abyss, we are losing everything: our bodies, dreams, language, and innocence. We are indignified and forcibly torn from our homes, our communities, our countries. We are slaughtered without a second thought at borders and in brutal camps. Destitute in refugee camps, we languish in indefinite exile, our bodies left to decay in deserts and dungeons. We sink into the seabed's coldest depths or drift, discarded, upon the restless surface, with our remains mingling with the detritus of shattered vessels. No one distinguishes our bones from the wreckage; no creature of the deep and shallow sea-camp hesitates to devour our flesh. Salt scours away every wound; the tides leave no trace of our bodies behind. We are rendered the rubble of racialised humanity, adrift and persecuted in an unyielding womb-abyss. Our broken bodies and screams linger as the ruins and displaced voices of a crumbling world. We seek refuge covered in open wounds, scars, and weary bodies, only to be invited into deeper dehumanisation within systems built on our constitutive exclusion from politics and from life itself. Yet we do not surrender to these losses, nor do we seek to conquer them or remain perpetually bound by their immeasurable weight. Instead, we must learn from these multifaceted and complex ordeals, embracing the new possibilities that loss unveils. Mbembe highlights two types of losses: those that 'liberate' and those that are tied to 'necessity' (2019, p. 29). Central to our invitation is a plea to relinquish the necessity of loss.

The invitation to address losses in order to heal and seek emancipation requires descending into the belly of the refugee abyss, confronting its open wounds and scars, as well as the displaced voices, cracks, and fissures recounted in this book, to harness poetic traces through which we can forge threads of acentric relations. If we view the world from within the refugee abyss, we will understand that the nation-state itself has descended into a womb-abyss. Within this abyss, we can recognise that its existence and dissolution must be suspended in a teleological sense, with the aim of overcoming our present precarious reality and rewriting and rebuilding the world anew. We have insisted that the work of world-writing and world-building cannot rest on particularities, singularities, homogeneities, or notions of articulation and transparency. These have long caused harm to human relations by offering 'one world' while denying the existence of 'many actual and possible worlds' (Mbembe, 2019, p. 113). The conception of universal rights and the imposition of a rights-based order, which seeks to reduce the vastness of human experience into a singular, irreversible path towards hegemonic existence, is not only totalitarian in essence but also fundamentally and structurally colonial. This is what the boat, the camp, the desert, and the border—each representing abyssal calamities—remind us to move away from. The belly of the refugee abyss is our allegory to reimagine shared vulnerability and relation beyond mere humanitarian relief.

Moreover, we invite you, dear reader, to attend to our displaced voices. Our voices are not merely shouts or screams in the wilderness; they are poetics that penetrate through cracks and new openings, heralding the birth of a world yet to come. These voices are not expressions of hope, for hope often becomes a perpetual escape into a predictable and tameable future. Instead, displaced voices demand entry into an unknown future with new light, a new possibility is born from shared vulnerability and responsibility. They seek to overcome stunned muteness in the face of the abyss. For the displaced voice, unlike hope, the future is not a distant dream but a resource for present action. We call for shared participation in shaping the origin and terms of the future, with the understanding that the origin of the future no longer lies in the future. The origin of the future depends on what the past and present hold and project, with all their unpredictabilities, opacities, and becomings. It is time to assemble threads of traces, crossroads of becomings, and movements essential to the emergence, restoration, and reconstitution of liveable lives and habitable places.

Our final invitation is to affirm that no one, entity or construct, owns the world. The world must not be subjected to human greed, capitalist obsession with dominance, or the drive to delineate (b)orders and assign value. The world is inappropriable to our desires, but through naming it, 'humanity as a whole delegates itself in the world and receives from the world confirmation of its own being as well as its fragility' (Mbembe, 2017, p. 180). From this perspective, Mbembe reminds us that humanity is in 'debt': 'sharing the world' (2017, p. 181). This underlines the brute fact that separation remains the price we pay for this debt. Borders are erected and fortified across the world, guarded by walls, weapons, drones, and fracturing societies. These barriers splinter the shared traces of life, ensuring that no one may pass from here to there and no hand meets another in greeting. No human delights in nature's gifts without the stamp of permission from the powers that divide us. No journey is freely taken, no presence freely given, and no one comes together with the Other face to face. These are but a few of the labours of separation and (b)ordering. We owe the world a greater debt—a debt to heal this rift, to embrace the world as one, and to create in-commons shared by all: humans and non-humans, beings and things alike. If we repay our debt, the world owes us a habitable world and shared living.

In closing, we have cast our demands and extended invitations seeking the quiet solace of release from the burdens of necessity, the weight of responsibility, and the relentless call of obligation. These emerge, unbidden, from the very marrow of our existence, from the ethical summons that comes with speaking as beings of flesh and bone, bound in the struggle and grace of living in-common and becoming-with, confronted by the trembling spectres of the existential, the political, and the moral. As we tremble with the tremors of the world, like Glissant, we choose to remain with poetry in poetry and the boundless imaginings of the poetic: 'We know ourselves as part and as crowd, in an unknown that does not terrify. We cry our cry of poetry. Our boats are open, and we sail them for everyone' (Glissant, 2009, p. 9).

We offer our calls and gestures,
not in pursuit of compliance,
but as gentle gestures,
poetic murmurs of the Other,
shared humbly from a place of mutuality,
where each of us exists
as a poetic trace within
the vast weave of Relation.
Let them be received as ethical calls,
fragile yet resolute,
resonating with the open wounds
and scars of shared existence.

It is in the spirit of Relation, resignation, and emergence that we share our poetics, always hoping to find yours reaching back.

Our poetic cries appeal not for naturalisation in the womb-abyss,
but for the inspiration of Relation.
Our yearning seeks not nationalities and flags,
but a multiplicity of human relations.
Our longing is not for bordered territories,
but for ruderal crossroads where life unfolds resplendently.
Our vision of time does not intersect in linear juridical constructs,
but in the interweaving of multiple entanglements.
Our sacred intuition is not reason,
but the abundance of imagination.

We have rendered our displaced voices open, speaking not with the piercing clarity of certainty but with a deliberate opacity, through which light and shadow entwine. In this quiet unfolding, our wounded and scared bodies, lost and found, breathe together.

References

Akomolafe, B. (2020) Coming Down to Earth • Writings – Bayo Akomolafe [online]. https://www.bayoakomolafe.net/post/coming-down-to-earth (accessed 1.9.25).
Badwan, K. and Phipps, A. (2024) *Keep Telling Of Gaza*. Berlin: Sídhe Press.
Fanon, F. (1963) *The Wretched of the Earth*. New York, New York: Grove Press.
Fanon, F. (1986) *Black Skin, White Masks*. London: Pluto Press.
Glissant, É. (2009). *Poetics of Relation*. Ann Arbor, Michigan: University of Michigan Press.
Mbembe, A. (2017) *Critique of Black Reason*. Durham, North Carolina: Duke University Press.
Mbembe, A. (2019) *Necropolitics*. Durham, North Carolina: Duke University Press.

Index

Note: *Italics* indicates figures in the text and page numbers followed by "n" refer to end notes.

Aas, K. F. 130
abnegation 158, 160
acentric relationality 157–161
Agamben, G. 41–46, 51, 53–54, 62–64, 83, 88, 113, 153–155, 158, 161
Alex story 13–14, 99
Anderson, B. 53
Andom, N. G. 88
Anzaldúa, G. 43, 140, 157
Arendt, H. 28–31, 34, 46, 63–64, 79, 101, 124, 161
assignment process 69
asylum colonies 7, 115, 123, 130
asylum process 3, 20, *91*, 91–92, 116, 121–123, 126, 130

Behrman, S. 36
Bellinger, A. 143
Bernal, V. 79
Betts, A. 36
bio-power/productive power 54
bios (political life) 41
Black man 167–168
bodily existence 138–146, 148, 152, 154, 161
borderization 56
Border Security Command 118
Bourdieu, P. 12
Bozzini, D. 80
Brekke, J. -P. 115
British Military Administration (BMA) 59
Brochmann, G. 115
Butler, J. 101, 130; *Precarious Life* 57

Cairo 90–91, 100, 106, 109, 135, 147
Canning, V. 121, 126
carceral humanitarianism 36, 92, 97
carceral state 50, 62, 71, 82, 100
carceral system 56–57, 72, 79, 82
Carpenter, D., *Magna Carta* of 1215 27
Cartagena Declaration on Refugees (1984) 29
chaos 10, 37–38, 55, 73, 110, 140, 165, 167
childhood adultification 119
coloniality 4–6, 29, 37–40, 42–46, 50, 54–55, 81, 84, 118, 128–129, 136, 138, 141, 154, 156–158, 161, 167–169, 171
colonial sovereignty 52
commandement 51–52
Commissions of Inquiry (COI) 32, 71–72
Court of Appeal 120
creolization 21
Cusumano, E. 113

datafication 40
death of asylum 37
Declaration of the Rights of Man 29–33
Declaration of the Rights of Man and of the Citizen 28
decoloniality 136, 150
dehumanisation 8, 11, 23, 25, 32, 36–37, 42, 58, 78–79, 81, 84, 99, 107, 116–117, 120, 122, 135, 154, 166, 172
desert 2, 5, 7–8, 10, 16–18, 23–25, 69, 84, 92–97, 100–102, 108, 111, 129, 134, 139–140, 142, 171
destituent power 154
detention and deportation 97–99

double negation 7, 115
Dublin Regulation 19, 114–117, 120

Edler, I. A. 113
Édouard Glissant: One World in Relation 22
Egypt 18–19, 91–92, 97–98, 101, 105, 114
Eritrea 1–2, 58; colonial violence 58–59; detention and deportation 97–99; detention and forced disappearance 70–73; forced displacement 82–84; Gedli/the struggle 59–62; national service 64–70; refugee camp 85–88; rule of no law and no rights 62–64; state violence 62
Esmeir, S. 42
Ethiopia 11, 58–61, 63, 65, 70, 78, 85, 87, 90, 92, 114, 166
EURODAC system 116, 118

face 148–152
face-to-face encounter 148–149
Fanon, F.: *Black Skin, White Masks* 149, 151; and humanity 2; and human rights 44–45; new humanism 151; open door of every consciousness 141–142; *turn white or disappear* 52; *The Wretched of the Earth* 21, 84
Farés story 17–18, 111, 154–155
fish, sustenance for 21, 23, 116
forced displacement/forced migration 1–4, 10, 21–22, 28, 35, 42–43, 58, 70, 77–78, 81–84, 138, 149, 162, 165, 171
Foucault, M. 71; body and mind 80–81; carceral system 56–57, 72, 79, 82; *Discipline and Punish* 56; optimism 54

Gallant, Y. 32
Gaza Strip 32, 46, 114
Gedli/the struggle 59–62
Geneva Convention (1951) 28–29
gifas 65–66
Glissant, É. 4, 7–9, 40, 50, 139, 148, 150, 162–163, 165, 170, 173; mockery of the image 151; *Poetics of Relation* 1, 20–23, 134, 165–170; Whole-World 159; womb-abyss, features of 53
Goldberg, D. T. 146
Gordon, L. R. 158–159
governmentality 7, 50, 56–57, 62, 64, 100, 118, 150, 153, 166–168
Great Depression 34
Greece 112–113, 117
Grovogui, S. N. 32–33

Hartman, S. 21
Hatem story 18–19, 98–99
Hedru, D. 70
Hirt, N. 69, 79–80
Hizbawi Serawit/people's army 66
Home Office 119–122, 126–127
human dignity 1, 22, 24, 42, 110, 158
humanitarianism 36–37, 39, 92, 97, 139
humanity 2, 6, 11, 21–23, 29–31, 36–40, 42–46, 54, 61, 77, 84, 96, 100, 114, 117, 121, 133, 135, 140, 148, 152–154, 156, 162, 167–169, 171, 173
human rights 27, 29–33, 39–46, 60–61, 112, 167
Human Rights Watch 31–32, 112, 117

Ignatieff, M. 28
incomplete death 138–140
indoctrination and servitude, domain of 80
inoperativity 153–154, 156, 158
integration concept 124–129, *125*
intermediary 89
International Court of Justice (ICJ) 32
International Covenant on Civil and Political Rights (ICCPR) 31
International Covenant on Economic, Social and Cultural Rights (ICESCR) 31
International Criminal Court (ICC) 32
International Organization for Migration (IOM) 25, 36, 40, 90
International Refugee Organisation (IRO) 34–35
Isin, E. F. 96
Italy 19–20, 58, 112–113, 115–116

Kibreab, G. 59, 65, 68, 88
Kok, W. 89
Kuhrt, A. 27

Lampedusa tragedy 15–17, 25, 108, 111, 114
League of Nations 30, 34
Levinas, E. 148–149, 151
Libya 2, 14, 16–17, 23, 32, 87, 90, 94, 96, 108, 110, 112, 114, 166

Lomba, S. d. 125, 127–128
Long, K. 34

Mackinnon, E. S. 29
Maldonado-Torres, N. 5–6, 21, 43–45, 78
mamet and hanetay 12–13, 82
'Man' and 'Human' 29–33, 42, 44–45
Mbembe, A. 1, 21, 42, 51–53, 56, 72, 143, 145–146, 149–151, 156–157, 162, 165, 167–168, 170–173; *Aesthetics of Superfluity* 55; panoptic fortification 71; *On the Postcolony* 1, 52–55, 146
McNeill, F. 125–126
Medecins Sans Frontieres (MSF) 113
Medhin story 11–13, 82
Mediterranean Sea 11, 15–17, 19, 22–23, 25, 96, 105, 107, 109–114
Mekonnen, D. R. 65–66
memory 152–157
Mereb-Belesa-Muna line 58
metropoles 2–3, 7–8, 23, 45, 52, 55–56, 73, 102, 106–108, 114–115, 118–119, 123–124, 128–130, 134–135, 140, 147, 153, 157
Middle Passage 22–24
Mignolo, W. D. 33
Ministry of Defense 65
mother country 51–53
Mountz, A. 37
movement 146–148
Müller, T. R. 68–69

National Charter 67–68
National Service Proclamation 82/1995 64–65, 70
nation-state as womb-abyss 51–57
necroethics 159
necropolitical reality 78, 123
necropolitics 34, 54–56, 78, 80, 83, 97, 101, 107, 121, 139, 159
Netanyahu, B. 32

ontological death 37
open boats 3, 7, 20–22
Organisation of African Unity (OAU) 29, 32

persecuted errantry 139
Petition of Right 27
physical death 37
Plato, *The Republic* 27
poetics of refuge 6, 8, 23, 40, 130, 133–137, 146, 152
poetic trace 3–5, 10, 130, 133, 137–139, 144–146, 152–153, 161–163, 170, 172
police city 88–92, 100, 134, 140
political death 37
postcolony 1, 52–55, 146
prohibition, domain of 80
Putin, V. 32

Quijano, A. 43

raciality 45–46, 54, 138–140, 157–158, 161, 168–169, 171
Rancière, J. 30–31, 33
recruitment 63, 65–66, 93
refugee camp 2, 5, 23, 36, 84–88, 90, 92–93, 100, 108–109, 113, 117, 171
Refugee Convention (1951) 28–29, 34–36, 90, 121–122
refugee, emergence of 34–40
refugee experience 77–82
refugee status determination (RSD) 35, 86, 90–91
refugee trafficking 88, 92–97, 101
Reisen, M. 87, 95
right of the rightless 40–44
Rygiel, K. 96

Sawa 65–69
sea-camp 7, 23, 107–116, 129, 134, 139–140, 152, 171
Shagarab refugee camp 85–88
Simon, J. 50
sovereignty 7, 27–28, 33, 37, 42–43, 45–46, 50, 52–53, 56–57, 59, 61–62, 64, 69, 73, 81, 100, 118, 150, 153, 162, 166–168
Spijkerboer, T. 112
Sudan 14, 17–18, 23, 32, 58–59, 84–85, 87, 90, 92, 96–98, 114, 166
Sudan Country Response Plan (Sudan CRP) 85–87
symbolic power 12

take life or *let* live right 81
Tigray/Tigray war 61, 85, 90
torture camp 36, 96–97, 100, 108, 134, 139
training, domain of 80
Tronvoll, K. 65–66
23 refugees story 14–15

UK 19–20, 40, 107, 114, 116–127, 130
Underhill, Justice 120
United Nations High Commissioner for Refugees (UNHCR) 25, 35–36, 40, 85–88, 90–92, 99, 113
United Nations Relief and Rehabilitation Administration (UNRRA) 34–35
United States Constitution 28
United States Declaration of Independence 28
Universal Declaration of Human Rights (UDHR) 28, 31

Warsay Yikealo Development Campaign (WYDC) 69
Webber, F. 118
Westgarth, W. 51, 74n1
white-masking 107, 124–129
Whole-World 21, 159–161
Woldemikael 58, 60
womb-abyss 3, 5–7, 20–21, 50–51, 73, 81, 99–100, 128–129, 137–140, 143, 147–148, 150–151, 153–162, 165–172; nation-state as 51–57; *see also* Eritrea
World War II 28, 31, 34–35, 58

Yacob, Z. 40
Yohannes, H. T. 136
Yonas, Zenawi, and Harnet story 19–20, 116, 123–124, 128

zoe (biological life) 41

FSC
www.fsc.org
MIX
Papier | Fördert gute Waldnutzung
FSC® C083411

Kolibri 360 GmbH
Ferdinand-Jühlke-Straße 7
99095 Erfurt, Deutschland
produktsicherheit@kolibri360.de